CITIES AND SOCIAL MOVEMENTS

Studies in Urban and Social Change

CITIES AND SOCIAL MOVEMENTS

IMMIGRANT RIGHTS ACTIVISM IN THE UNITED STATES, FRANCE, AND THE NETHERLANDS, 1970–2015

Walter J. Nicholls and
Justus Uitermark

WILEY Blackwell

This edition first published 2017
© 2017 John Wiley & Sons, Ltd

Registered Office
John Wiley & Sons, Ltd, The Atrium, Southern Gate, Chichester, West Sussex, PO19 8SQ, UK

Editorial Offices
350 Main Street, Malden, MA 02148-5020, USA
9600 Garsington Road, Oxford, OX4 2DQ, UK
The Atrium, Southern Gate, Chichester, West Sussex, PO19 8SQ, UK

For details of our global editorial offices, for customer services, and for information about
how to apply for permission to reuse the copyright material in this book please see our
website at www.wiley.com/wiley-blackwell.

Library of Congress Catalog Number: 2016028175

Hardback ISBN: 9781118750650
Paperback ISBN: 9781118750667

A catalogue record for this book is available from the British Library.

Cover image: © Salvador "Pocho" Sanchez: pochoone@gmail.com

Set in 10.5/12pt New Baskerville by SPi Global, Pondicherry, India

Printed and bound in Malaysia by Vivar Printing Sdn Bhd

10 9 8 7 6 5 4 3 2 1

"To our children who grew up while the book progressed: Emile J. Nicholls, Louise E. Nicholls, Imre D. Uitermark"

Contents

Series Editors' Preface

The Wiley Blackwell *Studies in Urban and Social Change* series is published in association with the *International Journal of Urban and Regional Research*. It aims to advance theoretical debates and empirical analyses stimulated by changes in the fortunes of cities and regions across the world. Among topics taken up in past volumes and welcomed for future submissions are:

- Connections between economic restructuring and urban change
- Urban divisions, difference, and diversity
- Convergence and divergence among regions of East and West, North and South
- Urban and environmental movements
- International migration and capital flows
- Trends in urban political economy
- Patterns of urban-based consumption

The series is explicitly interdisciplinary; the editors judge books by their contribution to intellectual solutions rather than according to disciplinary origin. Proposals may be submitted to members of the series Editorial Committee, and further information about the series can be found at www.suscbookseries.com:

Jenny Robinson
Manuel Aalbers
Dorothee Brantz
Patrick Le Galès
Chris Pickvance
Ananya Roy
Fulong Wu

Acknowledgments

We would like to thank Jennifer Robinson, Chris Pickvance, and Margit Mayer for constructive criticism and helpful suggestions. This book builds upon a series of articles we have published over the past couple of years. While the material in this book is by and large original, we have taken ideas, data, and some fragments from our articles published in *Antipode* (Uitermark and Nicholls 2014), *Environment and Planning A* (Nicholls 2011a; Uitermark et al. 2012), the *International Journal of Urban and Regional Research* (Uitermark et al. 2005; Uitermark 2014), the *Journal of Ethnic and Migration Studies* (Nicholls and Uitermark 2013; Nicholls et al. 2016), *Theory and Society* (Nicholls 2014), *Political Geography* (Nicholls 2016), a book chapter (Uitermark et al. 2014), Walter Nicholls's *The DREAMers: How the Undocumented Youth Movement Transformed the Immigrant Rights Debate* (2013), and Justus Uitermark's *Dynamics of Power in Dutch Integration Politics* (2012).

1

Sparks of Resistance

On Monday November 17, 2014, the US President, Barack Obama, addressed the nation in a live televised speech on immigration. After waiting in vain for Congress to pass an immigration bill, Obama announced that he would use his executive authority to protect almost 5 million undocumented immigrants from deportation. The responses to Obama's address were suggestive of just how controversial his actions were. The leader of the House of Representatives, Republican John Boehner, had warned Obama before his address. In Boehner's view, Obama usurped power like an autocrat and went against the will of the American people: "If 'Emperor Obama' ignores the American people and announces an amnesty plan that he himself has said over and over again exceeds his Constitutional authority, he will cement his legacy of lawlessness and ruin the chances for Congressional action on this issue – and many others." Michael McCaul, chairman of the House Committee for Homeland Security, echoed none other than Malcolm X when he stated that the Republicans were going to stop the executive action "by any means necessary." Yet another Republican politician, Senator Tom Coburn, said that Obama's move might result in bloodshed: "This country's going to go nuts, because they're going to see it as a move outside the authority of the president, and it's going to be a very serious situation … You're going to see – hopefully not – but you could see instances of anarchy … you could see violence."

Cities and Social Movements: Immigrant Rights Activism in the United States, France, and the Netherlands, 1970–2015, First Edition. Walter J. Nicholls and Justus Uitermark.
© 2017 John Wiley & Sons, Ltd. Published 2017 by John Wiley & Sons, Ltd.

Obama's decision to provide relief to millions of undocumented immigrants was unprecedented in scale, but it was not unique. Many of his predecessors had used their authority to the same ends. Earlier in his administration, in 2012, Obama had also granted temporary status to 600,000 undocumented youths who had arrived as children (Deferred Action for Childhood Arrivals, DACA). Nor is the regularization of undocumented immigrants unique to the United States. Countries as different as the Netherlands and France have occasionally enacted legislation and executive decrees to regularize the status of some groups of precarious immigrants. The Netherlands enacted a broad regularization in 2006, and in 2012 it passed a law to grant permanent residency status to groups of immigrants who had entered the country as minors and their families. France has also enacted large and small measures to regularize the status of tens of thousands of immigrants in 1997, 2006, and 2013.

These regularizations are remarkable on a number of levels. The literature on immigration suggests that, since the 1970s, governments in the global North have embarked on an immense effort to reinforce national borders through the construction of massive "deportation regimes" (De Genova and Peutz 2010; Kalir and Sur 2012; Menjívar and Kanstroom 2014). The United States, France, and the Netherlands, among many other countries, have developed an extensive infrastructure to monitor immigration flows and block the settlement of immigrants deemed unwanted. The US government in the 1990s allocated more resources to enforcement, expedited deportation procedures, restricted judicial discretion during removal proceedings, and reduced possibilities for appeals (Durand and Massey 2003; Varsanyi 2008). The Dutch government similarly introduced a range of laws and institutions to stop the flow of so-called non-Western working-class immigrants. It also developed a fine-grained infrastructure for monitoring, registering, and secluding immigrants, and increasing its administrative detention capacity from around 1,000 units in 1999 to almost 4,000 units in 2007 (Leerkes and Broeders 2010: 835). Likewise, France introduced restrictions on migrating families and asylum seekers, while also rolling out a massive infrastructure to facilitate the detention and removal of unwanted people in the country. After 1993, a series of laws eliminated automatic citizenship to those born on French soil (later rescinded), introduced stricter criteria for family reunification and refugee status, placed restrictions on public services to undocumented immigrants, barred most nonprofit associations from providing support to undocumented immigrants in need, authorized identity checks of suspect immigrants, and expanded detention centers at airports, ports, and cities (Hayward and Wright 2002).

These restrictive measures arose in response to public worries concerning the place of immigrants in nations being transformed by neoliberal globalization (Berezin 2009; Massey and Pren 2012). Prominent politicians and opinion makers suggested that immigrants drove down wages and further burdened the welfare state. They also argued that immigrants in Europe and the United States were so culturally different from nationals that they undermined social cohesion and posed a threat to national identity. There was extensive media coverage throughout Europe of immigrants "flooding" the region and living in inhumane conditions in camps, occupied buildings, and slum settlements. The "misery of the world," as former French Prime Minister Michel Rocard once said, was descending on these countries, presenting a major threat to national ways of life. Responding to this perceived threat, governments across the global North pursued restrictions and laid out the legal, moral, and physical basis for powerful deportation regimes.

Given the hostile climate facing immigrants and governments' frenzied attempts to secure their borders, one might have expected immigrants to adopt survival strategies that would allow them to remain hidden and under the radar. Engaging in assertive, highly visible, and sometimes disruptive political actions like protests, occupations, and hunger strikes would seem counterintuitive at best and unwise at worst. However, rather than hunker down and turn in on themselves, many immigrants have asserted their rights to have normal, visible, and equal lives in the countries in which they reside. While the general evolution has been in the direction of heated discourse and greater restrictions, some immigrant mobilizations have successfully swum against the tide and achieved important wins, including large-scale regularizations. How can we make sense of these seemingly irreconcilable trends: the general hardening of attitudes and policies toward working-class immigrants and the persistent struggles to extend rights and protection to this population? This book addresses the question by analyzing the geography of resistances and mobilizations in the United States, France, and the Netherlands over the past 40 years. We investigate the painful and contentious processes through which immigrants who were expected to work and disappear – Latino immigrants in the US case, North African and Turkish guest workers in the European cases – became resilient political subjects.

Where There Are Borders, There Are Resistances

One part of the answer is that the formidable efforts to close off the nation have generated resisting residues. If states want to seal their countries, they have to bring the border home and require local officials and citizens to take a direct role in rooting out "nefarious" foreigners from their daily worlds. This means that the acts of bordering and deporting people require thousands of street-level bureaucrats to assume frontline roles in carrying out exclusionary acts. The multiplication and localization of border enforcers are the only ways in which countries can close the cracks that allow unwanted populations to settle in countries. In the Netherlands, doctors are required to report on the legal status of patients and bus drivers are encouraged to keep an eye out for suspicious populations. In France, mayors have become responsible for granting "housing certificates" to immigrants applying for family visas and voluntary associations have been forbidden from providing assistance to suspected undocumented people. In these and many other instances, the proximity of street-level border enforcers to actual immigrants has allowed them to better survey suspicious activities and deny immigrants the resources needed to ensure their physical survival. As many institutions and professionals have assumed greater responsibility for ensuring *national* borders in daily life, the border ceases to be a distant frontier zone. Borders are no longer implemented by specially designated border police and mobilized against a foreign population we don't know or see. Maintaining and producing national borders now involves everyone – local police, housing officials, employers, teachers, voluntary associations – and is directed at real people engaged in countless daily practices. A border is no longer something that is geographically and socially distant but something that is proximate and carried out in daily life.

Many people assume their bordering responsibilities without second-guessing the rules. An employer rarely thinks twice about checking the immigration status of a prospective employee; public housing authorities and private landlords make it clear that they discriminate on the basis of immigration status; and so on. In these and many other instances, maintaining the exclusionary boundary between "legal" and "illegal" people becomes a banal part of one's work life. The border enforcer ceases to interrogate the moral or ethical rationalities underlying their exclusionary practices because it is just normal, reflecting what Hannah Arendt once called the "banality of evil" (Arendt 1977). When confronted with a "heartbreaking" or morally troubling case, street-level border enforcers oftentimes continue the assigned tasks but attribute moral responsibility to distant bureaucrats and government officials (Kalir and Wissink 2016). Too much proximity reveals the humanity of people and raises morally troubling questions, but this kind of tactical distancing helps assuage the moral ambivalences of street-level border enforcers.

While many people faithfully execute their tasks, others balk and resist. The paradox that haunts deportation regimes is that it is not only their efficacy that increases but also their vulnerability, as more and more local actors are called upon to participate in border enforcement. All these local actors may participate in border enforcement but they can also throw sand in the machine. Moral and professional ambiguities emerge when enacting exclusionary measures against real people who happen to be immigrants. The requirement to enact borders may conflict with other responsibilities associated with a job. Doctors in the Netherlands have pushed back on government measures, and some local police agencies in the United States have rejected partnerships with federal border enforcement agencies. Moreover, people who must witness the painful process of extracting and deporting people they actually know can produce moral shocks that spur resistances. Parents of school-age children in France, for instance, have had some of the most successful mobilizations to block the deportation of immigrant youths and their undocumented parents. The immigrant ceased being a distant Other on the outskirts of society but was now a friend or an acquaintance from school; somebody who had a face, a name, and a solid place in an actual community. Government policies aiming to extract immigrants thus have produced points of resistance and conflict with those being targeted by the measures (actual immigrants), those enlisted to carry them out (street-level border enforcers), and morally shocked friends, families, and supporters in communities. Thus, even – or perhaps especially – when immigration regimes are designed as hermetically closed systems, they generate countless local disturbances that can send tremors throughout the whole system.

One of our theoretical goals is to interrogate the limits of governmentality theory (Rose and Miller 1992; Rose 1999; Inda 2006) in the domain of immigration. Even though national governments try to reinforce their territorial power by developing deeply penetrating and far-reaching bordering strategies, we try to show that not all those involved in this process comply passively. Government measures to produce and enforce borders have had strong and somewhat unpredictable politicizing effects on immigrants and supportive nationals. Wherever power draws a line between the acceptable and unacceptable, the "legal" and "illegal" human being, those finding themselves on the wrong side of the divide can develop subversion tactics by evading detection, appealing decisions, or simply refusing to cooperate. Government strategies do not necessarily produce stable, clearly demarcated, and well-policed social orders where everybody has a neat place, as intended by governments. Instead, they produce a multiplicity of resistances and struggles, which can in turn have disruptive effects on the general order of things. "Where there is power," as Michel Foucault once asserted, "there is resistance, and yet, or rather consequently, this resistance is never in a position of exteriority in relation to power" (Foucault 1978: 95). Or, as Henri Lefebvre, concisely put it, "State-imposed normality makes permanent transgression inevitable" (1991: 23). Whenever powerful groups and institutions label outsiders as illegal and illegitimate, small resistances emerge and plant the seeds for larger struggles. We do not suggest that specific grievances and associated resistances alone explain large-scale struggles. However, they plant the seeds that can, under the right conditions, grow into larger and more complex mobilizations for rights and legal residency.

Where Small Resistances Take Root and Grow into Big Mobilizations

Our interest isn't to inventory countless forms of resistance. It is to examine the mechanisms in which some resistances concentrate in certain places, harness energies and countervailing powers, and grow into large mobilizations that eat into and sometimes alter the bordering practices and rationalities of modern nation states. The power to restrict and interdict produces countless seeds of resistance, but not all resistances take root and grow into disruptive political mobilizations. Understanding this process requires us to investigate the geographical terrains in which seeds of resistance are planted and grow into big, tangled, and disruptive struggles for rights and recognition.

Seeds of resistance are born at the specific points where restrictions are enacted: undocumented immigrants protest deportation orders by initiating hunger strikes in the places they live; immigrant day laborers fight for their right to work in towns that ban such activities; local mayors provide undocumented immigrants with homeless services in conflict with national laws; doctors treat patients in hospitals irrespective of their status; parents and school employees protest deportation raids in their schools and neighborhoods. Enacting restrictive bordering policies locally therefore localizes and multiplies seeds of resistances wherever they are enacted. We do not suggest that resistance is automatic, especially considering the ability of people to banalize exclusion. We do argue that attempts to seal borders produce many ambivalences and cracks, and that some of these can become a new point of resistance and conflict in the system. These local conflicts are often limited in scope and time but, under the proper conditions, they can grow into systemic challenges when immigrants collectively – with the support of allies and supporters – assert their rights in the face of attack and exclusion.

Resistances may be everywhere that power is enacted, but all places do not provide the support needed to grow resistances into tangled and disruptive political mobilizations. Social movement scholars have long asserted that certain resources (recruits, organizations, money, skills, trust, etc.) are necessary in transforming seeds of resistances into large mobilizations (della Porta and Diani 1999; McAdam et al. 2001). We also know that certain environments furnish more resources than others. Resistances may arise in places where specific government powers are enacted but not all places provide sufficient conditions to grow small seeds into big mobilizations. Immigrant detention centers and prisons, for instance, are important sites for producing seeds of resistance but these environments are not necessarily the best to transform early seeds into broad and sustained struggles. Detention centers in the Netherlands are home to hundreds of hunger strikes each year but these strikes are largely ignored by the media, public, support groups, and politicians because they take place in environments that do not possess the full range of resources needed to nurture their growth and maturation. These resistances end up passing largely unnoticed, presenting only minor and uneventful disruptions in the circuits of state power. In other instances, early resistances may find more supportive and enriching environments, providing them with conditions for further growth.

Certain environments may be richer and more supportive than others, but outsiders cannot simply tap into and make use of these resources automatically. They must develop *relations* with more established actors in these environments as a precondition to tapping into and making use of embedded resources, knowledge, and information. This book examines the relational qualities of places that make it possible for deprived and stigmatized outsiders to tap into rich resource pools and build powerful struggles for rights and equality in inhospitable countries. These relational qualities are heavily concentrated in certain large cities and, within them, in specific neighborhoods. These places function as incubators for early seeds of resistance and provide *relational opportunities* for outsiders to contest their exclusion. In places with abundant opportunities to create strong and supportive relations, marginalized activists can connect to sympathetic supporters and allies and eventually tap into the resources, information, and knowledge concentrated in strategic places. Relations provide access to a diverse range of strategic resources, which then facilitate the growth of small resistances into large and tangled mobilizations. We are aware that cities do not have a monopoly on resources, strategic mechanisms, and opportune relations but some do tend have a higher concentration of these attributes than other places. The concentration of these qualities in particular places produces environments that are better able to facilitate the growth of seeds of resistance into large and entangled struggles for rights, equality, and protections. This book investigates under what conditions cities do or do not perform this role of incubating resistance.

In the countries we investigate – the United States, France, the Netherlands – struggles for immigrant rights intensified in the 1970s in response to increasingly restrictive immigration policies. The fight for general rights of immigrants often emerged in response to deportations, police raids, the lack of decent housing, the unwillingness of officials to recognize residency claims, restrictions on selling labor or goods in public, and so on. While early struggles sprouted in many places across these countries, they took root and later flourished, especially in Los Angeles, Paris, and Amsterdam. These cities concentrated diverse resources and provided relational opportunities for pioneering immigrant rights activists to reach out and connect to a variety of supporters in possession of these resources. These supporters included leftist radicals, intellectuals, unionists, and humanitarians. Although these movements were national in scope and orientation, they relied on resources and relations that were spatially concentrated. In all three of our cases, immigrant rights activists in different mobilizations were able to assert their voice in the national political arena because of their ability to develop relations with people and organizations in possession of different kinds of resources. Cities are central arenas in the struggle for general rights and equality because they tend to be the frontline sites where exclusions are enacted *and* because they provide the resources and relational opportunities that can support emergent activists. While we show how these cities fostered large mobilizations in particular times, mobilizations morphed, collapsed, and re-emerged throughout the 40-year period under investigation here. The changing nature of struggles across time and cases provides us with unique insights into the factors that facilitate and block the contention in these cities.

The two central tasks of the book – explaining the persistence of immigrant rights struggles in spite of adverse conditions, and charting the geographies of these struggles – are two sides of the same coin. The mechanisms through which these immigrant movements (but not only immigrant movements) a rise or decline all have distinct and consequential spatial underpinnings. Our explanation for the evolution of immigrant rights movements thus examines *how* and *why* the networks constituting movements develop by tracing *where* they develop. By descending to the grassroots we hope to uncover some of the mechanisms by which movements take shape, grow, and fall apart.

Policing Resistance through the Urban Grassroots

Some cities provide rich environments for seeds of resistance to grow into robust mobilizations but activists in many cities do not always connect with others and develop productive political relations. Many factors impede such political relations. Some advocacy organizations may simply have sufficient resources of their own and may not need to develop partnerships with other organizations in their environment. Others may find themselves competing for the same recruits and sources of financing, which can exacerbate ideological and strategic conflicts. And still others may face institutional and discursive constraints imposed by local governance regimes. These different factors all play a role in shaping activism, but we draw specific attention to government efforts to rewire the networks making up the relational worlds of activists.

Los Angeles, Paris, and Amsterdam helped immigrant activists assert their rights in unpredictable and sometimes disruptive ways. In addition, anxious nationals demanded that government officials take action to protect public order against deviant groups and in unruly immigrant neighborhoods. Governments could not stand idle in the face of these demands because the demands called their legitimacy into question. Governments with more robust statist traditions (France and the Netherlands) became particularly active in rolling out new techniques to control the neighborhoods where immigrants concentrated and enlisted associations in efforts to integrate and police immigrant populations. While many organizations of immigrants had challenged discrimination, deprivation, and deportations in the 1970s, in the course of the 1980s governments attempted to enlist them as partners in efforts to promote integration and fight crime. Governments identified territories with elevated risks, monitored activities within them, identified influential organizations within these spaces, and introduced measures to control conduct and norms.

While recognizing that governments invariantly attempt to perforate and steer relations in civil society, we show that these efforts have been very uneven over time and space. In the United States, for example, the rollback of federal urban policy during the 1980s coincided with a tradition of laissez-faire immigrant integration policies. This resulted in rather weak control mechanisms to address the growing population of immigrant activists in Los Angeles. By contrast, France's control strategies targeted first- and second-generation immigrants, left human rights non-governmental organizations (NGOs) unscathed, and did not grapple with informal, undocumented activist groups. This resulted in a whack-a-mole approach by the state in which one segment of the immigrant rights movement was brought under state control while another segment was allowed to flourish for many years. Lastly, the flexible and pragmatic character of the Dutch state allowed it to respond to unanticipated threats by redirecting its attention from leftist radicals to Muslim organizations to counter radicalization and promote integration. Understanding the uneven strategies of government control helps account for differences in the form of national social movements and their power to achieve their goals.

Governments have a great capacity to disrupt productive relations between activists and supporters in the same city. However, the reach of government is always limited, even in a very effective governing context like the Netherlands. The constant enactment of bordering powers across a national space produces varied resistances. An effective and flexible government can anticipate, channel, and defuse many of these, but certain resistances inevitably escape its reach and give rise to destabilizing mobilizations. The book therefore draws inspiration from the governmentality literature because governments do reach into the life spaces and relational worlds of activists, modify subjective and strategic worldviews, and mediate exchanges. However, governments also produce resistance-generating interdictions, and some of these resistances can fester and grow beyond the gaze and reach of the state. Thus, the government asserts control over its national territory and activist relations in cities, but these measures are contradictory and imperfect, which provides interstitial openings for seeds to grow into potentially disruptive mobilizations.

Overview of the Book

This book stems from the individual and collaborative research performed by both authors since the early 2000s. For more than a decade, we interviewed many activists, political officials, and associations of various types. We used historical archives to discover new information and verify arguments made by informants. Archives from leading national newspapers (*New York Times, Le Monde, NRC*, etc.) were also used to provide information about conflicts, stakeholders, mobilization frames, and other details concerning different rights campaigns. Lastly, we made extensive use of secondary resources to provide greater context and detail for the campaigns and government measures in question. While we pursued our research projects independently over this period, since 2009 we have collaborated on a series of articles that form the foundation for this book.

This book addresses two major issues: how do precarious immigrants press for rights in increasingly inhospitable countries, and how do particular places help or block their ability to engage in these struggles? We address these issues by following the evolution of immigrant rights struggles in Los Angeles, Paris, and Amsterdam from the 1970s to the late 2000s. The book is divided into three, roughly chronological parts. Part I examines the birth of immigrant rights activism. In spite of important differences between our cases, the 1970s marked the emergence of this form of activism. We suggest that the similarities reflect the intensification of resistances against new government measures to restrict immigration and increase deportations. The closing of borders and the creation of deportation regimes provided the common structural push that inaugurated the battle for immigrant rights in all three countries. These restrictions concentrated in cities because all three of our cities had the highest concentrations of immigrants in their respective countries and all three cities possessed a high density and diversity of activist organizations. The density, diversity, and openness of local activist milieus provided a new generation of immigrant rights activists with relational opportunities to create new friends and supporters. These relations were used to tap and appropriate rich resource pools for struggles unfolding at regional and national scales. Thus, in spite of important differences between these cases, we continue to highlight the remarkable similarities in the first immigrant rights struggles of this era.

Part II shifts the focus and begins to examine government control strategies during the 1980s and 1990s. It suggests that differences in these strategies helped to restructure immigrant rights networks and place movements on very different trajectories. Whereas the first part of the book stresses the similarities between our cases, the second part identifies the government control strategies that contributed to producing differences in terms of immigrant rights activists' capacities and methods to assert rights claims.

Part III examines the effects of government control strategies on mobilizations. It suggests that efforts to exert political control have not extinguished struggles. Rather, these strategies have morphed grievances, resistances, and mobilizations over the past two decades. In the United States, we show that a rather weak strategy of political integration during the 1980s and 1990s provided the space for rights activists and their union allies to consolidate into a new hub of rights activism. Grassroots organizations in the 2000s and 2010s have been able to use place-based relations as a foundation to assert themselves in national debates and struggles over immigrant rights. In France, political integration essentially marginalized older left-wing immigrant associations and their second-generation comrades. Following this, the movement has been split between two factions: one faction made up of professional, mostly white, mostly male, and mostly national NGOs; and the other faction made up of informal, mostly undocumented, strongly female, and highly localized groups. In the Netherlands, political integration neutralized older left-wing immigrant associations and depoliticized the NGO sector. This has left a social movement field that provides aggrieved undocumented immigrants with a rather fallow field of support. Nevertheless, immigrants and their supporters continue to resist government restrictions but their battles have been highly individualized and scattered throughout the country. Thus, the third and final part of the book identifies the outcomes that result from the different government strategies.

Conclusions

There is a broad lesson that can be taken from this book. Resistance to exclusionary state power is not an exception but a constant. Even when confronted by sophisticated government strategies to pre-empt and neutralize resistance, our study finds that a pugnacious and forceful politics of rights persists. Every effort to silence or banish certain actors spurs innovations and alternative responses among targeted groups, producing constant struggles for rights and recognition. This does not mean that every configuration of resistance has the same chances of success. Under certain conditions, these resistances can evolve into struggles with greater reach and impact. Our exploration of the mechanisms that turn sparks of resistance into sustained mobilizations is a deeply interdisciplinary endeavor. Our own intellectual trajectories and the themes covered in this book span sociology, geography, political sciences, and urban studies. Our hope is that the book will speak to different audiences and serve as a bridge between the disciplines trying to understand how resistances emerge and why they succeed or fail.

2

Rethinking Movements from the Bottom Up

We enter into the study of immigrant rights mobilizations with the well-worn battle cry of human geographers: "space matters." People's living and working environments shape how they become politicized, how they mobilize their resources, what kinds of political opportunities are available to them, and how they construct their political wills and imaginaries. We cannot fully understand how movements evolve if we bracket them off from the lived geographies of people. Our study of immigrant rights struggles therefore places space at the center of the theoretical analysis and studies how geography is implicated in the emergence and decline of social movements. We develop a *relational approach* by examining *how* and *why* the networks constituting movements develop in specific *places* and evolve across *space*.

Immigrant rights movements, like all social movements, are composed of complex networks between many activists and stakeholders. We argue that cities potentially provide conducive environments for activist networks to form, diversify, and expand. Many authors have suggested that cities are relational incubators for powerful cultural and economic agglomerations (Sassen 1991; Storper 1997, 2013; Scott 2008). We suggest that, in a similar way, cities are potentially relational incubators for social movements. Cities can bring activists together in strong interdependent relations, transforming an aggregation of people into a potent political agglomeration. When this happens, activists within these hubs assume central roles in shaping the agenda, strategy, and discourses of

Cities and Social Movements: Immigrant Rights Activism in the United States, France, and the Netherlands, 1970–2015, First Edition. Walter J. Nicholls and Justus Uitermark.
© 2017 John Wiley & Sons, Ltd. Published 2017 by John Wiley & Sons, Ltd.

geographically extensive and complex social movements, enabling activists to puncture closed political arenas and make legitimate demands for rights and recognition. However, cities do not always spawn social movements. In addition to identifying the mechanisms through which movements emerge from the urban grassroots, we need to investigate the mechanisms that quell or channel contention.

The first two sections provide an overview of writings on space, social movements, and cities. The section that follows discusses four crucial mechanisms of movement evolution and explains why these mechanisms are especially likely to be effective within cities and specific neighborhoods within them. We then explain how governing authorities develop strategies to assert control over the urban grassroots. While the framework is inspired by observations of immigrant rights social movements, our hope is that it has wider applicability.

Rethinking the Space of National Social Movements from the Bottom Up

Thinking about geography in the social movement literature

The standard geographical criticism that social theory inadvertently portrays space as a passive backdrop instead of a constitutive force applies to social movement theory too. The national arena has often been taken as the principal spatial arena of social movements and local struggles have largely been viewed as reflections or variants of national trends. The "methodological nationalism" (Beck, 2000, 2007) of this literature has made it difficult for scholars to take apart national social movements and examine the geographical elements that constitute them. Over the past two decades, however, a number of important observers have investigated the geographical makeup of social movements by reexamining place and localities, and assessing how activists in various localities connect to and constitute national and transnational movements.

The first development in this direction is associated with the turn to network theory (Diani and McAdam 2004). Activists work through complex networks and the makeup of these networks affects their capacity to mobilize collective resources and achieve key political goals. Mario Diani, for example, argued that the "impact of collective action will be stronger where permanent bonds of solidarity have emerged during the conflict. It will be weaker, in contrast, where collective action has consisted mainly of ad hoc, instrumental coalitions, without generating specific new linkages" (1997: 136). The focus on networks precipitated a closer look at the spatial underpinnings of movement activities. Diani

(2004, 2005) has shown how engagement in local struggles over environmental concerns led residents to connect to national and transnational campaigns. He suggested that struggles in towns and cities functioned as extensions of larger-scale campaigns, with activists renewing their commitment and ties to the general struggle through the activities and connections made in their everyday lives. Local actors were conceptualized as nodes performing specific functions within global circuits of contention. In his classic study of the Paris Commune, sociologist Roger Gould studied the Paris Commune as the outcome of "the networks of social relationships in which potential protesters are implicated" (1995:12). Gould's analysis showed that the strong ties within Paris's working-class neighborhoods helped generate commitment among their residents and provided the relational conduits for collective actions like barricading. Relations formed in neighborhoods (rather than in artisanal guilds or along other occupational lines) played *the* central role in shaping the Commune: "Urban insurrections through the 1800s, both in France and elsewhere in Europe, were organized around the construction of barricades to seal off the popular quarters from the forces of order; thus *it is not surprising that insurgent mobilization should have depended on neighborhood rather than trade solidarity*" (Gould 1993: 748, emphasis added). Local social networks were also responsible for shaping the levels of solidarity between participating activists: "Social pressure to report for guard duty derived from the fact that one's fellow battalion members were also one's neighbors. Failure to participate in the insurgent effort was construed as a betrayal of loyalty to the neighborhood and was sanctioned accordingly" (ibid.). In a similar vein, Robert Sampson and Douglas McAdam have argued, on the basis of their research in Chicago, that "collective action events in the contemporary city are (a) highly concentrated geographically and (b) explained by systematic variations in community-level characteristics" (Sampson et al. 2005: 679; Sampson 2013). Perhaps most importantly, they suggest that it is not a single type of organization that is responsible for high mobilization capacities. Rather, it is the entanglement of diverse organizations in specific places that contribute to enhanced mobilization capacities (ibid.: 209). Such observations concerning the importance of place-based networks extend to broad and geographically extensive social mobilizations that make heavy use of social media. For example, in their analysis of interactions among Twitter users during the Spanish 15-M movement, Javier Borge-Holthoefer et al. (2011) found that the observed communities were largely geographically defined. Findings like these suggest that even in a hyper-connected world, activists continue to derive important advantages from the networks found in urban places.

A second development that has led some prominent scholars to address the spatial underpinnings of social movements has been associated with the renewed attention to emotions. In *Passionate Politics*, Mark Goodwin, James Jasper, and Francesca Polletta (2001) argued that social movement theory overreached when it emphasized that activists were rational actors and not an irrational mob. The "emotional turn" in the social movement literature has prompted some to think more carefully about the spatial underpinnings of powerful emotions. Randall Collins argued that face-to-face interactions are central to producing powerful emotions between activists. Intense interaction rituals producing collective effervescence hinge on the physical assembly of people and their mutual focus on symbols or acts like chanting and marching (Collins 2001: 28). These intense, face-to-face interactions produce solidarity, emotional energy, collective symbols, and moral sentiments and feelings, all of which are essential for sustaining mobilizations. Collins's theory therefore suggests that spatial proximity is a necessary condition for emotion-generating interactions in social movements (Collins 2004). His work invites us to direct our attention to the points where movement activities originate and develop.

A third development in the literature is associated with studies of transnational social movements. This interest contributed to a series of theoretical and empirical writings on how local activists "scale up" and connect to national and transnational networks. Saskia Sassen influentially argued that global cities have acquired central importance as sites for political contention, with new information and communication technologies enabling "a variety of local political actors to enter international arenas once exclusive to national states" (Sassen 2004: 649). Margaret Keck and Kathryn Sikkink (1998) explored how networks and political opportunities at different spatial scales (regional, national, international) influenced the capacity of movements to assume a transnational form. Sikkink (2005) went on to argue that the likelihood of movements extending beyond their national containers depended on international political opportunities and the possibilities of finding allies already mobilizing in the international arenas. In a similar vein, Sydney Tarrow and Douglas McAdam (2005) placed the issue of "scale shift" at the center of their theoretical analysis of transnational social movements. Scale shift, according to them, implies not only a geographical extension of activist relations but also an extension of organizations and sectors (2005: 125). Two mechanisms play particularly important roles in permitting the process of scale shift. First, "brokerage" is the mechanism that permits the spread of the movement through links between two or more previously unconnected actors (ibid.: 127). Brokers not only connect people but also introduce frames that allow strangers to see similarities in each other's different struggles. Brokered ties create new relations across geographical and organizational boundaries, which rapidly enhance the potential reach and diffusion of a mobilization. Movements that shift scale through brokerage tend to grow fast but they also collapse quickly as leaders and brokers lack the loyalty and influence to overcome internal friction. Second, "relational diffusion" concerns the spread of information, tactics, and goals through actors with pre-existing relational ties. Pre-existing ties facilitate scale shift and diffusion because distant actors are better able to identify with struggles and trust the actors engaged in them. This results in a diffusion process that is stable and well grounded but geographically and socially limited in reach. The geographical limits impede the ability of the mobilization to penetrate the national or transnational public sphere.

Although these and other scholars have begun to examine key spatial components of movements, there has still been little effort to synthesize these findings and develop a more elaborate theory to understand the spatial underpinnings of social movements. The literature reflects ad hoc insights into the different spatial elements of movements (place, proximity, distance, scale). These intermittent interventions reflect a side interest by several political scientists and sociologists rather than a full spatial turn in the literature. Nevertheless, these interventions are important in shaping our thinking about space and social movements. Local activist relations play important roles in far-flung social movement networks because they reinforce group bonds and commitments to large-scale political change. The strength of relations allows these actors to contribute their resources and energies to risky campaigns.

Thinking about social movements in human geography

Human geography is the natural home for thinking about the spatial makeup of social and political phenomena, but for a long time this discipline's strong critical tradition was largely informed by structural Marxism and poststructuralism. These theoretical paradigms examined why people (should) resist but not the nuts-and-bolts mechanisms involved in translating small resistances into large and sustained forms of collective action. This is not to say that human geographers failed to provide a theory of social movements but that the grand theories that many preferred (structural Marxism and poststructural philosophy) were too big, blunt, and abstract to identify the finer mechanisms that made it possible to grow small resistances into large movements. Whereas the "why" question was frequently addressed by critical human geographers, the "how" question of social movements remained under-explored until the late 1990s.

Paul Routledge and Byron Miller played pivotal roles in addressing the finer mechanics of resistance and social movement. These geographers provided a profound reflection on the centrality of *place* in social movements. For Routledge, a close analysis of place allows us to better understand the "'language of discontent', which motivates and informs social movement agency" (1997: 222). The language of discontent, according to Routledge's formulation, varies from place to place depending on the relations and cultures found in specific geographical locations. Language, resources, imaginaries, frames, and so on do not exist on the "head of a pin" but are firmly situated in context-specific relations. This gives rise to what Routledge called uneven "terrains of resistance" (1993, 1994). The unevenness of these terrains differentiates political socialization by geography, making people in certain places more prone to resistance than others. Routledge's early foray into the issue of place and social movements was followed by Deborah Martin's work on how community organizations "create a discursive place-identity to situate and legitimate their activism" (Martin 2003: 733). Activism becomes meaningful and legitimate by drawing upon discourses that oftentimes derive from local meaning structures (Martin and Pierce 2013).

These geographers of social movements did not view place simply as a location or site in a broader geometrical space. They drew inspiration from Doreen Massey's relational and global view of place. As Massey (1994: 154) argued, places are not constituted by "some long internalized history" but are "constructed out of a particular constellation of social relations, meeting together at a particular locus," and can be "imagined as articulated moments in networks of social relations and understandings." Understanding place in this relational fashion makes it possible to investigate how certain loci become nodes within larger movement networks. The theoretical insights of these place-oriented geographers have therefore been strategic because they have not only reinforced the centrality of place as central building blocks of social movements, but they have also inspired us to conceptualize social movements as geographically uneven terrains. Certain places are more propitious for political socialization and activism than others, and places are always shaped by *and* shaping activists in other spaces and scales through messy and complex relational exchanges.

Geographers have also examined how scale is implicated in movements (Miller 2000, 2001, 2009; Herod and Wright 2002; Miller and Martin 2003). Shifting between local and (trans)national scales requires dramatic shifts in a variety of repertoires as targets, allies and adversaries, and meaning systems undergo fundamental changes with the broadening geographical scope of a struggle. For instance, Miller's analysis of an anti-sweatshop campaign addresses this issue when he points out, "there is a dramatic jump in scale from the retail clothing corporation and its sweatshops to communities, if not a world, of consumers; dramatic shifts in mobilizing strategies, frames, and geographies are required if much broader and diverse constituencies are to be mobilized" (2004: 577). Routledge also identifies how networks mediate rescaling processes. He notes that "grassroots globalization networks forge an associational politics that constitute a diverse, contested coalition of place-specific social movements, which prosecute conflict on a variety of multi-scalar terrains that include both material places and virtual spaces" (Routledge 2003: 334). Activists within locally rooted and globally extensive networks interact with one another through what Routledge (2003) calls "convergence spaces" – that is, the concrete and virtual spaces where far-flung activists can meet, share experiences, and build common political imaginaries.

Seeking to build on the work of human geographers, we have made our own contributions to the literature by drawing on insights from economic geographers and urban sociologists (Nicholls 2003, 2008, 2009, 2011a; Uitermark 2004, 2012; Uitermark et al. 2012; Uitermark and Nicholls 2014). Economic geographers introduced an interesting research problem during the 1980s and 1990s (Scott 1988; Storper 1997, 2013): why do certain (economic) networks agglomerate in specific locations when global networks and mobility have become so prevalent? The economic geographers argued that advanced economic activities in certain industries (finance, technology, film and culture industries) agglomerate because proximity reduces transaction costs, enhances tacit knowledge, and improves the ability of actors to respond flexibly to fast-moving and uncertain conditions. The advantages afforded by economic agglomerations make the cities and regions where they are located into major centers of value and innovation (i.e. hubs) within dispersed and globalized networks. Rather than economic territories standing in opposition to global networks, territorialized economic relations were viewed by these geographers as propulsive forces that ground and drove the global economy. The observations concerning economic networks appeared transferable to social movement networks (Nicholls 2008, 2009). Proximity between diverse activists favors trusting relations, intensifies emotional solidarities, and reduces uncertainties. These "relational assets" (Storper 1997) improve the ability of diverse activists to work in complex and high-risk forms of collective action, enabling them to pool high-grade resources (economic, cultural, symbolic capital, etc.). Their ability to tap and deploy collective resources for different campaigns allows activists in these places to achieve powerful roles in geographically extensive social movement networks. Distant geographical networks allow locally generated resources and ideas to circulate across space. While distant networks help diffuse information and resources across space, they are also weaker (à la Tarrow and McAdam), prone to breakdowns, and have greater difficulty transmitting complex knowledge (à la Storper). As a consequence, the most productive centers of power within broad social movement networks are concentrated in geographically situated activist hubs, the places where resources are generated, pooled, and deployed in larger-scale struggles.

While these hubs are power-generating centers, the power they generate also introduces processes of geographic unevenness whereby hubs have power over the multiple peripheries constituting a social movement network. The unevenness of the network – a necessary condition for outsiders to produce countervailing power within a political system – is prone to center–periphery conflicts, as geographical centers capture more resources and legitimacy flowing into a social movement network than the many peripheries. This theory has therefore aimed to provide a broader framework to understand three basic questions concerning the geographies of social movements: why activists agglomerate in certain places; the function of agglomerations in broader social movement networks; and how the emergence of activist hubs creates uneven social movement networks that are structurally prone to conflict along center–periphery lines.

Both sets of literatures – the insightful contributions of social movement scholars and the conceptual work of geographers – reveal that social movements are modes of collective political action underlain by complex geographies. Coming from different disciplinary traditions, both lay out the basic topography of broad social movements: *the relations that constitute movements are fostered within places and across space. Distant networks connect locally situated activists into highly uneven spatial configurations with a few powerful centers (activist hubs) and many peripheral nodes.* This spatial configuration has a dynamic of its own: hubs generate higher degrees of power because of enhanced resource mobilization capacities within them. Extending a network beyond hubs is necessary to generalize a campaign but this comes with the risk of fragmenting and weakening relations between distant actors. And finally, hubs capture more resources, influence, and attention than peripheral nodes. This helps the hub to drive the general network forward but this geographical unevenness produces center–periphery cleavages because of the center's power advantages over outlying regions.

Social movement spaces are complex and dynamic structures. Their different components (hubs, nodes, connections, scales) enable the concentration and deployment of energies that propel politicized people into battles for political power. By mapping out the spatial structures and dynamics of social movements, our hope is to begin revealing the anatomy of contentious political struggle. Social movements are intrinsically spatial modes of collective action and understanding their multiple spatialities is essential for analyzing how they emerge, grow, move forward, and die.

Reconnecting Cities and Social Movements

Our attention now turns to a specific spatial form: cities. Our analytical approach is different from much of the literature on contentious cities because many of those writings focus on struggles for rights within specific cities. *Urban social movements* have more often than not been conceived as a specific type of movement alongside other types of movements (ecology, feminist, civil rights, etc.). Much of the literature does not examine what particular role cities play in broader struggles for a wide array of rights (e.g. immigrant, labor, civil rights, gay and lesbian rights), and not just the right to the city. The uptick in mobilizations in the early part of the 2010s (15-M in Spain, the North African Revolutions, Occupy, Gezi, etc.) sparked an interest in the role of cities (in particular "the square"), but this line of inquiry remains hampered by the theoretical blinders of the past. One of the central aims of this book is to demonstrate how cities have played important roles in fostering the struggles for the rights of immigrants in their receiving countries, and not just their right to the city.

The distinction between urban and other social movements finds its conceptual origins in Manuel Castells's seminal work in *The Urban Question* (1977) and *The City and the Grassroots* (1983). *The Urban Question* began its inquiry into cities and social movements by adopting the common Marxist distinction between spaces of production and reproduction (Saunders 1986; Pickvance 2003). While the urban reproduced the labor power of workers through collective consumption (e.g. housing, streets, education, parks, transit), the factory transformed this labor power into profitable commodities (Castells 1977: 237). As capitalism split the lives of the working class, urban spaces created distinctive types of grievances and struggles centering on collective consumption issues. For the young Castells, his interests were in how the grievances in the city and factory were structurally distinct from one another but also complementary and could connect into broad and revolutionary movements.

In *The City and the Grassroots*, Castells (1983) took some distance from structural Marxism and his earlier interests in the structural complementarity of productive (factory) and reproductive (city) spaces (Saunders 1986). He began to emphasize the qualities that made cities distinctive spaces for creating grievances and containing mobilizations. *Urban* structures, institutions, and cultures conspired to entrap mobilizations localities while taking their attention away from broader power structures. "Crucially," Chris Pickvance notes, "Castells argues that urban movements have lost their ability to bring about structural change in power relations in conjunction with other groups. The 'meaning' of the city is largely determined by macro forces, and urban movements are now condemned to be no more than 'reactive utopias'" (2003: 103). Urban activists in the 1980s and 1990s became more interested in defending their particular street or squatter settlement against the forces of global capitalism than in taking the offensive and mobilizing in broader battles for social and political change. Particularistic NIMBYism was the fate of urban social movements in the period of global capitalist consolidation rather than broad anti-systemic struggles, as he had hoped for in the 1970s. Castells's discussion of the territorial basis of San Francisco's gay rights movement is telling (1983: 140). He argues that control over physical territory was a precondition for the gay men's liberation struggle, but producing such a territory became an end-goal in its own right. This impeded the ability of activists to scale up their struggle and create connections to other liberation movements. Urban territorialization was therefore viewed as a trap that precipitated actors to turn inwards and fight defensively for their particularistic "spaces of place" instead of the general forces of power.

Following these important interventions, the scholarship on urban social movements focused on the highly localized and particularistic nature of city-based contention. Place-based militants were said to be mobilizing for the protection of lifestyles or mobilizing against outside threats (Davis 1990; Fainstein and Hirst 1995; Mayer 2000; Boudreau and Keil 2001; Harvey 2001). For example, in her article on the pacification of Berlin's social movement scene, Margit Mayer argued that collective action in the 1990s had given way to partnerships with the local government, self-help groups, or NIMBY-like struggles (Mayer 2000). This literature examined how civil society was aligned with authorities and came to serve as an extension of the government rather than as a counterforce. The pessimism that marked this cycle of scholarship shared Castells's principal theoretical assumption: urban processes produce distinctive urban grievances, claims, and identities, and these in turn lead to local forms of collective action prone to place-specific particularism that are detached from broader social movement networks. Conflicts often begin in cities but structural, institutional, and cultural barriers make it virtually impossible for them to escape the city walls.

The "urban social movement" framework of the 1980s and 1990s was largely supplanted by the "right to the city" framework in the 2000s. The theoretical starting point of this literature is Henri Lefebvre (cf. Lefebvre 1996) and its normative tone is optimistic. The right to the city literature maintains that urban capitalism elicits grassroots responses from people reclaiming their rights to the urban commons (Harvey 2003; Mitchell 2003; Purcell 2003; Brenner et al. 2011; Marcuse et al. 2011; Smith and McQuarrie 2012). *Urban* processes under capitalism precipitate specific kinds of grievances because commodification and rationalization alienate inhabitants from the "right" to appropriate and produce urban space. "The right to appropriation," according to Mark Purcell, "is the right to define and produce urban space primarily to maximize its use value over and above its exchange value." Purcell goes on to argue that "The notion of urban space as property, as a commodity to be exchanged on the market, is antithetical to the right to appropriation" (Purcell 2003: 578). These fundamentally *urban* grievances (the right to appropriate space) give rise to specifically urban mobilizations and struggles over who has the "right to the city." Such grievances are expressed as a "cry and a demand" for a "renewed right to urban life" (Lefebvre, in Purcell 2003: 564). Some contributors to the literature have now argued that capitalism has arrived at a stage of planetary urbanization, with the urban now spanning the globe and even extending into outer space (Brenner and Schmid 2015). In this new context, it is not exactly clear what "the city" or "the urban" is, but there is a hope that the fight for the right to the city can help transcend the differences among neoliberalism's victims and unite the city's inhabitants in a joint quest to recuperate space from the market and the state (Mayer 2009, 2013).

Although the literatures on urban social movements and the right to the city are different in tone and draw on different intellectual sources, they both focus attention on the city as a distinct grievance structure, mobilizing arena, and political target. In spite of the merits of these literatures, they have inadvertently disconnected research on cities and urban movements from research on broader social movements (e.g. immigrant, labor, feminist, gay rights). The assumption that the urban functions as a separate and separating space moved prospective scholars away from exploring how struggles that unfold in cities contribute to general and non-urban movements unfolding at regional, national, and transnational scales. Pickvance adds that "Castells's theorizing provided a lingua franca for them [urban movements scholars] which obviated the need to look more deeply into social movement theory" (2003: 105).

The urban-specific scholarship has provided important insights into contentious struggles *in* cities but has not furnished the theoretical tools needed to understand how cities are supportive environments for general social movements. If we were to follow Castells's lead on the gay movement, cities would be conceived as the graveyards of broader social movements because they turn activist attention away from broader issues like liberation and equality and toward the defense of "reactive utopias" for marginalized groups. The concept of planetary urbanization does move beyond the physical boundaries of the city. But in suggesting that everything is now urban, all struggles by default are now struggles about the rights to the city. The concept of the "urban" becomes too elastic and loses its analytical value for understanding how *some* cities play distinctive roles in facilitating the growth of social movements (e.g. immigrant rights, gay rights, labor) that are not specifically "urban social movements."

Our view is more closely in line with Doreen Massey's (1994, also see previous section) suggestive concept of a "global sense of place." She stresses that places like a street, neighborhood, or city are not structurally opposed and determined by spatial structures ("spaces of flows"). Instead they are intermeshed in and constitutive of broader spatial structures. We also draw inspiration from Castells's recent work (see especially Castells 2012; see also Castells 1996, 2009). While Castells's earlier work portrayed mobilizations within cities as local and isolated, in this recent work he emphasizes that activists create spaces within cities to connect within and beyond the city limits.

> Thus, the Occupy movement built *a new form of space*, a mixture of space of places, in a given territory, and space of flows, on the Internet. One could not function without the other; it is this hybrid spaces that characterized the movement. Places made possible face-to-face interaction, sharing the experience, the danger and difficulties as well as facing together the police and enduring together rain, cold and the loss of comfort in their daily lives. But social networks on the Internet allowed the experience to be communicated and amplified, bringing the entire world into the movement, and creating a permanent forum of solidarity, debate and strategic planning. (2012: 168–169, emphasis in original)

By joining together in online and urban settings, people overcome their fear, express outrage and hope, and become part of global mobilizations. This analytical perspective takes us away from the place–space dichotomy proposed by the earlier Castells (1983) and allows us to conceptualize positive-sum complementarities.

Cities as Relational Incubators

So far we have argued that several important steps have been made to understand the interplay between geography, cities, and social movements. Building upon these literatures, this section discusses four mechanisms – aggregating grievances, the formation of activist clusters, the making of connections between clusters, and the formation of hubs as propulsive units within an extensive social movement space – that help politicize urban inhabitants, agglomerate them, and link them to broader political struggles. Here we describe the mechanisms through which movements can emerge within places and extend across space, while the next section explains why cities often do not realize their potential for cultivating contention.

Aggregating grievances in everyday urban life

Grievances are key driving forces for any social movement. The "urban social movement" and "right to the city" literatures, in particular, have suggested that cities are grievance-generating spaces. Working-class and minority inhabitants face the unequal distribution of services (from schools to housing to transit) and rights, while neoliberal capitalism alienates them from the means of making cities of their own choosing. The city, in this sense, becomes the frontline space where inequality and injustice are experienced on a daily basis. When people see themselves as equal but are treated with disdain and derision by local authorities, employers, neighbors, and landlords, they may experience a profound feeling of "moral shock" that catalyzes their politicization (Jasper 1997). For instance, in her study of the political formation of the Third World Left in Los Angeles, Laura Pulido shows that most activists "shared stinging memories of racism that required them to analyze their place within the larger society at a tender age" (2006: 56). Exclusion and marginalization do not happen in the abstract but in people's everyday lives. Cities help aggregate individualized grievances because they are places where marginalized individuals amass in large numbers (Fischer 1975). Concentrated numbers matter because they provide the economies of scale needed to support overlapping organizations. The concentration of organizations in a place permits individuals to come out of their private spaces, connect to one another, form common imaginaries and solidarities, and begin to think of themselves as a group with distinctive cultural boundaries and political dispositions. While these groups may be minorities within national societies, in specific places they can develop a critical mass and see their plight as a public problem rather than a private issue.

When this happens, groups form "counterpublics." Counterpublics – that is, "parallel discursive arenas where members of subordinated social groups invent and circulate counterdiscourses to formulate oppositional interpretations of their identities, interests, and needs" (Fraser 1991: 68) – have distinct spatial underpinnings; they take on the form of counterspaces. For example, in the 1920s and 1930s, Harlem's extensive infrastructure of periodicals, theaters, and clubs allowed it to function as an incubator of political, cultural, and religious discourses that reconceived the position of African Americans within the United States (e.g. Eyerman 2001). Within these counterpublics aggrieved individuals come together with others like themselves, share their experiences, and begin to construct meaningful mobilizing frames. People share stories and ideas of what is wrong and unjust with the existing system and why it is in need of change (Polletta 2006). These counterpublics are also learning laboratories where aggrieved people learn the nuts and bolts of running campaigns. People learn how to identify political opportunities and targets, how to leverage their resources, and how to construct compelling discourses to express their political grievances to multiple publics. Within these arenas, newly politicized activists experience changes to their own political subjectivities, transforming demoralizing feelings of fear and anxiety into motivating feelings of anger and hope.

When groups experiencing aggravated forms of discrimination become politically active, their first targets tend to be those specific policies and practices that violate their rights. For example, early mobilizations of gay rights activists in the United States did not target federal laws and statutes but municipal laws that restricted their right to meet and assemble (Chauncey 1995; Armstrong 2002). Similarly, the civil rights movement was grounded in struggles against restrictive neighborhood covenants, segregation in local school districts, and racially segregated public spaces (McAdam 1982). The city in these ways is a place where people experience disenfranchisement, driving some to make it a frontline arena for battles for general rights. Thus, high concentrations of marginalized people in places provide a critical mass of recruits to sustain and power larger mobilizations. Once engaged, people target the specific institutions or people that are the immediate source of grievances.

Harnessing resources in specialized activist clusters

Social movement scholars have long maintained that grievances are important but so too is the availability of different activist resources (money, know-how, media access, legal knowledge, capacity to mobilize aggrieved people, etc.) and the organizations that possess them (Zald and McCarthy 1987). Larger cities have a higher likelihood of containing a greater diversity of resources and organizations with skills and capacities specialized in specific issue areas (legal advocacy, faith-based advocacy, media, education, service provision for new immigrants, etc.). Spatial proximity between like-minded organizations working in specialized issue areas (law, education, immigration, labor) provides many opportunities to collaborate with one another on a variety of projects. While the spatial concentration of local organizations sustains the involvement of individuals, well-developed ties ("strong ties") between organizations in the same issue area enhance their capacity to pool and deploy their resources in struggles and campaigns. For example, immigrant rights attorneys from different legal advocacy organizations may often come into regular contact with one another and develop working relations through different campaigns, enhancing their ability to harness resources, learn from one another, and provide specialized legal services. These spatially concentrated and well-networked organizations form what we call *activist clusters.*

Connecting specialized clusters

Strong ties between similar organizations (i.e. clusters) spur specialization and enhance the efficacy of activists. However, Mark Granovetter (1983) convincingly argues that strong ties alone can leave a strong community isolated from information and resource flows needed for success (see also Burt 1995). When an organization or specific activist cluster is well resourced, it can fulfill most campaign functions alone. It may have communication specialists, lawyers, money, and mobilization capacities of its own, which reduces the need to reach out to others for assistance and support. However, many organizations have limited resources and may be compelled to use the "bridges" provided by weak tie relations to request assistance and support for campaigns (Tarrow and McAdam 2005: 127). When organizations working on common issues meet repeatedly about their concerns, there is a greater likelihood that norms, trust, and interpretive frameworks will develop between them (Nicholls 2008). Norms provide representatives from diverse organizations with common expectations and morals (Coleman 1988: 106). Trust and sanctioning capacities (e.g. downgrading reputation and expulsion for free riders and cheats) provide confidence that one's contributions to a collective enterprise will be reciprocated by other members. Higher levels of certainty make it possible for network members to contribute valuable resources, energy, and time to collective and high-risk enterprises (Coleman 1988; Granovetter 1983; Portes 1998; Tilly 2005). Immigrant rights activists and squatters in

Paris during the 1980s developed such reciprocal exchanges and interdependencies, drawing squatters into battles for immigrant rights and immigrant rights activists into battles for the de-commodification of housing (Péchu 2004). Similarly, in Amsterdam in the 1970s and 1980s, squats became hotbeds of radical anti-fascism, environmentalism, anti-imperialism, and so on. Once bound by interdependencies and reciprocal ties, sanctioning capacities minimize the incentives of any single organization to violate agreements, obligations, and the goodwill of others (Coleman 1988; Portes and Sensenbrenner 1993). Networks serve as gossip chains that can spread information about defaulting organizations, sullying reputations and potentially denying the organization access to the rich array of resources offered by the network.

Urban activist hubs as central drivers of a social movement space

Social movements are intrinsically uneven: there are some people, places, and organizations that drive mobilizations and others that follow. Just as only a few cities become major hubs within the global financial system (Sassen 1991), only a few cities develop into activist hubs and become social movement superconductors. *Activist hubs* emerge when reliable exchange systems and common frames develop across activist clusters within cities, forming tangled webs that enable embedded activists to pool their different and specialized resources and deploy them for a variety of rights campaigns. Well-connected activists in hubs broker relations between local allies and geographically distant comrades (Tarrow and McAdam 2005; Borge-Holthoefer et al. 2011). The process of connecting distant struggles permits the diffusion of analyses, tactics, and repertoires across space. These extended networks function as conduits that enable a flow of practices, ideas, and resources between different urban hubs (Routledge 2003). These relations allow these cities to become major hubs of national and transnational activism. San Francisco and Mexico City in the 1960s, Paris and Amsterdam in the 1970s, and Los Angeles and Madrid today have assumed their status as the centers of broad social movements because of the complex and interdependent networks that developed between the diverse activists and organizations located in these cities. These urban-based networks allow activists to develop more sophisticated ideas and compelling political imaginaries, mobilize more resources and people in large and inspiring campaigns, and reinforce the feelings and passions of belonging to a "historical" movement and moment.

Activists across countries and the world are drawn to the hubs because of the excitement associated with them. They are also drawn to the greater chance of finding opportunities or employment in environments with a greater number and diversity of organizations. To borrow from Storper and Venables (2004), the complex networks and constant interactions between activists produce a "buzz" effect, which only heightens the sense that these are the "places to be." The spaces created by the movement become "magnetic" as they draw in activists from nearby and far away (Gerbaudo 2012). Funders, media, and politicians may prioritize activities and organizations unfolding in these areas. Following the logic of cumulative causation, the more these kinds of resources flow into these cities, the more powerful they become, and the more they attract activists, organizations, politicians, media, and funders.

The geographical concentration of resources reinforces the collective mobilizing powers of these activist places within the broader social movement space, enabling organizations within them to use their enhanced powers to bolster national-level campaigns. Leading organizations within them acquire the power to influence the agendas and strategies of the movement, develop and diffuse principal mobilization frames, engage in negotiations with influential politicians, and so on. By sponsoring campaigns in distant and less organized places, their organizational reach helps diffuse strategies, tactics, resources, and ideas to sites across space. When powerful organizations play this kind of role, they assume a major role in directly shaping the agenda of activists in a broader struggle. The enormous powers concentrated in these urban hubs enable activist organizations within them to assert their influence over the entire movement, which can generate tensions between central and peripheral activists.

In sum, this section has highlighted how the constitutive mechanisms of social movements rely on particular types of environments. We conceive of *social movement space* as the sum structure of the activist network. Sometimes a social movement space is dominated by a single dominant hub, which powers and drives much of the broader network. Other times a space may display multipolar features, with multiple cities playing complementary (and sometimes conflicting) roles in complex social movements. Still other spaces lack a strong hub altogether, characterized by the uneven distribution of wildcat mobilization and one-off altercations across a national territory with only tattered connections between them. One of the goals of this book is to map out and explain some differences across our principal cases.

Controlling the Grassroots

The previous sections outlined why cities provide conditions for movements to emerge, consolidate, diversify, and extend. However, our account is not deterministic. We do not claim that cities always and everywhere become hotbeds of movement activity; merely that they have the potential. There may be many reasons why this potential is not realized. The complex networking processes that make some cities into powerful activist hubs can be interrupted by countless factors, including intense competition between local activists, ignorance of complementary activities and skills, substantially different goals and strategies, general apathy, and so on. While recognizing this wide array of potential hindrances, we highlight the important role of governments in influencing and disrupting the formation of productive activist relations in cities. Exactly because the city is a generative space of mobilizations, it is also a frontline space where states (local and national) constantly create new governing techniques to produce and maintain social and political order.

Cities are frontline spaces for exerting political control

Liberal governments have an ambivalent position regarding the urban grassroots. On the one hand, they appreciate the value of a vibrant grassroots civil society because it contributes to creating trusting residents who take their civic responsibilities seriously (Putnam 1993, 2000). Authorities also appreciate the role that grassroots organizations play in extending their reach into poor and minority communities, helping them to incorporate these communities into mainstream politics and governance. The realization that top-down planning is often viewed as costly, illegitimate, and ineffective leads governments to embrace and support attempts of marginalized groups to address issues within their own communities. During the past 30 years, many different governments have initiated projects to encourage civic organizations and "partnerships" in different policy projects in economically deprived areas (Fung and Wright 2003; Nicholls 2006; Becher 2010; Silver et al. 2010). The aim of many of these projects has been to harness the energy of local civil society organizations to address social problems in deprived areas. In the early days, left-leaning governments embraced these "bottom-up" programs because they were viewed as democratic and non-bureaucratic vehicles to address social problems. In more recent times of neoliberal austerity, these measures have become the preferred means through which local and national governments address advanced marginality in large cities without having to engage in more costly redistributive measures.

On the other hand, granting civil society too much autonomy provides space and resources for alternative and oppositional cultures to take root and grow. When left unchecked, the urban grassroots can grow into a snarling tangle that can overwhelm the powers of local political elites and undermine their legitimacy. This can disrupt the existing order and place local authorities at the mercy of organizations or leaders deriving their power from below. In his study of the collapse of government in Chicago's South Side, Sudhir Vankatesh (1997) recounts how charismatic gang leaders helped fill the power void in these areas of the city. In other instances, weak government presence in fast-urbanizing working-class neighborhoods of Cairo provided a space for the Muslim Brotherhood to assume a prominent governing *and* political role in deprived areas (Munson 2001). Thus a central dilemma of urban government officials is in developing methods that allow them to harness the values of grassroots while at the same time containing the risks associated with an overly autonomous and oppositional civil society.

Techniques to control the grassroots

The scholarship on government control has drawn on different yet overlapping theoretical traditions. Weberian traditions stressed that states need to rationalize the sociopolitical process found in cities as a basis to effectively govern their societies, giving rise to bureaucratic controls to impose order on messy cities (Mann 1986, 1993; Le Galès 2002; Nicholls 2006). Marxists, by contrast, have suggested that government controls serve to facilitate social reproduction and block alliances between different fractions of the working class (Castells 1977, 1978; Katznelson 1981; Harvey 1985). Social movement scholars have argued that a process of co-optation is likely when radicals are subjected to repression and moderates are lured into governance structures with tangible rewards (like subsidies) and the promise of political influence (Kriesi et al. 1995; Mayer 2000; Pruijt 2003). In more recent years, the governmentality approach has extensively addressed how governments shape civil societies and govern through them. The key insight informing this approach is that the creation of an independent civil sphere outside of the government requires sustained effort and considerable skill. The governmentality approach examines the art of liberal governance or the ways in which the government facilitates and harnesses society's self-organization (cf. Foucault 1991; Cruikshank 1993, 1999;

Rose 1996, 1999; Raco 2003; Dean 2009). Our views are shaped by all of these theoretical traditions but we are partial to the governmentality perspective for one reason: whereas the other two traditions stress that governments achieve control by "caging" or "repressing" targeted populations, the governmentality perspective stresses that governments do this by trying to *produce* subjects that experience the world through the same categories, meaning systems, and practices of the state. The Foucauldian tradition stresses that targeted populations are not only caged into compliance, but they are made into subjects that help secure the social and political order.

In this book, we give the governmentality perspective a relational twist. While the governmentality perspective has extensively focused on the biopolitical rationalities and technologies through which governments act on populations (cf. Foucault 1976, 1991, 2009), we seek to bring out how governments intervene in the *connections* among governmental and civil players. While the conduct of individual organizations is a target of governments, the networks and relations between organizations are also subject to government intervention. Ordering, channeling, and limiting the relational exchanges between activist organizations enhance the likelihood that these organizations will conduct themselves in appropriate and orderly ways. Anticipating the charge that this amounts to conspiratorial thinking, we want to emphasize that governments are quite open about their intentions – they do not secretly mastermind plans to engineer civil society but instead develop elaborate policies and guidelines stipulating what kind of "partnerships" they seek to establish with and among civil society associations. Selecting reliable partners, ignoring questionable groups, driving wedges between good and bad actors, and stigmatizing deviants are *normal* parts of governing the trenches of urban civil societies.

Contrary to total institutions where complete surveillance by design is possible, the effective policing of the city's grassroots relies on the capacity of state administrators to enlist civil actors – such as associations, activists, and intellectuals – in their programs of government so that civil society becomes part of a web of governance rather than an uncontrollable and tangled site that nourishes multiple resistances. Policing is successful when civil society serves as an extension of the state by diffusing its categories and supplementing its actions. This occurs when civil associations forgo their roles as representatives of marginalized constituencies and become agents that police "problem groups" targeted by the state (immigrants, youths, homeless, etc.). One sign that this is happening is that actors put less effort into organizing constituents and focus instead on managing concrete social problems in cooperation with state administrators. Examples include resident groups who shift their attention from fighting gentrification to consulting with governments on how to manage citizen participation; development agencies ceasing resistance against structural dependency to help companies employ impoverished workers; anti-racist organizations which no longer protest structural discrimination but instead counsel the police on how to treat minorities. Such transitions are often brought about by incorporating organizations into governance networks; co-opting through partnerships has been a common method to incorporate civil associations into the state's policing strategies (see Mayer 2000; Sites 2007). Co-optation is typically an ambivalent process: organizations gain power as they are recognized as legitimate voices and allowed access to resources but they can only wield such power within parameters set by the government. As the material basis of civil associations becomes tied to government funding, the margins to argue outside the boundaries of acceptable dissent are significantly reduced (Mitchell and Staeheli 2005).

Successful governance (viewed from the government's perspective) shapes how organizations interpret, conceptualize, and articulate grievances. These organizations then help transmit the categories of the state to marginalized peoples, encouraging people to employ these categories as normal and natural ways to frame their political action. Certain "good" associations therefore come to dominate urban civil society, with radicals facing stigmatization and complete isolation. The result is what Michael McQuarrie (2013) called a "civic monoculture," in which a seemingly vibrant and diverse civil society comes to be dominated by singular rationalities, norms, and methods for addressing problems. This stifles the possibilities for innovation and contention within these urban spaces. Such a configuration enables the government to capture the benefits of civil society while at the same time containing the risks and uncertainties associated with it.

We refer to these attempts to incorporate potentially risky populations through civil society as *political integration*. Note that we do not use the term "integration" as a synonym for assimilation or acculturation. Instead, we view integration as a control strategy that aims to incorporate targeted populations into governance structures (Uitermark 2014). This strategy stands in contrast to "banishment," which conceives outsiders as a threat and develops measures to physically exclude the group from the established population. Our empirical chapters identify different ways in which governments aim to achieve political integration. Sometimes governments try to enlist brokers in civil society to represent ethnic groups (especially in Amsterdam in the 1980s); at other times governments prefer a territorially based strategy that recruits key neighborhood figures into governance structures. Regardless of the qualitative differences between these strategies, governments in pursuit of political integration aim to reach into the grassroots in order to enlist non-state actions in the governance of populations and places.

The uneven reach of the government

The propensity of civil actors to develop relations with one another and form challenging counterpublics and activist hubs decreases as their dependence on the state increases. Some access to state resources (from money to legitimacy) may bolster the fortunes of organizations but too much may result in subordination to government officials. Incorporation into governance structures propels civil actors to focus on specific territories where they form partnerships based on territorial proximity and functional policy domains instead of ideological affinity. As civil associations increasingly serve as the eyes, ears, and hands of the state, their horizons are truncated. Having committed to showing their effectiveness within a specific territory for a specific target group, they effectively become outposts of the state within urban civil society, focusing their attention on managing social problems in minority populations rather than denouncing wrongs, contesting the order, and projecting radical alternatives.

Methods of governmental control can be extremely pervasive, but they are incomplete and temporary. Government policies and institutions need the continual investment of resources and authority. These expenditures may seem to be less of a priority by governments facing budgetary constraints or embracing a hard rollback form of neoliberalism (Peck and Tickell 2002). Whereas a local government may have had the resources and capacity to extend its reach deep into the urban grassroots during one period, changes in governing priorities may impose limits on what it can do in a succeeding period. This, we argue, reflects the case of Los Angeles, where severe cuts in revenue during the 1980s limited its capacity to incorporate new clusters of challengers emerging beyond its reach. Other governments may have sufficient resources to reach out to targeted populations in particular territories but the methods and techniques employed may not be flexible and adaptive enough to address and incorporate new risks. This can result in the deployment of massive institutions in designated areas but large pockets of political autonomy that enable new forms of resistance to fester, evolve, and grow into system-threatening struggles. Thus, control through integration has indeed been effective in producing politically complacent urban civil societies but these controls are by no means total. Their partial collapse and inflexibility in the face of new threats leave open spaces for creative, disruptive, and innovative political projects to take root and grow.

Our thinking on government control is informed by the Foucauldian tradition but we choose to embrace that part of the tradition that stresses the cracks, disruptions, and unevenness of governing projects. States embrace certain rationalities to think about the populations and develop technologies to deal with the risks associated with these populations and methods to intervene through banishment and discipline, reaching deep into the grassroots. However, these governing strategies generate resistances and are inherently incomplete. There are many factors that limit the reach of government and make its grasp over society uneven, contingent, and open to constant disputes and negotiations. It is precisely the unevenness of government controls that precipitates differences in outcomes between countries.

Conclusions

In this chapter, we explored the literature in a search for answers to the questions of how and why movements matter to cities and, especially, how cities matter to movements. We provided a number of reasons why cities can offer a particularly conducive environment for the creation of movement networks, tracing the development of movements from the generation of individual grievances to the formation of urban hubs spearheading larger social movements. We argued that an analysis of urban space is crucial for understanding social movements but we did not claim that cities are the only spaces where strong movements develop, nor did we claim that all cities spawn strong movements. Movements are the contingent outcome of numerous and complex networking processes, which means that their presence or absence cannot be accounted for by deterministic theories pinpointing definite causes or factors.

Rather than providing an explanation for movements, we sketched a theoretical framework that can help to examine the rise and decline of movements in particular cases. We should direct our attention to the making or breaking of networks among (potential) challengers to explain the strong differences of movement strength through time and between cases. The following chapters chart how immigrants contested government policies by entering into relations with others in their urban environments. In line with the theoretical framework developed here, we examine how these immigrants established relations among each other and articulated their grievances, formed activist clusters, established relations to others, and ultimately spawned highly uneven social movement spaces. We use the case of immigrant rights activism as a prism. By examining how this specific type of activism changed, we hope to shed light on the more general mechanisms underlying the changing geographies of social movements.

Part I

The Birth of Immigrant Rights Activism

The 1970s marked the birth of mobilizations for the fundamental rights of working-class immigrants who had come to societies of the global North in search of employment. Immigrants had become part of these societies but most nationals considered them to be "foreign aliens" or "guest workers" to whom constitutional protections simply did not apply. Not only were immigrants not seen as rights-bearing human beings, government measures in the postwar period had been devised to render the population invisible; they were contained within the lowest echelons of the labor market; they were housed in secluded hostels; they were made temporary, mobile, and deportable; and they were blocked from access to the public sphere. Governments were not pursuing a biopolitics of making a risky population knowable in order to integrate and normalize it. This was a biopolitics of invisibility in which the technologies of the state were used to separate immigrants from the national population while simultaneously making their labor available for exploitative use. Immigrants were subjects outside the realm of political possibility (Ngai 2004; Raissiguier 2010). Although immigrants engaged in small acts of resistance or struggled to attain some protections through pre-existing organizations (e.g. labor, religious organizations, minority associations), few, if any, of these actions asserted that basic rights and protections should be extended to "foreign aliens."

This changed in the mid-1970s. At this time, the rights of immigrants became a legitimate subject of debate, and just as important, immigrants

Cities and Social Movements: Immigrant Rights Activism in the United States, France, and the Netherlands, 1970–2015, First Edition. Walter J. Nicholls and Justus Uitermark.
© 2017 John Wiley & Sons, Ltd. Published 2017 by John Wiley & Sons, Ltd.

themselves arose as people who were asserting their own rights in the public sphere. Immigrants asserted themselves into the public sphere as a subject of politics, unleashing fierce and ongoing debates over what kinds of rights should be accorded to this population. Whether or not one was favorable to the rights of immigrants, the mobilizations of the 1970s and 1980s permanently disrupted the prevailing assumption that immigrants were beings without rights, outside of the public sphere.

The chapters of Part I highlight the factors that contributed to this remarkable turn of events in the United States, France, and the Netherlands. While the proliferation of "new social movements" facilitated immigrant rights activism, these rights only became a big political issue as governments across the global North began to introduce restrictions on immigration flows and enact increasingly repressive measures. The rapid accumulation of these measures during the 1970s rendered tens of thousands of people "illegal" and "criminal" almost overnight. The process that illegalized the population also planted the first seeds of resistance and struggle by immigrants and their supportive allies. Rather than forcing this population out of national territories, government attempts at banishment made immigrants and their rights into a subject of politics, forever transforming national citizenship in the countries of the global North.

Politicizing the rights of immigrants happened in an uneven activist geography with a handful of urban centers and many peripheries. Cities like Los Angeles, Paris, and Amsterdam were particularly propitious environments for the growth of these kinds of mobilizations. In addition to being major gateway cities with large concentrations of immigrants, they were cities with diverse activist clusters that were well prepared to support these struggles. In spite of the huge differences between these three cities, the concentration of interconnected and entangled activist clusters allowed them to foster large and contentious responses to repressive government measures of the 1970s. The density, diversity, and connectedness of activists and organizations in these cities, in other words, provided contexts of mobilization that facilitated immigrant rights activism and made these cities into hubs of increasingly national immigrant rights movements. Part I therefore aims to identify the birth of the immigrant rights activism in the three countries and analyze how Los Angeles, Paris, and Amsterdam came to play major roles in incubating and supporting rights activism.

3

Making Space for Immigrant Rights Activism in Los Angeles

During the late 1960s and early 1970s, immigrants from Latin America faced worsening legal conditions in the United States. The Hart–Cellar Act of 1965 dismantled restrictions on many immigrants but it also introduced new restrictions that negatively affected people from Latin America. Mexicans constituted the largest numbers of immigrants in the country but they also faced the most important restrictions (De Genova 2005). This rendered tens of thousands of immigrants in the country "illegal" over the course of the 1970s. This status, coupled with growing border restrictions, contributed to ending circular and temporary migration and favoring permanent migration and settlement in large urban centers. In response to the rapid growth of undocumented immigrant populations in major gateway cities like Los Angeles, local and national governments introduced new measures to detect, detain, and deport people from their new communities.

The period in which tens of thousands of Latin Americans were being made "illegal" and criminal coincided with a renaissance of Latino political activism in eastern Los Angeles. The area housed a high concentration of diverse activist and service organizations, ranging from moderate Mexican American political organizations to Leninist Chicanos. Their concentration in this dense area of sprawling Los Angeles made the eastside into a buzzing center of new social justice politics, with different actors, ideas, slogans, and practices circulating within it. The diversity and complex connections between people and

Cities and Social Movements: Immigrant Rights Activism in the United States, France, and the Netherlands, 1970–2015, First Edition. Walter J. Nicholls and Justus Uitermark.
© 2017 John Wiley & Sons, Ltd. Published 2017 by John Wiley & Sons, Ltd.

organizations transformed East Los Angeles into one of the most vibrant political spaces in the country. Although there were other Latino activist hubs in California (primarily San Francisco) and the southwest (San Antonio and Denver), the density and diversity of Latino activism in Los Angeles made the city stand out as a major arena of political innovation and power (Valle and Torres 2000; Pulido 2006).

What is striking is that the issue of undocumented immigrants remained peripheral in the early1970s. Veteran activists focused much of their attention on political and economic opportunities for *documented* immigrants and their descendants. At best, undocumented immigrants were not a central concern. At worst, they were viewed as a threat to more rooted working-class Latinos (documented) and an impediment to their upward mobility. Rather than mobilize to expand the rights of undocumented immigrants, many Latino leaders argued that "wet-backs" (a derogatory term frequently used during the time) needed to be blocked at the border and deported from the country.

The indifference and antipathy displayed toward undocumented immigrants changed in the mid-1970s. This resulted from the efforts of long-time immigrant rights advocates like Bert Corona, and his good relations with a cluster of radical Chicano activists. They argued that established Latinos should stand in solidarity with new, undocumented immigrants in the face of increased government repression. Though these activists initially were on the periphery of Los Angeles's activist milieu, they eventually gained broader support for their views. They planted a pivotal seed of innovation and that seed grew into a major mobilization issue for Latino activists.

Los Angeles would go on to play a major role in the national immigrant rights movement but this was by no means automatic. The high concentration of *illegalized* immigrants and the high density of Latino activism were certainly important conditions that made this outcome possible. However, in and of themselves, these conditions were not enough. The slow and painstaking work of innovative activists played an essential role in framing the importance of this issue for the broader Latino population, and building bridges and relations between clusters of Latino activists. This early brokering work contributed to making the issue salient among established activists.

This chapter examines how Los Angeles developed into a nascent hub of immigrant rights activism. It provides an overview of government restrictions enacted during the postwar period. Following this, it describes the emergence of key activist clusters in Los Angeles and their connections to one another. The chapter then examines how the issue moved from a sideline concern of a small coterie of activists into a central issue of the Latino eastside. As the issue gained importance, leading activists were better able to draw upon supportive networks and fight off state and national-level efforts to enact more restrictions against this population.

Government Restrictions on Immigrants and Rights

Postwar migration flows to the United States from Mexico were largely governed through the Bracero Program, which ran from 1942 to 1964. The program provided immigrant workers from Mexico with temporary and renewable visas. During the 1950s, approximately 437,000 Mexicans worked under Bracero Program contracts, opening paths for thousands of other migrants without legal authorization to follow in their tracks (Gutiérrez 1991: 7). While the government introduced programs like "Operation Wetback" to curtail unauthorized migration, weak border restrictions and weak employer sanctions resulted in comparatively open migration flows (De Genova 2005).

The Bracero Program was originally devised as an emergency measure to meet labor shortages in agriculture but it became permanent as large employers found it useful for securing an army of workers with limited rights (Calavita 1992). Bracero contracts imposed sharp restrictions on the rights of immigrant workers. Dependence of workers on employers for visas also presented strong disincentives to participate in union activities. The Bracero Program channeled many new immigrants away from large urban centers and into agricultural regions like the Central and Imperial Valleys of California. Just as important, the new migrant labor force was temporary and circular (Massey et al. 2003). This favored male migration and transient populations more than family migration that would permanently settle in the country.

The Bracero Program was phased out in the mid-1960s and followed by the Hart–Cellar Act of 1965. This law introduced quantitative restrictions on immigration from Latin America, which adversely affected Mexican immigrants (Massey et al. 2003; De Genova 2005; Chavez 2008). Hart–Cellar introduced a method to grant legal residency visas on the basis of a quota system, with exemptions for family reunification, asylum seekers, and immigrants with specialized skills. The visa quota for the Western Hemisphere was originally set at 120,000 per year and the quota for non-exempt visas for Mexico was eventually set at 18,200 (De Genova 2005: 173). Mexico was the most important sending country and migration flows far exceeded the quota (De Genova 2005: 170). As hundreds of thousands of immigrants had already become integrated into US labor markets over the previous 20 years, the new visa restrictions transformed many of these people into "illegal aliens."

The border closure also raised the risks and costs of international migration, which in turn encouraged many migrants who depended on work in the United States to permanently settle without authorization (Massey et al. 2003; Massey and Pren 2012). The closure of the southern border did not lead to the curtailment of Mexican migrants but instead to a decline in circular, transient, and male migration, and an increase in the permanent settlement of unauthorized immigrants in cities. As male immigrants settled permanently, their families started to join them. This spurred the growth of the undocumented immigrant population, reaching nearly one million by 1977 (Gutiérrez 1991: 16).

It was at this moment that the issue of unauthorized immigration became prominent in public debate. Prior to this period, there were few, if any, media depictions of new immigrants as a threat to the national population (Chavez 2008; Massey and Pren 2012). The rapid growth of permanently settled, undocumented immigrants began to make this an issue that concerned broad swaths of the population. The recession of the early 1970s spurred many Americans to consider new immigrants as a particular threat to their prosperity. Media depictions emerged that framed immigrants, especially unauthorized ones, as a major threat to the country (Chavez 2008; Massey and Pren 2012). Chavez notes that the Immigration and Naturalization Service's (INS) commissioner in 1974 played a pivotal role in lighting the fuse of the "threat" discourse when he announced that up to 10 million "illegal aliens" were "flooding" the border at the time (Chavez 2008: 26). While this announcement was based on sheer speculation, it helped unleash a flurry of reports on "illegal aliens" "invading" and "flooding the country" in reputable press outlets like *Time* magazine and *U.S. News & World Report*, among others (ibid.: 26–28).

The concern with immigration by larger parts of the public prompted the federal and state government to respond. The US Congress paid little attention to the issue of undocumented immigration before 1965. Congress began to investigate undocumented immigrants as an object of public policy in 1969, one year after the Hart–Cellar Act was implemented (Genova 2005: 170). In 1972 and 1973, the INS introduced systematic "neighborhood sweeps" in which suspected undocumented immigrants were apprehended and deported (Gutiérrez 1991; Acuña 1996). While the sweeps were initiated and led by the federal INS, they inspired local law enforcement agencies to increase their own scrutiny of immigrant communities. The high level of media attention associated with these repressive actions helped spread fear and uncertainty in immigrant communities.

The state of California also introduced new anti-immigrant legislation. In 1970, Assembly member Dixon Arnett introduced a bill "to impose criminal sanctions against employers who 'knowingly' hired an individual 'not entitled to lawful residence in the United States'" (Gutiérrez 1991: 17). The bill was important for two reasons. First, it served as a prelude to state- and local-level legislative activism on immigration issues. While states and localities would become active on the immigration front in later decades, this was one of the first state measures in the post-1965 era to address the issue of immigration. Second, it outlined the use of strict "employer sanctions" in the fight against undocumented immigrants. Employer sanctions had in the past been floated as an option, but the Dixon–Arnett bill provided the language and methods to translate this idea into a concrete and enforceable policy. The California bill failed to pass, but it served as a policy template for federal legislation in subsequent years.

Thus, the growing fear and anxieties concerning immigrants prompted the government to initiate measures to restrict unauthorized immigrants in the country (Massey et al. 2003). This escalation of government powers and instruments targeted immigrants in their daily lives. Neighborhood and workplace sweeps became a normal part of the undocumented immigrant's urban landscape. Cities were transformed into treacherous landscapes, with any wrong or unlucky move prompting deportations and separations from families and community life.

The Activist Landscape in Los Angeles's Eastside

Local and federal officials began to invest more time and energy policing unauthorized immigrants from Latin America at a time when Los Angeles's eastside emerged as a thriving hub of Latino activism. Eastside activists and advocates focused on issues concerning older immigrant populations and did not invest extensive resources to support recent and undocumented Latinos. The eastside activist hub was made up of three clusters with distinctive yet overlapping histories: established Latino advocacy groups, labor activists associated with the United Farm Workers, and Chicano student groups and organizations. While the issues, repertoires, and histories of these clusters varied, they also had complex and interdependent relations that stretched out over many years.

Most Mexican American and Latino advocacy organizations in the early 1960s were quite moderate. They fought to advance the social and political mobility of Latinos in the United States (Gutiérrez 1991). The dominant organizations of the time were the Mexican American Political Association (MAPA), League of United Latin American Citizens (LULAC), and the Community Service Organization (CSO). These organizations were focused on providing established Latino residents the opportunities to enhance their economic and political power in the country (Muñoz 1989). The organizations were national in scope, but they were grounded in local branches and rooted in California's main urban centers of Los Angeles and San Francisco. MAPA, for example, was created in the early 1960s by Los Angeles-based activists disappointed with the Democratic Party's failure to provide opportunities to Mexican American politicians. Edward Roybal, Bert Corona, and Sal Castro, among others, sought to create a thriving organization by working with community organizations, political clubs, and other organizations in the Latino eastside. Allied organizations like LULAC[1] worked closely with church, civic, and social service organizations. LULAC members created their own clubs ("junior LULAC") and worked closely with other community organizations (Catholic Youth Organization, church programs, and city-sponsored youth organizations) to recruit youths into their network (Muñoz 1989: 52). Working parallel to and often in concert with LULAC, MAPA created student associations at area universities like California State University, Los Angeles and the University of California, Los Angeles. These overlapping organizations created an integrated political and civic infrastructure in this area of the city, providing multiple points to recruit and socialize local youths.

Alongside this advocacy infrastructure, many Mexican American leaders of the postwar period had direct and indirect ties to unions. Several Mexican American leaders (Bert Corona, Ernesto Galarza, etc.) had been politicized through their work with the left-wing Congress of Industrial Organization (CIO) in the prewar period. Their organizing work in the factories and fields continued into the 1940s and 1950s. The strong labor tradition among some Mexican American leaders helped influence a new generation of labor activists in the 1960s. Cesar Chavez emerged from this tradition and helped create the National Farm Workers Association in 1965, which was renamed the United Farm Workers (UFW) several years later. In addition to its other campaigns, the organization lent its support to striking grape pickers in northern California. The theater activist Luis Valdez joined the grape pickers' campaign and assumed a leading role in framing the union's messaging. His manifesto for the campaign ("Plan Delano") asserted that the UFW was struggling "for social justice" and was led by "the sons of the Mexican Revolution" (Muñoz 1989: 54). The UFW campaign and Cesar Chavez quickly gained prominence and captured the political imagination of thousands of Latino youths in rural areas and large urban centers. It resuscitated the labor-centered strategies of Latino activism and stressed the importance of engaging in high-profile and combative struggles. MAPA and LULAC continued to be the most influential advocacy organizations in Latino civil society but UFW allies and supporters in Los Angeles assumed increased prominence alongside them.

In addition to Latino advocacy and labor clusters, second-generation youths mobilized to demand recognition and rights for their specific group. In 1967 Rodolfo "Corky" Gonzalez, a long-time activist in Denver, Colorado, broke his affiliation with moderate MAPA and created a new organization: Crusade for Justice. Gonzalez played a critical role by introducing cultural nationalism and identity politics into Latino activist networks. This set up the foundations of the modern "Chicano" movement. His influential poem-essay, *I am Joaquin,* "captured both the agony and the jubilation permeating the identity crisis faced by Mexican American youth in the process of assimilation" (Muñoz 1989: 61). Mexican American youths were developing a new language to express pride in their ethnicity and identity, and this emergent identity became the basis for political mobilizations. Sal Castro, another disaffected member of MAPA and a Los Angeles high school teacher, helped organize the first large-scale student walkout from his school in East Los Angeles. Castro worked with local activists to coordinate the protest. This included disillusioned members of MAPA; student associations from UCLA and California State University, Los Angeles; members of the newly established Brown Berets; and members of local community organizations. Work on this and subsequent actions forged the backbone of an emerging cluster of Chicano activists in the city. They rejected the assimilationist aspirations of older Mexican American organizations and embraced the radical politics of identity reflected in slogans like "Viva la Raza" and "Chicano Power." The student walkout thrust the budding Chicano movement onto the national stage and Los Angeles became one of its hubs.

In response to the student walkout, the district attorney of Los Angeles indicted its leaders (the "LA Thirteen") for subversive communist activities. This move triggered countless solidarity demonstrations in the city and across the country. Rather than stifling the Chicano movement, efforts to repress it contributed to its fast growth and diffusion. These mobilizations were followed by national-level conferences in Santa Barbara and Denver to consolidate the Chicano movement organizationally and discursively. While the conferences were national in scope, the Los Angeles and San Francisco delegations exercised the most influence in setting the agenda and shaping the outcome (Muñoz 1989). As fast as the movement began to consolidate itself, splinter groups emerged on the left of the Chicano movement, with radicals arguing that the movement needed to embrace a more Marxist and anti-imperialist line (Pulido 2006).

By 1970, Los Angeles's Latino eastside had become a dense space of intermeshed political ideas, networks, and traditions. The older advocacy organizations like MAPA and LULAC continued to exercise important influence in this part of the city. UFW support groups also became rooted in the area, alongside a flourishing number of Chicano organizations and groups. It must be stressed that while these clusters were distinct from one another, there were thick and complicated networks that tied them together. Many of the Chicano leaders had been brought up through MAPA and LULAC's student organizations. MAPA also provided important levels of support to the UFW and assisted with its urban-centered campaigns. In addition to these intermeshed networks, the more radical activists of Los Angeles's eastside reached out to other Los Angeles radicals, including the Black Panther Party, Students for a Democratic Society, and communist organizations like the Progressive Labor Party, the Socialist Workers Party, and the Revolutionary Communist Party (Pulido 2006). Young activists navigating the circuits of this counterpublic space would have encountered community efforts to support the UFW, campus meetings held by Chicano nationalists, electoral campaigns organized by MAPA and LULAC, and evening lectures sponsored by Leninist Chicanos. Certain people became dedicated members of a single organization but most crisscrossed multiple organizations and activist spaces, holding multiple affiliations and ideologies simultaneously. Floating activists helped broker ties between many different organizations in this milieu and facilitated the circulation of different strategies, ideas, and cultures between them. This was not a political space that lent itself to coherency and ideological closure. Rather, it was a space of radical pluralism, one that facilitated experimentation and innovation in how the struggle for Latino rights should be fought.

While the eastside became the epicenter of a robust Latino activist infrastructure, the problems facing recent Latino immigrants (lack of authorization, repression, the rollback of basic rights and privileges) barely surfaced on political radars. The focus centered on the politics of settled Latinos rather than the politics of newly arrived Latinos.

Organizing for Immigrant Rights in Los Angeles

In the mid-1960s, many Mexican American leaders believed that recent and undocumented immigrants were *threats* to established Mexican and Mexican American communities. Leading voices argued that sealing the borders and keeping new immigrants out would improve the power of established immigrant communities to negotiate with employers. Others believed that the constant flow of new immigrants slowed processes of cultural assimilation for older immigrant communities. Advocacy organizations like LULAC and several Mexican American intellectuals came out strongly against new immigrants during the 1950s and 1960s. As early as 1949, the prominent University of Texas professor George Sánchez expressed the preoccupation with new and undocumented migrants: "More often than not each wetback displaces an entire resident family and causes those displaced persons to become migrants [and] inhabitants of the slums" (Sánchez, in Gutiérrez 1991: 8). In this context, the struggle of many Mexican American leaders was to improve the economic, political, and cultural conditions of established and legal populations *and* combat the flow of unauthorized immigrants.

The leadership of the United Farm Workers reflected the consensus of this generation. Employers often used newly arrived immigrants as strikebreakers to undermine UFW organizing efforts. If the union was going to expand the rights of established and "legal" immigrant workers, the UFW had to mobilize against recent "wetbacks" and "illegals." These concerns made the UFW one of the most vociferous critics of immigration and a strong advocate of employer sanctions and other enforcement measures. The UFW mobilized in support of California's Dixon–Arnett bill and other federal-level enforcement measures. Thus, some of the biggest advocates *against* immigration during the 1950s and 1960s were not white nativists but Mexican American intellectuals, civic organizations, and unionists who viewed new immigrants as a threat to their political power and economic status. The advancement of established Latino communities could only be achieved by barring new immigrants from entering the United States.

While older Mexican American activists spoke out against undocumented immigrants, most young Chicano activists ignored the conditions facing recent, unauthorized immigrants. They were not particularly concerned about new restrictions and the rollback of rights facing this population. Their struggle was about creating an empowered identity and their primary targets were educational institutions (high school and university). One prominent Chicano activist from the era remembers:

> The demands of the Chicano student movement were relative to educational issues. There certainly would always be students who were not native-born, so they would be considered immigrants in the sense that they weren't native-born ... But predominantly student demands were education-oriented, access to Chicano Studies Department programs, higher education financial aid, bilingual education, study of history, recognition of national heroes. (*La Hermandad Mexicana Nacional,* personal interview)

Chicano activists also believed that their activism should be directed at improving their neighborhoods, fighting discrimination, and combating police brutality. Although some sympathized with the plight of recent immigrants (documented and undocumented), most viewed them as a population apart from their own.

Although the largest organizations had not taken up the issue of new and undocumented immigrants (Garcia 2002), some took a different line. Bert Corona (former labor organizer and president of MAPA) and Soledad Alatorre created a branch of *La Hermandad Mexicana Nacional* in Los Angeles and subsequently formed the Center for Autonomous Social Action[2] (CASA) (Corona 1994; Garcia 2002; Pulido 2006). Corona was an important supporter of the UFW in the late 1960s but disagreed with the union's position on immigration. He and Soledad Alatorre believed that the best way to build up labor unions was by fighting for the rights of undocumented immigrant workers. They designed *Hermandad* and CASA as mutual aid organizations that provided legal and educational services to undocumented immigrants in Los Angeles. These were the first organizations in the city to advocate for this population. Corona resigned from MAPA to take on these new responsibilities and he used his good connections to this and other organizations for support.

Corona was able to recruit Chicano activists because of his ties to key leaders in that struggle. He established contacts with radical Chicanos through his involvement in various local campaigns. He took an active role in a defense committee to support three East Los Angeles youth activists who had been charged with shooting a Los Angeles police officer (*Los Tres* Committee). Through his work on this support committee, he connected to several leaders in the Chicano activist cluster, including the hugely influential Rodriguez family. This family had been involved in the campaign to create a Chicano Studies department at California State University, Los Angeles; helped form the Brown Berets; and organized the organization *Casa Carnalísimo* (House of Brotherhood). The family had established its credentials as a leading voice of Los Angeles's flowering activist scene.

Corona developed a friendship with the family and encouraged them to volunteer at CASA. Many of their friends and comrades followed suit, helping establish a durable bridge between CASA and Chicano activists in the city. Early Chicano volunteers at CASA went back to their own student and political organizations and introduced the issue of immigrant rights into their organizations. The issue of immigrant rights was diffused in the activist milieu through interpersonal networks. One early volunteer remembered that "A number of us in different universities began injecting it into the politics of the student movement, the broader issues of immigration, separation of families, the demands for visas, the rights of workers – how that related to the student movement: the need for student solidarity and student-worker alliances, and back to the question of identity" (*Hermandad Mexicana*, personal interview). As this issue gained legitimacy and prominence across Chicano activist networks in East Los Angeles, more youths came out and volunteered at CASA and *Hermandad.* The Rodriguez family and their friends began to see CASA as a vehicle to build a revolutionary movement. They argued that CASA should use its momentum to move the Latino left away from the "bourgeois reformism" of MAPA *and* the cultural nationalism of Chicanos. CASA was in a strategic position to steer the movement in a Marxist and anti-imperialist direction (Pulido 2006).

By 1972, *Hermandad* and CASA had several thousand members and were helping approximately 60,000 immigrant clients (Corona 1994). It opened branch offices across the Los Angeles region and began to open offices across the United States. The principal source of revenue was derived from a low membership fee and low fees for services. Just as important, activist volunteers staffed most of the positions in local offices. Many of these volunteers were youths belonging to Chicano student and community organizations in Los Angeles. "We needed and wanted the participation of our members," Corona remembers in his biography. He goes on to stress the centrality of volunteers in providing essential resources and services: "We needed voluntary services in maintaining our headquarters, gathering food and clothing, and in our public demonstrations against the INS and the Border Patrol. We were an extended family, which looked after the needs of all its members. All of this kind of assistance we got from our members" (Corona 1994: 294).

Brokering new ties did not simply result in introducing the issue of immigrant rights to Chicano groups it also involved efforts to reveal similarities between the struggles of Chicanos and undocumented immigrants. As CASA became more radical, it embraced a no-border position. Drawing a contrast to the nationalist ideology of many Chicanos, CASA activists articulated a position that they were all Latinos, and that the differences between recent and established immigrant communities were the result of categories imposed on them by the imperialist state (Pulido 2006). Rather than embrace ideologies that reinforced these false differences between Latinos, CASA argued that Latinos needed to dismantle the real and imagined borders that divided their population. Their national newspaper, *Sin Fronteras* (Without Borders), became a major vehicle for articulating their no-borders position. It defined its primary constituents as all "Mexicans in the United States," including long-term citizens *and* recent immigrants (undocumented and documented). "From CASA's point of view, the historical and ongoing exploitation of both Mexican-American and Mexican immigrant workers in the United States made them virtually indistinguishable" (Gutiérrez 1991: 17).

The brokering work of Corona, Alatorre, and the Chicano activists of CASA helped shift opinion in the broader activist milieu. Rather than framing recently arrived and undocumented immigrants as a threat to established Latino communities, they helped reveal the similarities between the groups and demonstrate how their struggles were connected and depended on one another. One Los Angeles youth activist in 1972 argued in the Chicano newspaper *Regeneración,* "'It is claimed that illegals cause high unemployment of residents; that they oppose the formation of unions; that they drain residents' incomes by adding to welfare costs; that they add to the tax burden by needing special programs. These are fake claims. [I]llegals ... do not create unemployment of Chicanos, employers desiring to pay the lowest possible wages do'" (cited in Gutiérrez 1991: 19).

The moderate Mexican American organizations like LULAC and MAPA shifted their positions as well. They were responding to pressures from those aligned to undocumented immigrants (CASA, *Hermandad,* certain Chicanos) *and* the realization that anti-immigrant measures (neighborhood sweeps, proposed employer sanctions, etc.) were negatively affecting established Latino communities (Gutiérrez 1991). Latino advocates began to push back on these measures out of concern for their adverse discriminatory effects on all Latinos in the United States, not just undocumented immigrants. The new consensus finally forced the leadership of the UFW to change its position as well. Chicanos and the moderate organizations in the mid-1970s vigorously lobbied the UFW against its past support of employer sanctions and repressive enforcement measures. Responding to this pressure, Cesar Chavez eventually announced in 1974 that the best way to address the issue of strikebreaking immigrants was to demand full legalization and recruit newly authorized immigrants into the labor movement:

> The illegal aliens are doubly exploited, first because they are farm workers, and second because they are powerless to defend their own interests. But if there were no illegals being used to break our strikes, we could win those strikes overnight and then be in a position to improve the living and working conditions of all farm workers. (Chavez, in Gutiérrez 1995: 199)

The UFW still sought to eliminate "illegals," but rather than do this through repression and banishment, they now believed that this should be done through a general amnesty. Chavez argued that the union's position was to support an "amnesty for illegal aliens and support their efforts to obtain legal documents and equal rights, including the right of collective bargaining" (Chavez, in Gutiérrez 1991: 24). For the UFW leadership, the rights of undocumented immigrants had now become a central issue to fight for rather than deny and suppress.

By the mid-1970s, the promotion and protection of immigrant rights became a cause for a unified political struggle. Initially only radicals had supported the idea that immigrants were rights-bearing subjects meriting support. But the position of the radicals spread through the eastside's relational circuits, eventually becoming a consensual position across its three main clusters. Overcoming divisions and seeking equality for all were viewed as a more effective strategy for improving the economic and political standing of the Latino community than insisting on the enforcement of immigration restrictions. By tapping into local activist networks, Corona and his Chicano allies changed perspectives on the issue of undocumented immigration and mobilized local resources for local, state, and national campaigns.

One of the first campaigns was directed against the Immigration and Naturalization Service's neighborhood sweeps. The INS raided workplaces, shopping centers, apartment complexes, and bus stops to detain and deport immigrants, oftentimes without due process. *Hermandad* and CASA provided immigrants with education and training concerning their basic rights when facing INS agents. "They [immigrants] were not aware that they had rights under the Bill of Rights of the U.S. Constitution. These rights offered protection from arrests without warrants and from arrests for merely looking like a class of people whom the INS and the Border Patrol defined as 'illegal'" (Corona 1994: 291). In addition to protesting these activities and providing educational workshops, *Hermandad* filed lawsuits against the INS and Border Patrol. "Our position was that the INS had developed an illegal policy, based on its unproven premise that most of the Spanish-speaking people who walked the streets were deportable and therefore had no rights to constitutional appeals or defense. We disagreed, and our position was reinforced by countless court cases, including earlier U.S. Supreme Court rulings" (Corona 1991: 293).

Hermandad and CASA invested heavily in several important legislative campaigns, including the campaign against California's Dixon Arnett bill in 1971. This campaign pitted them against some of the bill's most important union supporters, including Cesar Chavez and the UFW. *Hermandad* and CASA organized demonstrations in Los Angeles, mobilized caravans to the state capitol, and organized letter writing and media campaigns to oppose the law. CASA and *Hermandad* also led an effort against proposed federal legislation (Rodino bill) that would introduce employer sanctions at the national scale (Garcia 2002: 73). As part of this effort, Corona and Alatorre helped create the National Coalition for Fair Immigration Laws and Practices, which was the first national immigrant rights network in the United States. They organized one of the first national-level immigrant rights protests, with sizeable demonstrations taking place in cities across the country. The demonstration in Los Angeles drew 15,000 supporters, the largest immigrant rights demonstration up to that time. These relatively poor organizations achieved regional and national influence because they were able to draw on crucial levels of support from local networks (radical Chicano youths, Latino advocacy organizations, and later the UFW).

Conclusions

East Los Angeles in the early 1970s was a major hub of Latino activism. A diverse array of activists demanded more political and economic opportunities in the country. They argued that because of their background, they were being denied the resources needed to survive and thrive. Moreover, Chicanos argued that the empowerment of this community depended on its ability to take pride in its culture. They should view their culture as a source of power rather than an impediment to their incorporation in the country. Activists in this dense and diverse milieu addressed many issues but the issue concerning the specific rights of undocumented immigrants was still not on their radar screens. For most Americans at the time, the issue simply did not exist because many assumed that their "illegality" rendered them without rights in the country. New, undocumented immigrants were also considered by many to hurt the settled Latino population because they drove down wages and reinforced negative cultural stereotypes about Mexican Americans in the country.

In spite of this consensus, certain innovators in this milieu began the painstaking work of making the rights of immigrants visible and worthy of political attention. Bert Corona and his Chicano comrades reached out to one another, developed common understandings of the importance of this struggle, and expressed commitment to making this a central issue in Latino activist circles. They tapped their own networks, argued with friends and reluctant comrades, and produced frames that revealed the similarities between illegalized and settled Latino communities. This painstaking networking helped convince many, if not most, activists in this milieu that the fight for immigrant rights was indeed central to their own concern and an issue that needed to be addressed. Recognition of the issue allowed Los Angeles activists to initiate the first large-scale campaigns to push back on new anti-immigrant measures in the city, state, and country. These campaigns marked the beginning of immigrant rights activism in the United States, and Los Angeles stood out as one of the main urban hubs driving it.

4

Radical Entanglements in Paris

During the 1960s and 1970s, migrant workers in Paris lived in a state of enforced invisibility. The government and economy depended desperately on their labor. The postwar boom (commonly known as the *Trente Glorieuse*) was made possible by the tens of thousands of people that had been imported to build infrastructure, construct housing, and produce goods for an increasingly affluent middle class. Labor migrants were central to the life of the country, but the government viewed the foreigners (especially non-Europeans) as a major risk to French life. The puzzle for policy makers was how to extract and exploit the labor of immigrants while minimizing the risks associated with foreign people. Immigrants were allowed into the country but they were literally cast into the shadows. Many were housed in specially designated hostels. The managers of these hostels (many of whom had served as officers in postwar colonial conflicts) monitored the behavior of residents and imposed restrictions on their access to public space. The government restricted the labor rights of immigrants, limited their rights to assemble, banned their engagement in politics, and restricted their ability to express their opinions in public. Any disruptive act or statement made in the public sphere could be used as grounds for immediate deportation. The labor of these migrants was welcome in the country while their presence was not, resulting in measures to render them invisible from the public eye.

Cities and Social Movements: Immigrant Rights Activism in the United States, France, and the Netherlands, 1970–2015, First Edition. Walter J. Nicholls and Justus Uitermark.
© 2017 John Wiley & Sons, Ltd. Published 2017 by John Wiley & Sons, Ltd.

The economic and oil crises of the early 1970s reduced the need for immigrant labor. The government's strategy shifted from one of masking the presence of foreigners to blocking immigrants from coming to and settling in the country (the banishment strategy). The government during this decade introduced new policies and measures to raise legal entry barriers, roll back the rights and protections for those who obtained authorized residency, and deport those who failed to obtain authorization. This new level of repression exacerbated pre-existing frustrations among immigrants and spurred resistance in the places where this repression was enacted. Many, if not most, of these conflicts and resistance stayed rather small and local, but several grew into larger-scale mobilizations. They were able to penetrate the public sphere and make immigrant rights into an issue of national debate.

How was it that under the most difficult and hostile conditions immigrants were able to scale up their small resistances and create powerful mobilizations that called into question the government's restrictive immigration policies? This chapter addresses this question by suggesting that Paris in the 1970s provided a uniquely rich and supportive environment to transform small seeds of resistance into flourishing mobilizations with national-level reach. Resistances emerged throughout the country, but they took root in an urban context that was particularly well suited to nurture their maturation and growth. Once a left government was installed in power in 1981, new political opportunities opened up, spurring the rapid growth of immigrant activism and its formation into a truly national immigrant rights movement with the city of Paris standing at its center.

Government Restrictions on Immigrants and Rights

Recognizing the need for immigrant labor after the Second World War, the De Gaulle government laid the legal ground to expand the state's capacity to regulate immigration flows. The Ordinance of November 2, 1945 provided the legal criteria and instruments to control the terms of recruitment, residency, and naturalization. The National Office of Immigration (ONI) became the principal agency charged with identifying the economic sectors in need of migrant labor, developing bilateral agreements with countries for guest workers, and recruiting immigrants to France. Up until the 1980s, immigration as a policy issue was the exclusive domain of the Minister of the Interior and not the parliament, with the Ministry assuming principal authority in passing and enacting executive decrees and circulars (Hayward and Wright 2002). By keeping policy in the hands of the Ministry and outside the reach of the parliament, state officials hoped to keep the issue out of the political debate.

An early dilemma facing French policy makers was how to balance the need for immigrant labor with the need to "protect" the national population from possible disturbances accompanying mass immigration. Government officials recognized the need of immigrant labor but many also feared that immigration could unleash countless cultural and political problems. Demographers working for the government were concerned about North and West Africans, arguing that their cultural, political, and religious backgrounds presented important risks (Weil 1991; Wihtol de Wenden 1994). As a consequence, the government encouraged immigration from Italy and then expanded this to Spain and Portugal in the early 1960s. Private sector recruiters nevertheless continued to target North African workers (Hargreaves 1995). In spite of government efforts to regulate migration flows, by the late 1960s 80% of immigrants bypassed formal government channels and entered the country without authorization, regularizing their status after their arrival in the country (Ireland 1994: 26). The importance of non-European immigrants for the French economy led most officials to recognize them as a "necessary evil" that needed to be controlled and regulated (Hayward and Wright 2002).

French government officials were not only interested in controlling flows but also in controlling immigrant populations once they arrived. In the early postwar years, rapid industrialization and urbanization resulted in increases in immigration and an accompanying housing shortage. The explosion of large shantytowns (*bidonvilles*) on the outskirts of large cities concerned residents and local politicians (De Barros 2004). As these settlements became negatively associated with immigrants, immigration emerged as an issue in public debate in spite of government efforts to silence it (Weil 1991; Hayward and Wright 2002). Officials in 1958 created a new welfare agency – Social Action Fund for Immigrant Workers and their Families[1] (FAS) – to regain control over the immigrant settlement process. FAS was charged with providing a range of welfare services, including employment services, literacy classes, and housing, with housing accounting for the vast majority of FAS resources (70% of expenditures between 1959 and 1970) (Heins 1991: 595). While public funds for immigrant housing were channeled through FAS, a semi-public housing corporation, the National Society for the Construction of Housing for Workers[2] (SONACOTRA), actually produced, distributed, and managed immigrant housing.

SONACOTRA hostels were designed to control the lives of immigrants settling in France by micromanaging their conduct and bodies. Restricting housing to single-male occupancy reduced the possibilities of family migration and reinforced the temporary character of immigration. Hostels were also designed as total institutions that could ensure the social and spatial isolation of this group from French nationals. The social and living functions of residents were contained in the hostel (i.e. housing, religious, social activities, medicine). This minimized the need for migrants to venture into the city in search of services. As total institutions, immigrant residents were placed under intense surveillance and disciplinary control by former military personnel who had served in the Indochina and Algerian wars. "By recruiting senior non-commissioned officers in great numbers (who had participated in Indochina and Algerian wars) as managers, the aim was both to discipline these immigrants – as they were former colonized – and to 'civilize' them into a new social institution which would meet all their social needs (housing, work, religion, etc.)" (Hmed 2006b: 2). Thus, the state devised welfare measures that allowed it to better control this population and steer it away from disruptive interactions with local communities.

According to the Ordinance of November 2, 1945, immigrants were officially designated "foreigners." As such, they were legally barred from engaging in politics on the principle that foreigners should remain neutral in national affairs. Violating the principle of foreign neutrality was grounds for deportation. Moreover, officials could use the amorphous label "menace to the public order" as further justification for deporting unruly immigrants. Immigrants were barred from creating their own associations unless the Minister of the Interior gave them special permission. This last restriction stemmed from a 1939 decree that sought to block the potentially seditious activities of the country's German immigrant population (Wihtol de Wenden and Leveau 2001: 27). Immigrants were also restricted from starting or running their own newspapers. Though immigrants were allowed to join unions, they were not allowed to hold leadership positions or participate in courts designed to assess employee grievances.

While the government set up barriers to political incorporation in France, it encouraged foreign consulates (e.g. Morocco, Algeria, Tunisia) to play an active role in the ideological and cultural lives of immigrant communities. Consulates offered religious and educational programs to their nationals (and offspring) while sponsoring "friendly societies" (*Amicales*) to play an active part in shaping their social and civic lives in France. By encouraging immigrants to retain their foreignness, French officials hoped to minimize their involvement in domestic affairs. This reflected a common practice of racialized states to separate "polluting" populations from "virtuous" citizens.

The French government's efforts to cordon off immigrants and exert control over them created a legal and administrative space that made it difficult for many to interact with French nationals. They were restricted from entering French civic and political life and the welfare regime channeled them into self-contained housing complexes. By isolating and containing immigrants, the national community could prosper from cheap labor while reducing the risks associated with North and, increasingly, West African immigrants. These methods were not only seeking to confine the spatial, social, and political movement of immigrant bodies but they were also directed at shaping their souls. Through the hostel system, immigrants were subjected to instructions on how to become good guests in French society, with hostel managers (former colonial officers) training immigrants to conform to this subordinate and docile status (Hmed 2006a, 2006b). France didn't simply have a "guest worker" policy, it also sought to make immigrants easily removable "guests."

The deep economic recession in the early 1970s led to an important shift away from the guest migrant policy of the postwar period. The Minister of the Interior introduced the first of many directives to close down labor migration. The Marcellin-Fontanet circular of 1972 made the acquisition of a visa dependent on proof of permanent employment and housing. Thousands of people unable to meet the criteria or provide adequate documentation were stripped of permission to reside in the country. In 1974, this circular was followed by the suspension of all labor and family migration to the country. The effort to ban family migration violated international treaties and the Council of State required the government to rescind the ban. The Minister of the Interior signed a decree that recognized the right to family reunification but also introduced a long list of requirements to qualify for family visas. Among other things, sponsors applying for family visas had to demonstrate stable employment and a "certificate of decent housing" issued by the mayor of the municipality. The sponsor was expected to earn enough income to rent an apartment large enough to house all expected family members in relative comfort (Péchu 2004: 129). For many working at the bottom end of the labor market, this proved to be a difficult, if not impossible, task. The state therefore recognized the right to family reunification in accordance with its international obligations, but income and housing restrictions made it difficult for many working-class families to realize this right. Restrictive conditions placed on working-class immigrant families encouraged many family members to arrive on tourist visas and attempt to regularize their status after their arrival in the country (Péchu 2004: 126). Lastly, a ministerial decree in 1976 stripped visas from immigrants who found themselves "without employment or regular resources for six months" or who had spent more than six months outside the country (Siméant 1998: 184).

As was the case in the United States and the Netherlands, restrictions played an important role in producing a new population of illegalized immigrants. Growing restrictions on labor immigrants deprived legal status to thousands of immigrants who had been working in the country for years. Immigrants who did not meet new restrictive criteria, who could not furnish adequate documentation of employment or housing, or who found themselves out of a job for more than six months, were made "illegal." The growing number of illegalized immigrants – the consequence of government policies – "compelled" the government to introduce new measures to forcefully remove them from the country. In 1977 the Minister of the Interior, Lionel Stoléru, initiated large-scale deportation raids that targeted immigrant neighborhoods while providing financial aid for the "voluntary return" of compliant immigrants. In 1980, the Minister of the Interior, Christian Bonnet, introduced the first legislative bill to amend the Ordinance of 1945. The law tightened conditions for legal residency visas, lowered the deportation threshold, and facilitated the detention of undocumented immigrants. The Peyrefitte Law of 1981 legalized identity checks for people "suspected" of being undocumented immigrants, essentially making all minorities and immigrants liable to police interventions. The Peyrefitte Law also tightened the housing requirements for family reunification, increased minimum salary requirements, and required new supporting documents (including a letter from the mayor) to prove that minimal criteria were met. This law essentially made mayors the gatekeepers of family residency visas.

Thus, during the 1950s and 1960s, the government responded to the growing population of risky immigrants (i.e. North and, increasingly, West Africans) by developing a strategy to render them invisible. The hostel system was designed to keep them out of public view and restrictions on civic and political life aimed to block their entry into public debate. France could prosper from immigrant labor without having to expose the nation to the cultural, social, and political risks associated with this population. The economic downturn of the 1970s prompted the government to sharpen the boundaries between immigrants and nationals by barring new immigrants into the country, criminalizing established immigrants, and deporting immigrants who had been rendered "illegal" by restrictive government measures.

The Activist Landscape in Paris

Massive political restrictions on immigrants provided few channels to express grievances in the public sphere. French officials encouraged the consulates of sending countries to take an active role in dealing with the grievances of their nationals. These countries were happy to comply as this provided a way to monitor the activities of their citizens and develop supportive clients in France. As noted above, consulates from sending countries (but especially Morocco, Algeria, Tunisia) developed "friendly societies" (*Amicales*) with the approval of the Minister of the Interior. Consulates also ensured religious instruction for their citizens by providing government-trained imams, and they provided a range of legal services. In assuming these roles, foreign consulates served as brokers between their nationals and the French state.

Foreign governments – with the encouragement of the French state – dominated the associational life of immigrant communities through the *Amicales*. Postcolonial consular offices used the *Amicales* to assert their control over political activities in France. These associations helped newly established postcolonial governments to monitor the activities of their nationals and mobilize support for the governing party. By 1970, 10% of all Algerians (approximately 100,000) in France were members of the Amicale of Algerians in Europe[3] (AAE) (Ireland 1994: 38). While the scope and reach of the AAE was impressive, other sending countries pursued similar efforts to dominate the associational and political lives of their citizens in France. In spite of this influence, control of the *Amicales* was by no means total and dissenters continued to operate in immigrant communities. In the absence of formal and autonomous immigrant organizations, dissenters were mostly informal networks of friends and comrades concentrated in urban centers (mostly in Paris). Thus, major restrictions on formal immigrant associations and the dominance of government-dominated *Amicales* limited the formation of a robust activist cluster in immigrant communities.

This contrasted with the radical renaissance unfolding in Paris in the late 1960s and early 1970s. A variety of Maoist new left parties emerged in opposition to the historical dominance of the French Communist Party. While these small and radical political parties continued to mobilize for a proletarian revolution, other activists mobilized against specific forms of exclusion that affected women, minorities, tenants, prisoners, gays, and patients, among others (Eribon 1991; Duyvendak 1995). Moreover, following Israel's occupation of the West Bank and Gaza Strip, Palestine solidarity committees sprang up throughout the city.

Radical Parisian intellectuals displayed heightened levels of activism during this period and became important contributors to the city's social movement milieu. These included prominent sociologists like Henri Lefebvre, philosophers like Jean-Paul Sartre and Gilles Deleuze, and writers like Jean Genet. Louis Althusser's long-time position at the *École Normale Supérieure* helped produce a tightly knit generation of politicized intellectuals, including luminaries like Michel Foucault, Alain Badiou, Étienne Balibar, and Jacques Rancière. The diverse range of activist organizations (some of which were formalized, while others remained informal) and intellectuals operating in this dense milieu created a radical "counterpublic." This milieu provided many opportunities for people to attend common social and political meetings, read similar radical journals and newspapers, and engage in regular face-to-face debates over the tactics, strategies, and meanings of radical politics in "monopoly capitalist" societies.

The concentration of radical activists and their networks in northeastern Paris provided emerging dissident immigrant activists with important opportunities for political socialization (Siméant 1998). Some immigrants had previous experience as activists in their home countries, but they lacked familiarity with the French political field, which made it difficult to activate pre-existing "activist capital" (Siméant 1998). Their incorporation into radical networks introduced them to the local "rules of the game" and helped them to readjust their activist skills and experience accordingly. The Palestinian solidarity committees were particularly important places where young North Africans came out, connected to one another, and interacted with Parisian radicals. Many of the immigrant activists undertook their politicization through these committees and their participation in far left parties like *Gauche Prolétaire* (Proletarian Left). Their activist backgrounds in home countries, and their knowledge of French, facilitated their entry into radical networks and enabled them to assume leadership roles in subsequent mobilizations.

As North African dissenters engaged in different mobilizations during the course of the 1970s, they began to develop their own organizations that stood in opposition to the *Amicales*. The most prominent among these was the Movement of Arab Workers[4] (MTA), which was started by Paris-based immigrant activists in 1973. The MTA was a way to provide immigrants with greater autonomy in shaping their political voice and begin to develop claims targeting both the sending *and* receiving countries. It stressed the distinctive character of the immigrant voice but also emphasized its connections to the general anti-capitalist and anti-imperialist struggles of the native working class.

The MTA served as a model for a new generation of immigrant groups from Morocco, Algeria, Tunisia, and Turkey. They were Marxist, oriented toward French politics, highly secular, and vehemently opposed to *Amicales*. Other immigrant organizations flourished alongside it, including the Association of Moroccans in France (AMF), the Union for Tunisian Immigrant Workers, the Movement for Mauritian Workers, and the Association for Turkish Workers.[5] In spite of the diversity of the associations, the MTA retained its prominence in this emerging cluster and served as an important broker between immigrant activists and other radicals in Paris. While differences permeated across them, they shared a common ideological background rooted in Marxism and a common interest in the struggle for immigrant workers. This was reflected in the use of "workers" in the names of immigrant associations emerging during this period. As one activist with a Turkish association noted, "We had the idea: we are revolutionary communist proletariats. Who cares about whether a worker has papers?" (Siméant 1998: 84).

These associations provided a new generation of immigrant activists with an ideological, social, and political space to organize and forge their own distinctive interests. However, they were informal, poor, and officially outside the law. Because these associations could not gain legal recognition from the Minister of the Interior, they did not have a legal right to exist and were ineligible for support by the state and other funding agencies. Lacking access to resources and the authorization to represent the interests of immigrants, early immigrant associations depended on French allies for basic operational resources and support.

A variety of human rights and anti-racist NGOs in Paris stepped forward to provide support and advocate on behalf of immigrants. Among these organizations, the Human Rights League (LDH) was the oldest, dating back to the early twentieth century. The Movement against Racism and Anti-Semitism and for the Friendship of Peoples (MRAP) emerged soon after the Second World War and was closely aligned to a national trade union and the French Communist Party. Different Catholic organizations that had been supporting immigrants during the 1960s formed the Federation of Associations in Support of Immigrant Workers (FASTI). Protestants formed a similar organization, the Inter-movement Committee Close to Evacuees (CIMADE), during the war years to support displaced populations but extended its work to new immigrants in the 1960s and 1970s. Lastly, a new generation of activist lawyers allied with new left currents formed the legal advocacy association the Group for Information and Support to Immigrants (GISTI) in 1971.[6] GISTI embraced Michel Foucault's concept of the "specific intellectual," which posited that intellectuals with practical skills (lawyers in this instance) should lend those skills to the struggles of marginalized people rather than seek to speak on their behalf (Artières 2002). These different organizations, all located in the immigrant-rich neighborhoods of northeast Paris, had a similar function with respect to the cluster of immigrant activists: provide support and representational assistance in their fledgling struggles.

Mobilizing against Government Repression

A new generation of immigrant activists began to openly resist restrictive government measures in the 1970s. While resistances emerged throughout the country, the concentration of activists, networks, organizations, and clusters in Paris made it a particularly rich environment to support early mobilizations. However, the lack of established immigrant and minority organizations favored wildcat mobilizations more than organized demonstrations and formal campaigns. These mobilizations often emerged in direct response to repressive government measures (restrictive housing, deportations, raids, etc.). Handfuls of immigrant activists often responded to government restrictions with small struggles. Some of these small resistances were able to draw upon the support of comrades from their immediate support networks, which in turn enabled them to grow and extend their struggle beyond the original point of conflict. French radicals were disposed to providing first-line support to emergent and unscripted struggles of immigrants. Many viewed immigrants as a proletariat unsullied by "trade union mentality." Immigrant workers symbolized the excesses of capitalism and a proletariat ready to pursue the class struggle in a revolutionary rather than reformist direction. As a result of this heroic representation of immigrant workers, early immigrant struggles became a *cause célèbre* in radical Parisian circles and attracted a variety of supporters. Once small resistances had grown into larger mobilizations, human rights NGOs (LDH, FASTI, MRAP, etc.) often came in and provided additional levels of support.

There were many small struggles during the mid- to late 1970s, but two in particular evolved from small conflicts into major regional and national mobilizations. In 1973, residents of a housing dormitory for guest workers launched a campaign against SONACOTRA (Ireland 1994; Siméant 1998; Hmed 2007). Initially, the residents of a single hostel launched a rent strike. The goals were narrowly focused on high rents, poor living conditions, and the repressive regulations imposed on the tenants. Three of the four leaders of the campaign had extensive "activist capital" (Péchu 2004). Two had been Maoists in Portugal and Algeria and the other had been a prominent anti-government activist in Senegal's student movement. While these leaders built support for their struggle among the residents of the hostel, they also developed contacts with other radical activists in the Paris region. By attending meetings and socializing with other Parisian militants, they established direct connections to French Maoists, pro-Palestine groups, and activists within the Senegalese community. As this handful of immigrant leaders gained the trust and confidence of individuals within these clusters, early supporters brokered relations to friends and comrades in their own networks and helped extend support through these relational chains.

French supporters provided professional skills, including legal and architectural expertise. These resources provided the rent strikers with the knowledge to challenge SONACOTRA practices and present policy alternatives. Parisian activists also introduced the immigrants of SONACOTRA to tactics that were well suited to the French political context, including advice for negotiating with the police, and the use of petitions and letter-writing campaigns (Hmed 2006a). Parisian activists also won the support of respected Parisian personalities, including Jean-Paul Sartre and Simone de Beauvoir, helping to further extend the visibility and legitimacy of the campaign. This rapid extension outward from the original point of conflict enabled the immigrants of SONACOTRA to penetrate the public sphere and assert their fundamental right to have rights in spite of their foreign status. The support also allowed them to widen the campaign to 120 hostels across the country.

In this instance, connections to different activist clusters in Paris permitted the flow of resources to strengthen the initial struggle, amplify their capacity to make powerful public claims, and shift their struggle from a single hostel in Paris into a national-scale campaign. The mobilization shifted to the national scale but the hub remained Paris. Thus, a handful of rent-striking immigrants were able to connect to other activist clusters in Paris through connecting points like meetings and events, and through a string of friendly brokers. These first-line supporters helped extend relations with others across the city's activist milieu, unleashing the resources contained within the city's activist networks and channeling them toward rent-striking immigrants. This process of networking, diffusion, and resource pooling transformed an obscure and invisible skirmish into one of the most contentious political events of the 1970s.

In addition to mobilizing against SONACOTRA, several pockets of immigrants began to mobilize against national policies that restricted the rights of immigrants. In 1972 and 1973, small numbers of immigrants across the country launched hunger strikes (Siméant 1998). In the northern town of Valence, a young Tunisian immigrant activist began a hunger strike to protest his deportation for having violated the principle of foreign "political neutrality." His "crime" was to have attended meetings of a small left-wing group. Two other hunger strikers in Paris, members of a pro-Palestine group, were also targeted for deportation on the same grounds (Wihtol de Wenden 1994). By stepping out of the shadows and engaging in political speech, the activists challenged laws and assumptions that immigrants did not have basic rights to free speech and association. "For the immigrant, ... speaking out was already a very political act in a country where they didn't have the right to speak politically; a country where they lacked the right to vote, the right to create an association, or the right to publish articles or newspapers without special authorization from the state" (Zancarini-Fournel 2002: 53). French intellectuals and activists came out in support of the hunger strikers and formed the Defense Committee of the Life and Rights of Immigrant Workers.[7] The defense committee was heavily influenced by Maoists and activist intellectuals like Michel Foucault, Jean-Paul Sartre, Roland Barthes, and Jean Genet (Cordeiro 2001; Artières 2002). Once the defense committee had gained strength, several human rights NGOs provided additional legal, representational, and material support (LDH, GISTI, FASTI, MRAP). The growing prominence of the campaign prompted other immigrants to join the hunger strikers. This helped expand the number of strikers to 28 at the highest point of the campaign.

The French activists played a crucial role in elevating the struggle. They employed their cultural and symbolic capital to represent the claims of immigrants through frames that resonated with French political culture. French radicals framed the "immigrant worker" as a part of the working class willing and able to pursue revolutionary goals. They were represented as a heroic, vanguard element of the proletariat, unsullied by the petit bourgeois aspirations and appetites of the French working class. Being represented in this way, the figure of the "immigrant worker" gained great prominence within the radical currents of the French left. The country's second largest union (CFDT) came out in support of the campaign with the slogan "French and immigrant workers, same boss, same combat." The more French sympathizers wrote and spoke of immigrants in these ways, the more they attracted the support of other left intellectuals, activists, and workers to the immigrant cause (Wihtol de Wenden and Leveau 2001).

The growing prominence of the Paris-based hunger strikers triggered similar actions in Lille, Montpellier, Marseille, Toulouse, Lyon, and Nice. In each of these cities, aggrieved immigrants replicated the repertoire and tactics of the core group: they occupied public buildings and churches, launched hunger strikes, and denounced the increasingly restrictive turn in French immigration policy. In each city, local support committees made up of radicals, local branches of the national human rights NGOs, and church activists sprang up to support their efforts. While smaller mobilizations emerged throughout the country, they remained connected to the hub in Paris, with many activists commuting regularly between the provinces and the capital. "We can find in most of the struggles during this period militants commuting between Paris and the provinces, organizing successive meetings, actions, and hunger strikes across the country" (Siméant 1998: 75). By 1978, human rights NGOs, activist intellectuals, and several unions had created a national organizing committee (SOS-*Refoulements*). Based in northeastern Paris, the coalition coordinated the struggles against the national government's increased restrictions and more aggressive deportation campaign.

Thus, the state's efforts to repress populations and forcefully repatriate immigrants precipitated resistances. Aggrieved immigrants tried to push back on increasingly repressive government measures. While these early resistances unfolded throughout the country, northeastern Paris provided a particularly propitious context for early seeds of resistance to flourish into regional and national mobilizations. This area possessed a high density of radical activists and human rights NGOs. The existence of a range of connecting points and brokers made it possible for very different activists to establish connections to one another. The spatial proximity between activists facilitated repeated meetings between previously unconnected people. The extension of these struggles further into the Parisian social movement milieu allowed radical immigrants to tap local resources (money, office space, symbolic capital, legal knowledge, architectural skills) and grow their struggles into nationwide campaigns for immigrant rights. For the first time in the postwar period, immigrants were able to pierce the public sphere and assert their presence as human and political beings with inalienable rights. The relations built up in these urban places enabled them to fight their way out of the shadows and into the public sphere, struggling against the government measures that were designed to render them invisible, illegal, without rights, and deportable.

The Flourishing Immigrant Rights Movement in the Early 1980s

The election of a left government in 1981 introduced a break with the policies of the past. The parties making up the governing coalition (Socialist and Communist parties) were not at the forefront of immigrant rights struggles but these struggles had gained the support of large parts of the French left by 1981. Immigration and immigrant rights had become a litmus test within the left electorate. Just as important, some immigrants began to obtain citizenship through naturalization and their children started to reach voting age. Socialist leaders became interested in developing a reliable electoral constituency from this population. The risks of pursuing pro-immigrant policies were also not very high. Segments of the French population started to display some anti-immigrant sentiments, but the extreme right party (the National

Front) was still marginal in 1981 and could not tap into and harness the public's fledgling xenophobia (Berezin 2009).

Soon after 1981, the newly elected government introduced a large-scale amnesty, which resulted in granting legal status to approximately 200,000 immigrants over a two-year period. The government also legalized immigrant associations and removed all restrictions on political speech. Lastly, the government simplified the visa application process, lowered the eligibility criteria, and introduced a 10-year residency visa for eligible immigrants (up from one year). The new government also removed most restrictions on immigrant political speech and actions (e.g. legalized immigrant associations, political speech by immigrants, union participation, etc.). Prominent political officials spoke about discrimination, injustice, racism, and the structural forces precipitating exclusion of immigrants and their offspring (Dikeç 2007). This period therefore provided unique opportunities for immigrant activists to grow into a prominent political force.

From 1982 to 1984, first-generation immigrants were at the forefront of highly disruptive strikes at the Talbot-Peugeot factory in the Paris region (Gay 2014). The early strikers quickly gained the support of unions, members of left organizations, and the leading Paris-based immigrant associations. The newly legalized immigrant associations played a crucial role in supporting these struggles and tying them to North African communities. These associations included the Association of Maghrébin Workers of France (ATMF, the new name of the 1970s association MTA), Association of Tunisians in France (ATF), Federation of Tunisians for a Citizenship of Two Banks (FTCR), and Citizenship Assembly of Turkish Origins (ACORT).[8] The strikers also gained strong support from left-wing unions, which framed them as part of the workers' struggle against capitalism:

> André Sainjon, General Secretary of the Federation of Metallurgy Workers, … focused on workers' cohesion. Stressing that unskilled immigrant workers did not want to remain so forever, he compared their struggles with 'people's liberation', which mingled diverse nationalities, all united in the working class. Therefore, the conflicts were not described as immigrants' struggles, but rather as 'a struggle for workers, for unskilled workers to undermine old forms of Taylorism'. (Gay 2010: 10)

The strikes became another *cause célèbre* and fomented visions of an autonomous, bottom-up, and radical political agenda driven by immigrant workers. Initially this frame struck a chord with some members of the newly installed left government and it reluctantly supported the strikers. However, as the strike wore on and the left-wing government veered toward the political center,[9] the strikes became an embarrassing reflection of the government's inability to control its left flank in general, and immigrant organizations in particular.

While first-generation immigrants engaged in this mobilization, second-generation immigrants also exploded onto the French political scene in the early 1980s. Soon after the election of 1981, many youths participated in series of large-scale riots in the Lyon suburbs of Vaulx-en-Velin and les Minguettes. Participating youths were incensed by continued police repression and the death of one of their peers at the hands of a police officer (Wihtol de Wenden and Leveau 2001; Dikeç 2007). These riots were the first major disturbances involving second-generation youths, and they unleashed a political renaissance for this sector of the population. New associations grew rapidly across urban areas. They provided youth services, and they also sought to express a new political voice on behalf of this group. They denounced the economic conditions found in these neighborhoods and the discriminatory practices that blocked their social and political mobility. They abandoned the label "second-generation" and embraced the resolutely political identity of *Beur*.[10] They also created two new radio stations (Radio Beur in Paris and Radio Gazelle in Marseille), which provided a site where youths could express ideas and concerns and develop a distinctive culture of their own (Wihtol de Wenden and Leveau 2001: 39).

These activities culminated in the famous "March for Equality and against Racism" in late 1983. The march began in Marseille and ended at the presidential palace in Paris, with 150,000 people coming out in support of the marchers. The March for Equality was initiated by youths, but more established immigrant associations (ATMF, FTCR, ATF, ACORT, etc.) also played an important role in organizing and coordinating this massive undertaking. The peaceful character of the protest, the demands for equality, and favorable media coverage produced relatively strong support across France. The murder of a young Moroccan by a racist mob in November 1982 further magnified the resonance of the campaign's anti-racist message (Cordeiro 2001: 12). In light of this broad support, the Socialist Party threw its support behind the march and President Mitterrand personally received a delegation of youth activists.

The political and legal openings introduced in 1981 helped fortify a new round of mobilizations in the early 1980s. Once-illegal immigrant associations were now asserting their independence in the political field, playing an active role in supporting the campaigns of striking workers and second-generation youths. For many involved in these activities, this marked the emergence of an autonomous immigrant rights movement – fueled by immigrant grievances and directed by immigrants themselves (Wihtol de Wenden and Leveau 2001). While the change of government policies helped open the door to this development, it was nevertheless built upon the actions and relations constructed over the previous 10 years. That work by Paris-based activists provided the relations, organizational infrastructure, knowledge, and repertoires that made this new and expanded round of mobilization possible.

Conclusions

The center-right governments of the 1970s devised policies to banish immigrants from the country and national political life. Workers who had developed transnational lives and crisscrossed borders with relative ease were now made "illegal." As this population became the target of government repression, many fought back and struggled to assert their rights and presence in the country. Resistances were common in many places but they took root in cities with favorable mobilizing environments. Paris and its northeastern neighborhoods were particularly favorable in this regard because of higher concentrations of immigrants, activists, and organizations. The lack of resources and political legitimacy of early immigrant activists meant that they depended greatly on their French allies. These allied supporters provided material resources (money, office space, etc.), cultural and symbolic capital, and specialized knowledge (architecture, legal knowhow). Tapping local activist networks and channeling the resources of these networks to early mobilizations helped grow the struggles far beyond the original point of conflict. The momentum built up during the 1970s combined with the new political opportunities in 1981 to unleash potent, autonomous, and far-reaching immigrant rights mobilizations.

In 1970 most French people could not understand how "foreigners" could be recognized as human beings with many of the same rights as themselves. They were conceived as "guests" who should dutifully perform labor, not make a fuss, and leave once the task at hand was done. By law, a disruptive guest could and should be removed from the country for overstepping the line of acceptable behavior. The common sense of the people and law was that immigrants were somehow less than fully human beings and had no legal or moral standing to make rights claims in the country. Ten years later this assumption had come to an end. Not all French people recognized the equality of immigrants but it was now an issue of open public debate. The denial of very basic human rights was no longer taken for granted. Immigrant activists, advocacy organizations, lawyers, and politicians had mounted a decade-long struggle to assert the rights and humanity of immigrants. By doing so, the issue of the rights of immigrants had become (and have remained) a central issue in the public debate.

Thus, as we have argued so far, pushing the rights of immigrants into the public sphere did not occur in a geographical vacuum. State repression was enacted and experienced in concrete places (hostels, city streets, meeting places, etc.). Some immigrants (a minority of dissident activists) translated early feelings of outrage into concrete struggles by tapping into support networks in surrounding environments. Because cities like Paris had a high density and diversity of potential supporters (from radicals to human rights NGOs), this made the city a propitious environment for translating early seeds of outrage into actual mobilizations. Brokers and multiple connecting points in the city made it easier for new immigrant activists to connect to Paris-based supporters. As this local networking process gained momentum and extended outward, activists were able to tap into a wide range of localized resources found in the Paris region (money, legal knowhow, legitimacy, cultural capital, etc.), pooling and deploying these resources to support national-level campaigns. The struggle for rights in France therefore had a distinctive geography and Paris stood out as a singular and powerful hub within this national social movement space.

5

Placing Protest in Amsterdam

In the 1970s, the Dutch government became increasingly anxious about foreign workers who had come to the Netherlands without a work permit. The presence of these clandestine workers had not been considered a major problem during a period of continued economic growth but just after the oil crisis of 1973 the government was looking for ways to get a grip on unregulated immigration. In an effort to draw a sharp line between legitimate and illegitimate immigrants, the Dutch government proceeded to regularize all guest workers who had been working for at least a year and who had contracts for at least another year but declared guest workers not fulfilling these criteria to be unwanted aliens subject to deportation.

Just after November 1, 1975, the day the illegalization took effect, 100 Moroccans who had failed to achieve regularization started a hunger strike in the Mozes and Aäron church. They claimed that they fulfilled the formal obligations but that their employers refused to provide them with the required documents out of fear they might be persecuted for not paying taxes or violating labor laws. Soon after the 100 Moroccans had initiated their action, a further 82 Moroccans went on hunger strike in The Hague and Utrecht. This was the beginning of a protracted campaign that captured the headlines for months and involved a large number of organizations and prominent figures expressing their support. After initial talks with the government did not result in legalization for all

Cities and Social Movements: Immigrant Rights Activism in the United States, France, and the Netherlands, 1970–2015, First Edition. Walter J. Nicholls and Justus Uitermark.
© 2017 John Wiley & Sons, Ltd. Published 2017 by John Wiley & Sons, Ltd.

Moroccans, a new hunger strike was initiated, this time in De Duif, another church in Amsterdam's canal district.

The hunger strikes were a foundational act as they brought into view guest workers who had until then largely remained in the shadows. By making themselves visible, the hunger strikers politicized their presence and pushed the immigration issues onto the political agenda. For example, the parliamentarian Andrée van Es and her colleague Bram van der Lek visited the hunger strikers with the intention of convincing them to stop using this action method because it was "very bad for them." But once they were in the church something happened. They found that the hunger strikers were very motivated to carry on. Rather than convincing the hunger strikers, the parliamentarians ended up being convinced by them: "When we left late in the evening we had committed our full solidarity and support. We stopped going to the Binnenhof [i.e. the parliament] and instead visited the church every day to help people explain why they couldn't prove they had been working here for over a year."[1] The presence of the hunger strikers also stirred up discussions among churchgoers. Many people felt alienated by the sight of the Moroccans but they also were forced to reconsider their practices and beliefs. The church's priest used the sermon to critically interrogate religion and culture:

> Many people are disturbed by the way our Duif [church] looks: beds on the floor, banners on the pillars, strange stuff all around, all sort of activities, typing, watching television – in short, it's a mess. This is disconcerting for many people. I have to say: I'm one of them. Because I'm a religious person and that type of person appreciates tidiness and order, especially in a church.[2]

He went on to argue that "religious people are dangerous" as they so much "yearn order, regularity, loftiness, and ritual that they sometimes sacrifice people." Jesus, the priest said, warned against religious people and was in fact killed by them. The religiously inclined, he said, "respect the rich, the powerful, those who made it and became famous. But Jesus demands reverence for the poor, the defective, the scorned, the banished."[3]

Physical co-presence was essential to these processes of reflection and politicization. The priests, parliamentarians, and countless others who attended the church were deeply impressed as they sensed the hunger strikers' motivation and became embroiled in their action. Proximity brought the immigrants into the spotlight and allowed emotionally intense exchanges. The churches became centers of activism. For instance, when the activists at the Mozes and Aäron church discovered that the *Amicales,* an association loyal to the Moroccan government, had planned a protest in Hilversum to demand an end to criticism of the Moroccan regime, the church activists immediately arranged buses, drove to the protests, and engaged in a confrontation in which several people were wounded and which was ended, with difficulty, by the riot police.

The hunger strikes were ultimately successful. All hunger strikers received a permit. The hunger strikes also marked the beginning of radical immigrant activism. They were the first public campaign of the Committee of Moroccan Workers in the Netherlands (KMAN),[4] a radical left immigrant organization that would come to play a central role in Amsterdam's movement milieu. Turkish guest workers did not participate in the hunger strike but the wave of activism also spawned several radical Turkish organizations that would engage in a high number and wide range of campaigns through the 1970s and 1980s.

The hunger strikes were in some respects foundational but they could only emerge and obtain their significant effects within particular sociospatial configurations. Understanding the place where protests erupted and the relations within and among them is crucial for understanding why Amsterdam's movement activity exploded in the 1970s and 1980s. This chapter starts by examining how the government began to curtail immigration in the late 1960s and 1970s. The chapter goes on to argue that guest workers were initially enveloped in a tutelary regime but were able to break out of that regime through their disruptive actions in the 1970s. Initially these mobilizations were ad hoc and fragmented, but over time an activist cluster around immigrant rights consolidated, achieved recognition and received subsidies from the state, and became an integrated part of Amsterdam's movement milieu.

Government Restrictions on Immigration and Immigrant Rights

In the 1950s and 1960s industrial corporations and the Dutch government felt that the recruitment of Mediterranean workers was the only way to resolve the shortages of employees willing to do hard work for a low wage. Recruitment began in the Southern European countries (especially Italy) and later expanded to Morocco and Turkey. Economic motives dictated policies to guest workers: they were recruited because they were considered indispensable for continued economic growth. This does not mean that the guest workers were welcome rights-bearing citizens. The Ministry of Justice in particular was anxious about the recruitment policies as it feared that guest workers would remain in the country and bring over their families. In 1969, Minister Polak expressed his suspicion that foreign workers would develop into "an alien body within our population" (cited in Bonjour 2009: 88). In 1970, Minister Roelvink declared in a memorandum on foreign workers that "The Netherlands is most definitely not a country of immigration. With all due respect, one cannot do anything else than conclude that our country needs workers from other countries and not the settlement of families from abroad" (Minister Roelvink, cited in Bonjour 2009: 87). In response to these fears, guest workers could only bring over their families after they had worked in the Netherlands for a certain period of time and had arranged proper housing. Such conditions proved difficult to enforce in practice. Whenever the Ministry announced it would deport a guest worker's family, a storm of protest erupted in the media and in parliament (Bonjour 2009: 95). Until the mid-1970s, policies towards guest workers were thus shaped by a perceived necessity to recruit foreign workers to fill places unacceptable to native Dutch workers and the impossibility of preventing foreign workers from settling and forming families. While the government and corporations had assumed that guest workers would return to their countries of origin, it became increasingly clear that many of them would stay. Although many Southern European foreign workers returned, many Moroccan and Turkish immigrants settled indefinitely and formed or brought their families (van Beek 2010: 163–164). The government nevertheless denied that the Netherlands is an "immigration country" and warned of the risks of ghettos, uprooting, frictions, and isolation (Bonjour 2009: 92–93). These fears were compounded by immigration from Suriname; many immigrants moved to the Netherlands before independence in 1975 and before they lost their right of settlement in 1980, increasing the number of Suriname-born Dutch citizens from 50,000 in 1972 to 155,000 in 1980 (ibid.: 110).

As the economic crisis deepened in the 1970s, the government intensified its efforts to restrict immigration. The government faced the dilemma that it did not want to restrict the right to family unification and family formation but nevertheless felt it was necessary to stop immigration (see also Joppke 1998). This dilemma could not be fully resolved and for a long time the government grudgingly accepted that immigrants, including former guest workers, settled in the Netherlands and formed families. The Netherlands would eventually develop one of the most restrictive immigration regimes in Europe (Entzinger et al. 2013), but it was not until the 1980s that the government imposed serious restrictions on family unification and family formation (Bouras 2012). Instead, the government focused its efforts on the stricter selection of guest workers. It wanted to ensure that all immigration of guest workers took place through "official recruitment by Dutch selection centers" and introduced measures to curb "spontaneous entrance" (Penninx 1979: 172). The first steps were taken in the late 1960s by obliging foreign workers to apply for a permit for a temporary stay and the first comprehensive law was enacted in 1979 (the Labor Law for Foreign Workers[5]).

Initially the obligation to carry a permit was not enforced and many foreign workers moved to the Netherlands clandestinely. Fears of a clash of cultures or the formation of a subproletariat were sidelined while there was a strong demand for cheap labor. The economic crisis of 1973, however, convinced the national government that it was necessary to enforce the permit obligation. Raids on immigrants without the proper papers had occasionally taken place since the mid-1960s but they intensified in the early 1970s. The police organized large-scale nightly operations, searching hostels and detaining and deporting workers without proper documentation. The 1975 decree aimed to draw a sharp line between legitimate and illegitimate immigrants but it also sparked the first explosive conflicts over immigration policies discussed at the beginning of this chapter. Thousands of foreign workers and sympathizers took to the streets to protest the policies and series of hunger strikes discussed at the outset of this chapter took off.

The Activist Landscape in Amsterdam

Just after the Second World War, the Netherlands's political, social, and cultural landscape was organized into different ideological blocs, the so-called pillars. The Protestants, the Catholics, the Socialists, and the Liberals each had their own infrastructures: they had their own newspapers, schools, shops, civil associations, and political parties. None of these ideological blocs had a prospect of attaining an absolute majority and through a series of compromises they created a system of subsidized autonomy: each bloc managed its own services and received funding to do so from the central government. Although the pillars were certainly not total institutions in a Goffmanian sense, the religious pillars in particular zealously organized social control over their constituents and guided them from cradle to grave (literally: hospitals and graveyards were pillarized too).

Pillarization began to erode in the 1960s and 1970s as the baby boom reached maturity. The rapid expansion of the welfare state (Cox 1995) made people less dependent on local institutions and communities and tied their fate more directly to the institutions of the national welfare state. In the growing cities and rapidly expanding institutions for higher education, the social control of the pillars was comparatively weak. Amsterdam in particular was a refuge for people escaping from the pillars' social control and became a space for social experimentation. Social movements were exceptionally vibrant in Amsterdam in the 1960s and early 1970s.

The Netherlands in general and Amsterdam in particular experienced a wave of protests against authoritarianism, wars, sexism, and paternalism. In 1969, students occupied the Maagdenhuis, the seat of the University of Amsterdam's administrators, to protest the university's rigid hierarchies and demand participation at all levels of decision making. In the early 1970s, the feminists of Dolle Mina (Crazy Mina) initiated a series of protests demanding the right to legal and safe abortions and criticizing sexism. Psychiatric patients protested against forced treatments and their isolation in closed institutions (Tonkens 1999). Residents of urban neighborhoods spoke out against demolitions and demanded the right to stay put and decide on renewal plans (Draaisma and Hoogstraten 1983; Pruijt 1985; Mamadouh 1992; de Liagre Böhl 2010). Professionals like teachers, psychologists, and community workers felt that they had been complicit in the suppression of their students and patients and redefined their loyalty as they heeded and stimulated calls for self-determination and democratization.

Although these developments were certainly not unique to Amsterdam, the city became a focal point for protests in the Netherlands. While more traditional, middle-class households rapidly moved out into newly constructed suburbs, the city itself concentrated an increasingly young and secularizing population that used the city as a terrain for experimenting with new ways of organizing society, as manifested in paintings, designs, pamphlets, and communes. Students, housing activists, hippies, communists, and feminists each socialized in their own circles but there were many ties between these different activist clusters, as they came together in struggles against Apartheid, (the Vietnam) war, and modernistic urban renewal. Intellectuals and activists drew inspiration from struggles across Europe, and Amsterdam itself became one central node where intellectuals – including urbanists like Henri Lefebvre, Guy Debord, and members of the COBRA group – flocked to exchange ideas and articulate hopes of a free, egalitarian, and exciting city. Groups and parties inspired by utopian anarchism and socialism engaged in direct actions like squatting, proposed a bewildering number of alternative plans for topics ranging from urban renewal to child care, and successfully participated in the elections (with the utopian Leprechaun Party winning 5 out of 45 seats on the local council).

These experiences of experimentation and emancipation of Dutch youth contrasted sharply with the experiences of guest workers. Guest workers were recruited from Mediterranean countries (Southern

Europe, Morocco, Turkey) to perform filthy, dangerous, taxing, and poorly paid work. Most of the guest workers had low levels of formal education, many were illiterate, and virtually none spoke Dutch. They were expected to do the work and return to their home countries. The very last thing that was anticipated or planned was that the guest workers would settle in the Netherlands and be recognized as members of the polity. However, considering the huge language barriers and cultural differences, it was considered crucial that the guest workers receive counseling after their arrival in the Netherlands. Such counseling was provided by charities, foundations, and associations that operated in the long tradition of pillarization.

While many of the generation of native-born baby boomers threw off the yoke of conformity associated with the Dutch pillarized landscape, pillarized institutions were revamped to incorporate guest workers in networks of tutelage. Jan Rath (1991) shows that the institutional response to guest workers was strongly conditioned by earlier efforts to discipline and educate families considered "asocial" or "maladjusted." Such families were put in programs involving frequent inspections or forced to move into designated residential areas where they were under the continual supervision of wardens. The tutelage exercised by civil society organizations intensified as the welfare state expanded in the 1950s, but in the early 1960s critics increasingly argued that the programs amounted to intrusion, moralism, and stigmatization. The institutional framework created around the treatment of asocial families was not dissolved but reorganized to cater to new target groups, including postcolonial immigrants and especially guest workers. When the first guest workers immigrated from Mediterranean countries like Portugal, Spain, Italy, and Greece to the Netherlands, they were welcomed by committees consisting of employers, local government officials, hostel managers, and civil society organizations like churches and charitable institutions. The committees felt that their most urgent task was to manage the social conflicts arising from the putative cultural differences between the immigrants and their new working and living environment. Such cultural differences between the native Dutch and guest workers were perceived to be considerable for Southern European immigrants and enormous for Turks and Moroccans.

In a memorandum published in 1970, government officials expressed fear of an "alien proletariat" and stated that this "danger is all the more present since especially non-Europeans have strongly deviating societal, cultural and religious patterns, making integration into our society, if not altogether illusory, ... a very difficult ideal to achieve" (cited in Bonjour 2009: 76). The local committees provided professional guidance to groups of Mediterranean immigrants to ensure they knew what behavior was expected by employers, landlords, governments, churches, and unions. The tutelage of foreign workers became the provenance of specialized professionals working for newly established local "welfare organizations for foreign workers" that were increasingly funded by the central government; the Ministry of Social Work initially covered 40% of their budgets, and this increased to 70% in 1969, to 95% in 1972, and to 100% in 1975 (Rath 1991: 157). Guest workers were therefore incorporated into a specialized sector and placed under the direction and supervision of specialized professionals. Their subordination was further buttressed by their dependence on professional interpreters and spokespersons for communicating with the native Dutch, local governments, landlords, and employers.

In Amsterdam, guest workers became the responsibility of the Foundation for the Welfare of Foreign Workers (SWBW),[6] which had been established in 1972. SWBW had emerged from the private initiative of charities and associations from the pillarized civil society, whose primary concern was to ease the plight of the uprooted workers and smooth their relationship with the alien environment. While in other places these foundations operated without too many difficulties for many years or even decades (e.g. in Rotterdam – see Uitermark 2012), in Amsterdam the SWBW immediately became the site of intense conflict between the culture of paternalism fostered by pillarization and the counterculture fostered by the social movements of the 1960s and 1970s. In Amsterdam, new employees at the SWBW were dismayed by the lack of commitment of more senior employees and the board of directors to a more radical understanding of the marginalized position of guest workers. Amsterdam's SWBW was riven by conflicts from the moment it was established. These conflicts were won by employees who shared the democratic imaginations of the new social movements and favored a radical course of action. They successfully called upon the municipality to fire the director and four staff members, which enabled the radicals within the organization to take over.

After the coup by the radicals, the SWBW declared that "it principally rejected migratory labor (*trekarbeid*) as a form of exploitation" and the local organization set itself the goal of "improving the situation of the foreign workers' home countries in such a way that thousands of people no longer are forced to earn their living abroad" (SWBW 1973–1974: 1). And as long as this ultimate goal was not achieved, it endeavored to ensure that foreign workers had the same rights as their Dutch colleagues and that foreign workers could represent themselves optimally. The organization refused to engage immigrants individually and instead opted for a strategy of community development that not only involved the immigrants but also mobilized the support of volunteers and organizations. In their view, the SWBW had marginalized itself before the coup, "especially by the refusal to cooperate with most action, neighborhood and ethnic groups" (ibid.: 5). In response, the renewed organization would grant "first priority to group work. Not in a 'paternalistic' way in which the SWBW keeps control over the management and organization of the groups in question, but much more based on self-determination. Initiatives and the organization and execution of activities should be taken up by the group in question, with or without help from the Foundation's group worker" (ibid.: 7). While the SWBW was fully funded by the national government, its activities were highly contentious. It vehemently protested against the municipality's decision to close down hostels without offering satisfactory alternatives, it united employees against their employers, and it participated in demonstrations against measures targeting undocumented immigrants. Although the SWBW was very explicit in its support of self-determination through group work, it was a specific and selective kind of self-determination that it supported: it renounced "undemocratic" associations and only granted its support and solidarity to "progressive" organizations. In a typical SWBW newsletter, one could gain practical information about language courses or housing permits but also, for instance, an analysis of the position of Turkish workers in the international division of labor by Nihat Karaman, who would later develop into a legendary organizer for the communist-aligned organization HTIB (SWBW 1975).

These developments indicated that institutions originally established to guide and manage guest workers were increasingly becoming tools of mobilization in the hands of leftist immigrants and their native Dutch sympathizers. While initially the immigrants were regarded only as backward target groups in need of supervision and guidance, calls for emancipation and self-determination grew louder over time. The most vocal among the immigrants – often dissidents who not only came to the Netherlands to work but to escape persecution by their home country's regime – demanded direct representation. Rather than having a government-directed foundation look after their welfare, they argued that immigrant self-organizations and immigrant councils should be established. At least some professionals wholeheartedly agreed. They wanted to be in the service of immigrants and not in a position of supervising them. Such pressures against paternalism were heard throughout the Netherlands but especially in Amsterdam. In Amsterdam, the vocal and critical immigrants eventually got what they demanded: the SWBW was dissolved and immigrant self-organizations received funding as well as formal recognition as representatives of their communities.

Organizing for Immigrants' Rights in the 1970s and 1980s

The hunger strikes, the protests, and the flourishing of radical leftist immigrant organizations were highly remarkable considering the guest workers' position within the Netherlands. A largely undereducated group specifically recruited to undertake the most taxing of work without complaining suddenly manifested itself with demonstrations and radical actions that grasped the nation's attention. When we look closer, the mobilizations are even more remarkable. One might expect that a large and successful operation like the hunger strikes (involving contacts within the press, politics, and innumerable solidarity groups) would be orchestrated by activists with long careers in Dutch social movements well-versed in public relations and community organizing. In fact, the leader of the hunger strikes, Abdou Menebhi, had emerged onto Amsterdam's social movement scene only just before the hunger strikes took off.

Menebhi had first visited the Netherlands in December 1974. The occasion of his visit was the establishment of the *Amicales* of the Netherlands. Hundreds of Moroccans had gathered in a conference hall in Utrecht to hear speeches from notables and celebrate the creation of an association that would harness their ties to the home country. But Menebhi had not come to join the celebrations. He took the stage unannounced and launched a tirade against the *Amicales*, stating that they were imposters and rogues in the service of a fascist regime and ending his speech by saying, "If the Moroccan government is so concerned about Moroccans, let them care about Moroccans in Morocco first" (cited in Cottaar et al. 2011: 213). Menebhi's hatred of the *Amicales* had been cultivated during his time at the Association of Moroccans in France (AMF),[7] a Paris-based association established by Moroccan dissidents and vehemently opposed to the Moroccan government (see Chapter 4). Paris offered an extraordinary environment of politicization around that time, spawning a breadth of radical organizations, including the AMF and ATMF, among others. The AMF had been fighting the *Amicales* since they were founded in France in 1973 and Menebhi had been sent specifically with the purpose of undermining a smooth start for the *Amicales* in the Netherlands (Cottaar et al. 2011). Less than a year later, Menebhi would lead a series of hunger strikes of Moroccans in the Netherlands. How is it possible that radicalism among Moroccans suddenly surfaced in the mid-1970s? How is it possible that Menebhi – who was a very recent immigrant to the Netherlands and did not speak Dutch – could become the leader of a massive movement that brought the suppressed rights of guest workers to the attention of the public?

The answers to these questions can be found in the context in which Menebhi and his comrades operated. The city of Amsterdam, and particularly its historical center and the surrounding nineteenth-century neighborhoods, offered fertile soil for grassroots challenges in the 1970s and early 1980s. City planners had attempted to modernize the city center but their plans largely failed to materialize as a result of residents' opposition and budgetary constraints (Pruijt 1985). The opposition to the modernization of the city reached its peak in the early 1970s when residents and activists successfully resisted the government's plans to demolish the Nieuwmarkt neighborhood to make room for a metro line, a highway, and high-rise office buildings. Other neighborhoods in and just outside the center also saw intense resistance from residents to plans to demolish affordable housing and modernize the city. These areas had experienced a huge exodus of Dutch families to new towns and garden cities, leaving behind old-time residents who embraced the somewhat chaotic and diverse character of these neighborhoods and freeing up space for people in search of affordable housing in vibrant urban environments. Many people dissatisfied with the old buildings and narrow streets had been happy to move out into the garden cities and new towns, just as the government had anticipated and planned. But the people remaining in the city increasingly rejected the government's plans and the rationales underlying them (Uitermark 2009).

As the state and corporate capital had failed to redesign the city according to modernist and functionalist precepts, a space of political possibility opened up. The squatter movement became a powerful force in the city: it housed thousands of people[8] and operated a number of large social centers, as well as dozens of smaller community centers. The 1970s also saw the unfolding of an extensive infrastructure for community work, largely financed by the central state. Community centers provided everyday services and organized activities for local communities but were often staffed by radicals involved in social movement activities, including conscientious objectors performing their substitute service. This environment provided the conditions under which campaigns like the hunger strikes could take place and be effective.

Interestingly, the group had initially attempted to organize their campaign in a mosque. At this point, the Moroccan activists protested the Moroccan government because it refused to provide irregular immigrants with passports, which meant that they could not meet one of the crucial conditions for regularization, namely a valid passport. However, the activists were not welcome in the mosque. The first hunger strike by Moroccans was in the Mozes and Aäron church, located right at the spot where the Nieuwmarkt resistance blocked the highway through the neighborhood. The church had become a vibrant social movement center at this time and accommodated, among many other initiatives, office hours for irregular immigrants looking for a permit. De Duif, another site for the hunger strikes, is another example of grassroots mobilizations re-appropriating space. The Catholic clergy had decided to close De Duif in 1974 but a number of parishioners disagreed and squatted in the building to organize their own sermons and activities in defiance of the church authorities.

Grassroots resistance found its flashpoints in concrete settings like the Mozes and Aäron and De Duif churches where people aggregated, overcame fears, drummed up hope, and articulated desires for other, better futures (cf. Castells 2012). These sites were embedded in strong, place-based networks that had evolved in previous rounds of mobilization. The revolutionary sentiments flared up most intensely in the areas where modernistic urban renewal had backfired: the historical city center and the nineteenth-century ring surrounding it. Among the groups filling the places of the Dutch families who had moved to new towns or garden cities were guest workers. When Mediterranean guest workers first arrived in the 1960s they lived near the big industries that had recruited them and that were obliged to provide housing (Musterd 1981: 315), but over time more guest workers found their way to Amsterdam. Around 1970 guest workers lived mostly in overcrowded hostels and concentrated in the city center, while in the course of the 1970s they increasingly moved to (the least wanted segments of) the social housing stock in the nineteenth-century ring (Musterd and Ostendorf 1993). These areas provided the fertile soil in which Amsterdam's immigrant rights movement could flourish.

Neighborhood groups had formed during the resistance to demolitions and consolidated as residents came together (with the help of professionals) to participate in community affairs and decisions regarding urban renewal. Different kinds of neighborhood provisions – community centers, community theater, child care, neighborhood cinemas – were thriving and provided contact points for immigrants in search of services and a progressive social milieu. Anti-fascist and anti-authoritarian groups were also largely locally organized and rooted in this progressive milieu but they were oriented to national and international politics. Within these local networks leftist immigrant organizations could emerge, connect, and flourish. Originally the initiatives for immigrants were mostly taken by native Dutch sympathizers. For instance, the Foreign Workers' Collective (BAK)[9] had been established by groups in various neighborhoods in the center and the nineteenth-century ring and it held office hours for foreign workers, legal as well as illegal, in various community centers throughout the city. BAK provided individual assistance to guest workers who faced difficulties with their employers, landlords, legal status, or benefits but it also – and emphatically – sought to address "structural issues." A typical newsletter included reports from meetings, detailed explanations of regulations with respect to foreign workers, a report on the situation of Turkish guest workers living at the ship-yard, and a manifesto on how the mobility of guest workers undermines capitalism (BAK 1972). With regards to the latter, the newsletter states that "The result is the formation of an increasingly important mobile international industrial proletariat. Perhaps this proletariat is the first really fertile breeding ground for the emergence of an international revolution."

Permeating all the newsletters, minutes, and reports was a sentiment that it was not up to native Dutch sympathizers to decide what was best for immigrants. One potential solution to this problem was to involve foreigners in the organizations but organizations like BAK experienced difficulty recruiting and retaining foreigners. Support groups for for-eigners like BAK increasingly reoriented their activities and focused on assisting immigrants with forming their own leftist organizations. The formation of such groups is far from trivial. Many guest workers did not see themselves as the main protagonists in a socialist revolution, did not speak Dutch, did not have experience setting up organizations, and were generally less inclined to collectively organize to promote their own interests through contentious political action than to improve their position by adapting to the difficult situation they found themselves in. When immigrants did set up organizations, these were often quite con-servative (like the Moroccan *Amicales*, the Turkish Grey Wolves, or the Turkish and Moroccan mosque associations). Only a very specific seg-ment of immigrants were willing and able to profile themselves as a revolutionary vanguard. These immigrants were for the most part dissi-dents who had fled their country of origin to escape from persecution because of the disruptions they caused to authoritarian regimes.

The organization HTIB was founded in 1974 by Osman Candar. Candar had been a political scientist at Ankara University and fled to the Netherlands in November 1973 to escape persecution for his pub-lications in the communist student magazine *Aydinlik*. He moved back to Turkey in October 1974 after the Turkish government declared an amnesty. Although he spent less than a year in the Netherlands, his organization would take root in the Netherlands. Branches of HTIB were established in Rotterdam, Delft, and Amsterdam. While HTIB ini-tially had more members in Rotterdam than in Amsterdam, the latter branch was more active and visible, not least because of strong support from BAK and later its own support group (appropriately named HTIB support group). Shortly after HTIB had been established, the wife of

HTIB's main organizer, Nihat Karaman, established a sister organization specifically for women from Turkey. She explained, in a newsletter of the SWBW, that proletarian women from Turkey were often not free to choose the work they wanted to do and did not profit from the gains of middle-class women. HTIB became an important organizational node for leftist Turks and their sympathizers and participated in demonstrations against immigration restrictions, nuclear weapons, and wars. It also, again with the help of native Dutch supporters, campaigned against the fascist Grey Wolves associated with the Turkish MHP party. KMAN formed through the hunger strikes and was formally established in 1976. Abdou Menebhi became chairman and five of his comrades took up the other positions on the board. Like HTIB, KMAN spawned a sister organization (MVVA). Like HTIB, it participated in many demonstrations specifically for immigrant rights but also on other issues like war.

The founding of these organizations represented an important moment in the politicization of the immigrants involved. They could develop so quickly and strongly because they were embedded in networks that were not of their own making. KMAN was formally established in a squatted canal house in the historical Jordaan district and later opened its headquarters on Ferdinand Bolstsraat, just outside the historical city center in the nineteenth-century neighborhood De Pijp. HTIB was based on the Lijnbaansgracht, just around the corner from the Bloemgracht, and later moved to Weteringsplantsoen, just around the corner from Ferdinand Bolstraat. An examination of the activities of the early years of organizations like KMAN, MVVA (KMAN's sister organization), HTIB, and KTKB (HTIB's sister organization) shows that their contacts with neighborhood groups and anti-fascists were especially strong. Such contacts and supportive relations allowed radicals among the immigrants to carve out a large niche for their organizations. They provided a competing infrastructure to that provided by organizations mostly concerned with religion or loyal to dictatorial regimes. The competition between conservative and progressive organizations occasionally turned violent. KMAN and the *Amicales* had several large-scale street fights as different factions confronted each other during protests or events. But most of the time competition between different ideological currents was at a distance, with left-wing organizations building their base with support from local subsidies and local sympathizers while conservative organizations built theirs with support from home countries or supranational federations.

Leftist organizations could, in short, flourish because they could take root in a fertile movement milieu. The organizational base of leftist minority organizations expanded rapidly in the late 1970s and early 1980s with the help of state-funded professionals sympathetic to their causes as well as subsidies for organizations. The vanguards within these organizations formed a small group, but with the intense support they received they could establish satellite organizations, including various neighborhood-based platforms, youth organizations, and women's organizations. These organizations provided counseling, gave Dutch, Turkish, and Arabic language courses, organized information meetings, hosted large cultural events, published magazines, made radio broadcasts, and so on. The left-wing organizations did not only build an organizational base for their constituents they also cultivated ties to organizations within the local social movement space. As they mobilized their ethnic communities for progressive and radical causes, they increasingly gave and received solidarity – they turned from recipients into partners and came to function as a central node in a densely woven web of activists, associations, and intellectuals. The radical dissidents within leftist minority organizations were uniquely positioned to frame immigrants in ways that resonated with the new social movements blossoming in Amsterdam at the time. The minority organizations improved legitimacy of struggles around racism, imperialism, war, housing, and labor. While immigrants were expected and keen to emphasize their cultural particularities, the radical left minority associations also framed guest workers and their families as fighting the same fight as other activists in the city and around the world, emphasizing how people of all backgrounds should fight together against injustices. The integration of the radical left minorities in the movement milieu and the mutual adjustment of frames created relations of generalized reciprocity with left-leaning political parties, progressive broadcasting associations, activist journalists, and many prominent people (presenters, intellectuals, church leaders) eager to show their support for these disenfranchised groups. The repeated hunger strikes spearheaded by KMAN in 1975, 1977, and 1980 are just one example of mobilizations that were strongly rooted in the Amsterdam movement milieu but directed at national politics. Both Moroccan and Turkish leftist organizations in Amsterdam were driving numerous national campaigns against racism, for Palestine, against war, and against the deportation of specific immigrants or groups of immigrants, among other issues.

In addition to building their local organizational bases and kickstarting national mobilizations, left-wing organizations (like their opponents) were engaged in transnational activism. The close ties between leftist minority organizations, local sympathizers, journalists, funders, and politicians allowed this cluster to pool their resources to create international networks and bring people to Amsterdam. For instance, KMAN organized many meetings and campaigns with the Morocco Committee

(*Marokko Kommittee*) in support of people imprisoned, tortured, or banished by the Moroccan government. The strong tie between the two organizations was formed by Abdou Menebhi, a dissident who had escaped from Morocco's regime and chairman of KMAN, and his partner, a community worker active in urban renewal and minority policy. Dissident thinkers, musicians, and poets performed at cultural and social events organized for KMAN constituents but the organizations also often held meetings in high-society institutions like De Balie or De Rode Hoed to bring dissident thinkers to the attention of journalists and politicians. These centers for debate, and the concentration of journalists and intellectuals in Amsterdam generally, helped to amplify claims by radicals and translate them for Dutch audiences. The organizations also reached out as they participated in international campaigns to mobilize the dissident segments of the diaspora in coordinated international activities (e.g. to press the European Parliament to adopt policies strengthening the Moroccan resistance), in support of Palestine, or against racism in Europe. All these international campaigns required both extensive international networks for coordination and strong local networks for pooling resources and managing logistics. Similarly, prominent figures in leftist Turkish organizations teamed up with local activists and researchers to document the activities of the fascist Grey Wolves in Amsterdam and the repression of activists and intellectuals by the Turkish government. They also participated extensively in international federations that sprang from the leftist movement in Turkey.

The expansion of local organizational bases, the consolidation of ties to social movement clusters, and participation in international campaigns were facilitated by a vibrant social movement milieu but also by government subsidies. With the introduction of the so-called minorities policy in 1983, the national government provided local governments with the means to set up structures for minority consultation and fund organizations. Turks and Moroccans initially formed one council but in 1991 each group had its own council. The resources and influence within this unfolding field were strongly concentrated in the hands of the leftist minority organizations. A detailed examination of subsidies shows that leftist associations received well over 70% of the organizational subsidies between 1985 and 1995 (Uitermark 2012: 175). Leftist organizations also dominated the councils for minority representation. The government demanded that the councils represented all organizations of a specific ethnic group and so conservative organizations were also included, but leftist organizations typically took the lead and spoke on behalf of their respective ethnic groups. The dominance of the radical left was definitely not an expression of their support among minority communities. Although contemporary discussions about the religious conservatism of the Turks and Moroccans may lead to an underestimation of support for progressive and radical goals, many immigrants had no interest in radical politics and many participated in conservative organizations. The radical left's dominance was largely an expression of the strength of their networks and their lobbying efforts. In particular, KMAN and its satellite organizations were successful in monopolizing government-funded service provision and government-sanctioned representation: not a single conservative organization received funding in the 1980s. The leftist Turkish associations had to concede some ground to their conservative competitors but nevertheless claimed the bulk of the subsidies.

Conclusions

The developments in the 1970s and 1980s represent an impressive, even spectacular, consolidation of a movement hub in Amsterdam. Within a decade, a highly marginalized group consisting largely of people lacking formal education and occupying the very bottom ranks of the labor and housing markets had become highly visible. Small groups of dissidents who had been marginalized and repressed in their home countries took on the role of vanguards in Amsterdam, rapidly expanding their organizations, cultivating ties to activists in other sectors, and using their local networks as springboards for their participation in national and international campaigns. While there were some key individuals and organizations taking the lead in these campaigns, they could only make the impact they did because they were embedded in rich and diverse movement networks. These movement networks had grown through a series of mobilizations against the Vietnam War and the occupation of Palestine and in favor of causes like women's rights and university democracy. Mobilizations against the plans to modernize the city through draconian demolitions were especially important because they not only brought different groups together in protest but also protected the urban environments where radicalism could flourish. The networks arising from such mobilizations functioned as conduits that helped catalyze contentious politics: even small-scale or marginalized groups could, in the right conditions, gain the power to organize large-scale campaigns and communicate to national and international audiences. The importance of these place-based networks is also reflected in the socio-spatial logic of contentious politics: it moves from the urban core to the urban periphery. Hunger strikes, for instance, started in Amsterdam's city center and then spread to other cities. Similarly, immigrant organizations were established in Amsterdam's city center and then created offshoots in more peripheral neighborhoods and other cities. The tightly knit movement and community organizations in Amsterdam's historical neighborhoods cultivated strong immigrant organizations which subsequently developed into city, national, and international hubs of immigrant rights activism.

Although the leaders of these leftist immigrant organizations were much more radical than most members of their ethnic communities, they could nevertheless come to be seen as the legitimate voice of their communities. Their ties to other progressive Dutch organizations and political parties allowed the leftist immigrant organizations to occupy a place within the government and keep out rival organizations by stigmatizing them as undemocratic. At least until the early 1980s, the leftist immigrant organizations could profit from state resources without compromising their radical goals and ideologies. In spite of the state support they received, these organizations maintained an antagonistic stance toward the Dutch government as they incessantly protested against discriminatory policies and accused politicians and civil servants of choosing paternalism over involving the minority communities (i.e. the leftist organizations representing them) in handling their problems. The government thus supported opposition against itself, providing minority organizations with resources to create movement spaces where oppositional discourses could flourish. Such a contradictory situation could persist as long as social movements were strong enough to pressure the government, but after the 1980s the radical left would lose much of its power and appeal.

Part II

Urban Landscapes of Control and Contention

By the end of the 1970s, activists in the United States, France, and the Netherlands rallied to push for the rights of immigrants. Within these countries, Los Angeles, Paris, and Amsterdam had established themselves as hubs of national mobilizations, with activists in these cities using their networks to mobilize resources, create mobilizing frames, and set the agenda of broader campaigns. Moving into the 1980s and 1990s, immigrant rights mobilizations in these cities evolved in very different directions. Los Angeles remained a potent hub of immigration rights activism. The first generation of activists in Los Angeles moved to the margins while a newer generation emerged and consolidated itself into a major hub of activism. In Paris, immigrant activists were depoliticized and replaced by two other activist clusters: NGOs advocating for human rights and informal networks of undocumented immigrant activists (*collectifs des sans papiers*). These clusters mobilized, but cleavages and conflicts between them eventually put great strain on their working relations and eventually limited their effectiveness. Lastly, Amsterdam experienced a remarkable and *almost* total process of depoliticization. Radicals, NGOs, and later religious activists all underwent this process. This placed severe limits on the ability of actors to defend the rights of immigrants in the face of a major anti-immigrant backlash in the 2000s. Thus, while our three cases start from quite similar origins in the 1970s, they move in different directions over the course of subsequent decades. How do we account for this parting of the ways in our three cases? Part II suggests that strategies

Cities and Social Movements: Immigrant Rights Activism in the United States, France, and the Netherlands, 1970–2015, First Edition. Walter J. Nicholls and Justus Uitermark.
© 2017 John Wiley & Sons, Ltd. Published 2017 by John Wiley & Sons, Ltd.

of government control, in the form of "political integration," played a major role in shaping the activist networks that unfolded in these cities.

Local governments in large US cities had the resources and capacity to penetrate and exert control over the urban grassroots in the 1970s and early 1980s, but these resources dried up in the late 1980s as a result of federal cuts to big city budgets and cuts to local property taxes ("rollback neoliberalism"). Just as important, the government embraced a "laissez-faire" approach to immigrants in large cities and did not embark on large-scale "integration" and normalization projects as was the case in Europe (Bloemraad 2006). The light footprint of the state in immigrant neighborhoods opened a political space for new activist organizations to take root, experiment with new organizing methods, and eventually flourish.

While we account for blossoming rights politics in Los Angeles by stressing the veritable collapse of an integrating and normalizing state, we account for depoliticization in Europe by highlighting the renaissance of state technologies, tools, and tactics to integrate and normalize immigrant populations settling in these countries. Political integration became the preferred strategy of government control for our European cases, but we also show important differences between integration strategies. The Dutch state has shown impressive capacity to flexibly adapt and respond to points of rebellion that it had not anticipated. The French state has been good at laying out institutional and discursive controls for targeted populations (first- and second-generation immigrant associations) but it has lacked the flexibility needed to respond to unanticipated challenges. The French state has therefore lacked the same level of agility and adaptability that has made the Dutch state so effective in depoliticizing and containing the immigrant grassroots, permitting small spaces in which new seeds of resistance could take root and grow.

Thus, political integration is conceived here as a government strategy introduced in the 1980s and 1990s, alongside the tried-and-true strategy of banishment. Whereas expulsion was introduced to enforce the boundary between licit and illicit immigrants, the strategy of political integration was introduced to exert some control over the political activities of immigrants who had come to settle in the country. These two government strategies combined in various ways in US, French, and Dutch cities, setting the mobilizations in these places on three very different political paths in the years that followed.

6

The Laissez-Faire State
Re-politicizing Immigrants in Los Angeles

During the 1980s and 1990s, Los Angeles's social movement milieu remained vibrant but it also experienced significant changes. Established players like the radicals of CASA and *Hermandad* declined in importance while a new generation of union militants socialized in the struggles of the 1970s exploded onto Los Angeles's political scene. In addition to these activists, well-trained activists from Central America quickly emerged as they fled government repression and civil wars. These changes in the milieu's composition were also reflected in a change in its geography. The center of gravity shifted: East Los Angeles experienced a decline in contentious politics while central Los Angeles experienced a surge.

This chapter sets out to analyze the decline of older forms of activism in East Los Angeles and the rise of new forms in central Los Angeles by highlighting the uneven control strategies of the local government. It suggests that the availability of revenue and federal grants during the 1970s made it possible to ensnare some East Los Angeles organizations and stimulate them to professionalize their activities. However, the subsequent period of "rollback neoliberalism" in the 1980s (Peck and Tickell 2002) deprived the city of the means to reach out and channel the new buzzing cluster of activists in central Los Angeles. Moreover, the laissez-faire tradition of immigrant integration in the United States (Bloemraad 2006) reduced government efforts to micro-manage the political incorporation of new Central American immigrant activists.

Cities and Social Movements: Immigrant Rights Activism in the United States, France, and the Netherlands, 1970–2015, First Edition. Walter J. Nicholls and Justus Uitermark.
© 2017 John Wiley & Sons, Ltd. Published 2017 by John Wiley & Sons, Ltd.

This stood in sharp contrast to Western European countries where powerful government controls were rolled out to manage and channel the political conduct of new immigrant communities. Weaker government controls in central Los Angeles provided enough breathing room for new autonomous clusters to emerge, take root, and form new connections between them.

The chapter addresses these issues by first describing the changing landscapes of political control in the city. The uneven application of these controls stifled activists in one part of the city while permitting the growth of new activist clusters in central Los Angeles. As these clusters emerged in this area of the city, crosscutting concerns over the conditions of working-class immigrants encouraged some activists to reach out of their own particular clusters and build bridges with others. We suggest that this networking process contributed to creating a strong activist agglomeration, whereby members developed an aptitude to pool collective resources in a wide variety of campaigns. Such an agglomeration would go on to transform Los Angeles into a hub of immigrant activism in the late 1990s and 2000s. Before it assumed this position, however, relations needed to be built between different actors, trust needed to be nurtured, and common ways of seeing and doing things needed to be created. Only after this painstakingly slow process could the diverse activists in the city create the networks needed to pool and deploy high-grade resources for a range of collective ends.

Government Constraints on Eastside Activism

In the 1970s, CASA and *Hermandad* were positioned to assume leadership over the fledgling immigrant rights movement. These two organizations didn't only support the rights of recent immigrants, they had also pushed their allies in Los Angeles and elsewhere to do the same. Their early leadership on the issue was also helped by the shift in the demographics at that time. The population of immigrants grew from 8% to 27% between 1960 and 1990 (Waldinger and Bozorgmehr 1996: 16). By the end of the decade, the Los Angeles metropolitan area had become a major gateway of immigration from Latin America and Asia. In spite of these favorable conditions, political changes in East Los Angeles weakened these organizations in the late 1970s and limited their abilities to assume leadership roles in the 1980s and 1990s.

CASA grew rapidly in the early 1970s because of its embeddedness in East Los Angeles's activist networks. CASA leaders were able to draw upon a rich, motivated, and increasingly university-educated pool of local

Chicano volunteers. Access to these resources allowed CASA to perform higher-end functions like running communication campaigns, developing legal analyses, and so on. Moreover, CASA's good relations with local Latino and community organizations enabled it to partner up on projects, campaigns, and coalitions. While there were certainly differences between organizations in East Los Angeles, there were also many connections, reciprocal exchanges, and mutual obligation. CASA used these networks to draw on localized resources and become an important local *and* national organization. If CASA's growth can be explained by its embeddedness in East Los Angeles's activist networks, its decline can also be partially explained[1] by local institutional changes that affected activist networks.

Tom Bradley's campaigns to become mayor of Los Angeles in 1969 and 1973 gave many local activists hope that there would be greater opportunities for minority communities in the city, including Latinos. Bert Corona, the founder of *Hermandad* and CASA, supported Bradley in 1969 and 1973. Corona became one of the campaign managers and assumed responsibility for running the "Spanish-speaking campaign." He worked with MAPA, *Hermandad*, Brown Berets, MECHA, and other organizations in East Los Angeles to build a powerful electoral machine. While mobilizing local support for Bradley, Corona pressured Bradley to campaign in Latino and immigrant neighborhoods:

> We countered the racism and scare tactics [employed by Bradley's adversary] by getting Bradley to campaign very heavily in the Mexican barrios. He supported all our efforts. He went out to Estrada Courts, Pico Gardens, Aliso Village and other neighborhoods, and he campaigned among the *mexicano* poor. Besides targeting specific neighborhoods, we also had Bradley walk the downtown streets where *mexicanos* congregated and shopped. (Corona 1994: 270, emphasis in original)

Corona was successful in mobilizing the Latino vote in 1969 but this support was not enough to win the citywide election (Sonenshein 1994).

Bradley went on to win the 1973 election by assembling a coalition of economic elites, Latino and African American communities, white liberals, and unions. Bradley held together this motley coalition through the use of "selective incentives" (Stone 1994) for different blocs of supporters. His aggressive urban development strategy pleased downtown elites and many trade unions. He gained the support of minority communities by increasing public support for community organizations and introducing affirmative action programs in government hiring (Sonenshein 1994). Like other liberal big-city mayors during the 1970s (Sonenshein 1994; Stone 1994; McQuarrie 2013), Bradley made use of federal funding for grants, welfare, and infrastructure projects to incentivize the loyalty of key constituent groups. Federal funding for these programs increased dramatically during the early to mid-1970s, with the "urban" part of the federal budget growing from 2% to 12% between 1968 and 1973, and remaining at these levels until the end of the decade (Florida and Jonas 1991: 374). The growth of these funds was an extension of the Johnson administration's "War on Poverty" and a response to massive unrest in the country's largest cities (Piven and Cloward 1978; Castells 1983; Mollenkopf 1983; Florida and Jonas 1991; Cruikshank 1993).

In East Los Angeles, city officials and private foundations began to encourage community organizations to assume a greater role in providing services and adopt more professional methods to perform service functions. This was by no means unique to Los Angeles, with community organizations across the country facing similar pressures (see Castells 1983; Cruikshank 1993; McQuarrie 2013). Local government agencies expected community organizations to rationalize their operations, identify clear issue areas (property redevelopment, youths, drugs), and set well-defined and measurable goals. Organizations that failed to professionalize their operations could be deprived of financial support from the city. Community organizations that had started to depend on government funding had little choice but to comply with the new rules and expectations. As they did, their goals, strategies, and operating norms increasingly reflected those of the city government.

Not only did this blunt the contentious character of community organizations in East Los Angeles, it also resulted in what Michael McQuarrie (2013) called a "civic monoculture." By this he meant the homogenization of organizational models, norms, and goals within cities. The drift toward organizational conformity in East Los Angeles made it more difficult for subversive organizations with innovative and oppositional ideas to emerge and take hold. The hard-working staff and volunteers in eastside community organizations had difficulty enough keeping their operations running, let alone lend their support to revolutionary Chicano organizations like CASA. For organizations playing by the new rules of the game, there was no reason to establish partnerships with others that veered from the status quo and put their access to legitimacy and government resources at risk. Drawing on the language of counter-insurgency, the new partnerships between the government and civic associations during the late 1970s "drained the sea" of East Los Angeles, leaving leftwing radicals isolated and unable to tap into the resources of a local and supportive activist milieu.[2]

By 1978, East Los Angeles was on its way to civic pacification vis-à-vis the process of professionalization and the creation of a civic monoculture. The few remaining radical organizations like CASA were isolated and cut off from most organizations and people in the area. CASA members remained committed radicals and dedicated to immigrant rights, fighting against borders, and supporting revolution. But their continued radicalism in an increasingly depoliticized environment contributed to further alienating them from other organizations in the area. Revolutionary discourses failed to resonate with the newer professional norms of community organizations. These discourses were viewed as "noises" from unrealistic and unreasonable radicals. With a dwindling pool of allies and volunteers, CASA soon lacked the essential resources to service and advocate for undocumented immigrants. This resulted in the loss of the organization's members and membership dues, which precipitated a further decline in revenue from fees for basic services. Without volunteers, allies, revenue, and a base in the immigrant community, CASA could no longer survive and closed its doors in 1979.

Hermandad faced a similar political environment. However, its less radical and non-sectarian stance, its good relations with the Bradley administration, and the excellent reputation of Bert Corona in the city and beyond allowed it to draw continued support from local allies and the political establishment. *Hermandad* faced some of the same challenges as CASA. It had benefited from a highly politicized and charged activist milieu in the early part of the decade but now it focused more on service provision and less on contentious advocacy. The depoliticization of the milieu limited its abilities to draw upon local resources to mount bold local, state, and national campaigns. In spite of these limitations, *Hermandad* continued to provide services and support to undocumented immigrants and assumed important roles in national coalitions against the restrictive Simpson-Mazzoli bills of 1982, 1984, and 1986. By the end of the 1970s, the two major Los Angeles organizations that had led the way on immigration rights faced a challenging environment. Whereas one organization (CASA) failed to overcome these challenges and closed its doors, the other (*Hermandad*) adapted and continued its efforts to assist undocumented immigrants and campaign on their behalf.

The resources that enabled the Bradley administration to penetrate and steer the urban grassroots in a more professionalized direction dried up in the 1980s during a period of rollback neoliberalism (Peck and Tickell 2002). This required leaner governmental controls in traditional minority communities (i.e. East Los Angeles), which accelerated the depoliticization and destruction of local organizations. The funding that supported community initiatives in Los Angeles's low-income and minority areas dried up during the 1980s. The urban part of the federal budget fell from approximately 12% to 7% between 1978 and

1984 (Florida and Jonas 1991: 374). Federal funding for urban programs nationally declined during the decade, with annual funds being reduced for Community Block Grants ($6.3 to 4 billion), Employment Training ($14.3 to $4.2 billion), and Assisted Housing ($26.8 to $8.9 billion) (Eisinger 1997: 3). This meant that the "average federal share of the municipal income stream declined from 22 per cent in 1980 to a mere 6 per cent in 1989 while the share of funding from states remained constant (on average)" (Davis 1993: 11). To make matters worse in California, Proposition 13 in 1977 cut revenue from property taxes. By 1990, the average resident of California paid 38% less in property taxes than the average resident of New York (ibid.).

The decline in revenue from federal funding and property taxes induced the Bradley administration to prioritize policy areas that would stimulate economic growth and generate tax revenues. This precipitated an aggressive effort to attract elite businesses and middle-class residents to the city. The Bradley administration invested approximately $1 billion to make Los Angeles into a "world-class city" during a period in which services to low-income communities were being dramatically cut (Davis 2000). As scarce public resources were diverted into projects that benefited the upper middle class and elite businesses, the city cut economic development programs in low-income areas by 82%, housing programs by 78%, and job training programs by 63% (Davis 2000: 245). The city and county sought additional savings by outsourcing some social service functions to professional nonprofit organizations (Wolch 1990, 1996). Traditional community organizations were compelled to compete with new, non-local, and highly professionalized nonprofit organizations for declining government resources. Many of the smaller community organizations disappeared, while the larger ones held on through patronage ties with politicians or increased professionalization.

East Los Angeles activists therefore faced a pincer movement of government constraints: whereas many community organizations were encouraged to professionalize their activities in the late 1970s and early 1980s, dependent organizations were then confronted with much weaker levels of government support in the 1980s and early 1990s. This had the effect of precipitating community organizations to focus on service provisions to "troubled" groups (youths, immigrants, drug addicts, mothers), and it spurred intense and deleterious competition for a diminishing pot of public resources. Those organizations that could professionalize their activities the most survived and thrived in this environment. By contrast, contentious activist organizations were pushed further to the margins and isolated in East Los Angeles. In spite of the limits imposed on contentious organizations like CASA and *Hermandad*, individual activists who had been socialized through them and similar organizations in the

1970s continued their activism into the 1980s and 1990s. Some certainly tried to continue their activist work in community organizations in East Los Angeles, but others became incorporated into the new activist clusters that started to emerge in central Los Angeles. They helped form a bridge between two generations of activism, permitting the transmission of ideas, frames, cultures, and repertoires from one time-place (East Los Angeles in the 1970s) to another (central Los Angeles in the 1980s and 1990s).

The New Landscapes of Activism in Central Los Angeles

Leaner government controls helped to accelerate the depoliticization of East Los Angeles's grassroots but rollback neoliberalism made it difficult for the city to create new controls in the emerging immigrant communities of central Los Angeles. Just as important, the national and local government showed little interest in developing programs to "integrate" immigrant communities, reflecting the "laissez-faire" approach to immigrant governance in the United States (Bloemraad 2006). The combination of rollback neoliberalism and this laissez-faire approach to immigration limited the government's reach into new immigrant communities. This provided an opening for new and creative grassroots activities in this part of the city.

New immigrant organizations in the 1980s were also able to offset dependencies on government resources by depending on volunteers, private foundational support, and membership dues. The city government in the 1990s would provide more support to certain local immigrant organizations (day labor organizers in particular), but the diverse sources of revenue and support (e.g. allies, private foundations, fees for services, dues-paying members) and weak government surveillance provided these organizations with some autonomy to continue their more politically contentious work. The relatively light footprint on the local grassroots therefore allowed enough independence for the proliferation of diverse organizations with innovative ideas concerning how to service, organize, and politicize new immigrants in the city. Three clusters became particularly prominent during this time: immigrant organizations, unionists, and politicized academics from area universities.

A new generation of immigrant organizations

The 1970s and 1980s sparked an important influx of Central Americans to central Los Angeles. Whereas the combined population of El Salvadorans and Guatemalans stood at 13,300 in 1970, it ballooned to 99,600 in 1980 (Hamilton and Chinchilla 2001: 45). This remarkable growth continued into the 1980s as civil wars in these countries unfolded. A substantial number of these new immigrants were well-trained, left-wing activists seeking refuge from extremely repressive governments. Their settlement in Los Angeles changed the city's activist milieu in considerable ways. These immigrants brought different motivations, repertoires, and discourses to the scene, which made them an important source of political innovation. In particular, immigrant activists cultivated radical ideas and practices of self-organization under extremely repressive conditions.

Central Americans faced unique difficulties gaining refugee status. Because the US government supported the governments that repressed them, their applications for refugee status had a high rejection rate. Recognizing the legitimacy of refugee status would inadvertently undermine White House claims that its Central American allies were beacons of freedom in a battle against encroaching Soviet tyranny (Menjívar 1997; Coutin 2003). Only 3% of El Salvadorans and Guatemalans gained refugee status compared to approximately 40% of asylum seekers from socialist countries during the 1980s (Menjívar 1997: 111). Without legal status, Central Americans could not draw on most government services, which resulted in heavy dependence on nonprofit service providers, churches, and local activist networks. Several service organizations in Los Angeles, including the Lutheran Social Services and Refugee Resettlement, Catholic Social Services, and the Los Angeles Free Clinic, played important roles in providing the Central American population with basic legal, housing, and medical services (Hamilton and Chinchilla 2001: 122). Activists from solidarity networks, churches, and local organizations also played important supportive roles during this early transition period.

These organizations provided life-enabling support to new immigrants, and the immigrants in turn provided support for new organizations. Left-wing activists from El Salvador had extensive experience in building organizations under very difficult political conditions. In Los Angeles they employed a "base community" model to create one of the first immigrant organizations in the city, *El Rescate* (1981). This organizing model aimed to raise the political consciousness of the poor and strengthen solidarities within geographically bounded communities. Once a "base" of committed activists was formed in a community, it could then connect to other bases and extend their struggles outward. *El Rescate* provided legal and material services to the Central American community of central Los Angeles and went on to provide medical and educational services through its sister organizations *Clínica Oscar Romero* (1983) and *Clínica de Las Americas* (1989). It also created another organization (Santana Chirino Amaya Central American Refugee Committee) to play a more direct political role. This latter spinoff fostered political solidarity and consciousness-raising by hosting community events (meetings, information sessions, parties, dances, football clubs, musical bands, etc.) in Central American neighborhoods. It held weekly assemblies consisting of political speeches, information updates from the home front, concerts, and meals in the backlot of the *Clínica Oscar Romero.*

Other El Salvadoran activists who were affiliated with different left-wing parties in their home country created Los Angeles-based affiliates, largely in central Los Angeles. These political organizations held meetings, rallies, parties, fundraisers, and even revolutionary "Sunday schools" for the children of their members (Hamilton and Chinchilla 2001). Some of these organizations (the Popular Revolutionary Block) worked with their local allies to create the Committee in Solidarity with the People of El Salvador (CISPES). This organization assumed a leading role in the struggle against the Reagan administration's foreign policy in Central America. While CISPES quickly evolved into a national organization, two of the organization's first national directors, Heidi Tarver and Angela Sanbrano, were the founding members of the Los Angeles chapter. In addition to fighting against US foreign policies, CISPES helped launch a campaign to win refugee status for El Salvadoran and Guatemalan migrants (Coutin 2003). After several years of organizing support networks, launching lawsuits, and lobbying the House and Senate, CISPES and its allies finally pressured the government to provide many of these immigrants with Temporary Protected Status in 1990.

Alongside CISPES and *El Rescate*, other El Salvadorans created the Central American Refugee Committee. This organization worked with religious supporters (Southern California Ecumenical Council) to create the Central American Refugee Center (CARECEN). While CARECEN was rooted in central Los Angeles, its supporters also created branches in other cities with large concentrations of Central Americans, like Washington, DC (Hamilton and Chinchilla 2001). CARECEN provided many of the same legal and social services as *El Rescate* but it also introduced new services to address problems with exploitative employers and landlords. These included informing its members of their rights ("know your rights" pamphlets and workshops), instructing members on how to use the legal system against landlords and employers, and occasionally organizing small protests against problematic employers. It must be stressed that CARECEN played a pivotal role in transitioning immigrant activism away from home country and refugee issues and toward the rights (labor and housing) of new immigrants in their places of settlement. Its director in the late 1980s and early 1990s, the UCLA-trained lawyer Madeline Janis, pushed the organization further in this direction.

The passage of the Immigration Reform and Control Act (IRCA) in 1986[3] destabilized the lives of many immigrants (Coutin 2003). IRCA provided a path to legalization for undocumented immigrants, but only for those who had arrived before 1982 or who were working in agriculture. Recent immigrants (after 1982) living in cities did not qualify for this measure. By 1990, this left 60% of El Salvadorans without legal status (Menjívar 1997: 109). IRCA also introduced employer sanctions and augmented resources for immigration enforcement (Coutin 1998, 2003; Massey et. al. 2003). This meant that the government now had more resources to police a smaller population of undocumented immigrants, many of whom were Central Americans.

The Coalition for Humane Immigrant Rights of Los Angeles (CHIRLA) was created in response to IRCA (Coutin 2003; Patler 2010). CHIRLA formed as a coalition of immigrant rights organizations and allies. It was firmly rooted in the Central American district of central Los Angeles, but its aim was to service all immigrants in the Los Angeles metropolitan area. CHIRLA's first task was to provide legal counsel to immigrants and assist processing applications under IRCA's amnesty program. It was also drawn into labor rights disputes that resulted from IRCA's employer sanctions. Greater involvement in workplace disputes prompted CHIRLA to provide education and outreach programs to immigrant communities while simultaneously creating new programs to advance the rights of immigrant workers. Thus, like CARECEN, CHIRLA's service and advocacy work came to focus on both fighting for the legal status of new immigrants *and* fighting for the workplace rights of immigrants (documented and undocumented) who were settling in the country (Patler 2010).

This cluster of immigrant rights organizations continued to fight against US foreign policy and for the extension of residency status for Central American refugees. However, CHIRLA, CARECEN, and others moved to support campaigns for the rights of immigrants living and working in the country (Milkman 2010). CHIRLA began its Workers' Rights Project in 1991, with a metropolitan-level campaign to organize day laborers as a cornerstone of this project (Patler 2010). It expanded its efforts to assist immigrants in workplace disputes while beginning to provide more specific support to day laborers, domestic workers, and street vendors. It established a Domestic Worker Outreach Program in 1991, which eventually evolved into the Domestic Workers' Association. As part of this project, CHIRLA actively lobbied the California legislature to expand the protections and rights of domestic workers who had been exempted from many federal and state labor laws. In the mid-1990s, CHIRLA took a leading role in advocating against anti-solicitation measures targeting day laborers.

Pablo Alvarado, an El Salvadoran activist who had been inspired by the "base communities" model, took a leading role in creating and managing CHIRLA's day labor workers' centers. He used the centers to build solidarity among day laborers, educate them about their rights, and raise political awareness and consciousness. CARECEN also began to play a role in extending the rights of immigrant workers. In addition to creating their own day labor workers' centers, CARECEN addressed working conditions in the tourist industry and lent its support to the street vendors campaign in the 1990s. In this way, immigrant rights organizations continued advocating for legalizing immigrants, but they also embarked on projects to assert the rights of immigrant workers.

It must be stressed that this new generation of activists did not work in isolation from one another. They were embedded in tight interpersonal and interorganizational relations, and they were located in close proximity to one another in central Los Angeles. In addition to working intensively with one another, they went to each other's parties, attended weddings and baptisms, and frequented the same social establishments. They were allies as much as they were friends. Moreover, the exclusion and hostility facing Central Americans by the US government helped create a sense of "bounded solidarity" and "enforceable trust" among activists (Portes and Sensenbrenner 1993: 1335). Solidarity enabled individuals to conceive of themselves as a distinctive community in a fight to protect and extend their rights in hostile legal, political, and cultural environments. Trust enabled these resource-poor organizations to work with one another and contribute their scarce resources to projects and campaigns over an extended period of time.

The more they worked with one another and developed complex interdependencies, the more they became dependent on the resources provided by the activist cluster and the more sensitive they were to the cluster's sanctioning capacities. Cultivating a good reputation and respecting obligations to others, in other words, became necessary means to avoid exclusion from the unique resources and support provided by the activist cluster (Coleman 1988; Portes and Sensenbrenner 1993). These relations strengthened throughout the 1990s, with one long-time funder remarking in a 2001 interview:

> There is a lot of support, engagement, and organizing among the groups we are funding. We find them in response to that question: "With what other organizations do you work and to what extent?" We find that they mention each other. And they are not just mentioning each other but that

they are meeting or are a part of the same coalition. I'm talking about people who are engaged in actual work, who connect, and who actually collaborate with other organizations for very specific needs. You have IDEPSCA, CHIRLA, CARECEN, and KIWA working with each other around particular immigration projects. (Liberty Hill, personal interview)

Accruing solidarity and trust enabled partners to invest more in longer-term and more complicated advocacy projects.

The new unionism in Los Angeles

Alongside the cluster of immigrant rights organizations, a new and innovative generation of union activists emerged (Milkman 2006). They embraced a strategy to organize low-wage immigrant workers in the service and manufacturing industries. The offices of the most innovative unions were also located in central Los Angeles. These union activists were ensconced in the new immigrant communities.

Unions in Los Angeles faced a unique juncture in the 1980s (Milkman 2006; Soja 2010). Subcontracting and outsourcing in service and manufacturing drove down the working conditions and wages of workers. Globalization made matters worse. Firms that could leave left and those that stayed counteracted union organizing efforts with the threat of exit or through subcontracting (Cox 1997; Storper 1997; Bonacich and Gapasin 2001). The low-paid workforce of Los Angeles was also being remade by the influx of new Latino immigrants, a population that labor leaders had traditionally scorned. Most national unions during the 1980s believed that new immigrants (especially undocumented) were unorganizable, competitors for American jobs, and strikebreakers (Milkman 2006). This view led the AFL-CIO to endorse the punitive employer sanctions of IRCA in 1986 (Moody 1988: 283). Some national unions like the United Farm Workers and the Service Employees International (SEIU) had changed their position on immigration by the 1980s, but most others continued to view immigrants as threats to the American working class.

In this context, a new generation of young labor activists – politicized through the social movements of the previous decade – argued for a dramatic change in strategy: rather than just reassert the union's power in areas like durable manufacturing, they argued that unions should also organize workers in booming low-wage sectors. The service industry was particularly strategic because these jobs could not be outsourced to the developing world (Soja 2000). Moreover, they believed that migrant workers in flexible workplaces were organizable and capable of supporting high-risk campaigns (Milkman 2006). They drew inspiration from the UFW's two-prong strategy of building up committed union activists in workers' communities (not just the workplace) *and* gaining the support of broad sectors of the public through media campaigns (Needleman 1998). For this new generation of union organizers, the union movement's survival depended on changing from the traditional strategy of privileging durable manufacturing and the "traditional" working class (white, male). As UCLA urban planner and long-time housing activist Jacqueline Leavitt remarked, "If they didn't do this, they would die … I think it [the new strategy] was really a matter of survival" (personal interview).

John Sweeney, president of the SEIU, was an early and strong advocate of the new strategy and sponsored a national campaign to organize janitors – Justice for Janitors – in the 1980s (Waldinger et al., 1998; Milkman 2006). The campaign proved to be effective because it combined resources from the national organization (research, legal support, money, and media support) with efforts to build support in workers' communities and from the general public. It embraced direct action mobilizations such as occupations, demonstrations, public shaming of employers, and disruptions of employers' events. These early efforts revealed themselves to be effective in recruiting new workers, increasing union densities, reversing declines in wages and working conditions, and making low wages an issue of public debate. The strategy also demonstrated that undocumented immigrants were organizable and that many possessed experience that made them very effective union militants. According to the SEIU international vice president, "Immigrants from Central America have a much more militant history as unionists than we do, then the more militant they are, the more the union can do" (cited in Hamilton and Chinchilla 2001: 86). Rather than new immigrants being a threat to the labor movement, they were increasingly viewed as a source of labor's revival.

Other union organizers in Los Angeles agreed with the importance of organizing immigrants in the city's low-wage economy. The local leaders of International Ladies' Garment Workers Union (ILGWU) began their efforts to organize immigrant workers in the late 1970s. As more garment workers came from Latin America, the union hired Spanish-speaking organizers and made a concerted outreach effort to this community. After the passage of IRCA in 1986, immigrant garment workers faced new threats because of employer sanctions. Some employers began to discriminate against Latino immigrants irrespective of their legal status out of concern of violating the law; others threatened to report them to the Immigration and Naturalization Service (INS) in response to union organizing efforts; and still others employed more exploitative ways (homework; outsourcing to smaller contractors; etc.) to escape the reach of federal law enforcement agencies.

In response to the growing distress of garment workers, the union provided educational programs and legal advice on the basic rights of immigrant workers. In an effort to formalize and continue their outreach efforts, the union created Justice Centers to inform immigrants of their rights, file complaints against employers, and provide English and citizenship courses (Milkman 2010). ILGWU would evolve into UNITE (United Needle Trades, Industrial and Textile Employees) and launch an anti-sweatshop campaign in the 1990s. Alongside the path-breaking work of UNITE, Maria Elena Durazo, president of the Hotel and Restaurant Employees (HERE) union, pushed a similar strategy for her union. Before she assumed the leadership of the union, she argued that the old union leadership ignored the needs of immigrant workers in the hotel and restaurant sector and that the union's survival depended on extending its reach to the mostly immigrant and female workforce.

While SEIU, UNITE, and HERE began targeting low-wage immigrant workers, they also were interested in organizing outside traditional workplaces and developing support in immigrant communities. "The fluidity of their work lives makes organizing around the job a temporary thing, at best. As a result, the social structures of community become more important to the individual than the social structures connected with the job" (Bonacich and Gapasin 2001: 351). In order to gain access to immigrant communities and enhance their legitimacy within them, union organizers sought to develop connections with immigrant organizations proliferating throughout the city. There was also a concerted effort to gain the support of clergy and faith-based organizations for their various efforts (Hondagneu-Sotelo 2008). Maria Elena Durazo (president of HERE) and Madeline Janis-Aparicio (former director of CARECEN, current director of LAANE[4]) recognized the importance of clergy and created a new inter-faith organization in 1996, Clergy and Lay United for Economic Justice (CLUE).

> At that time, she [Janis-Aparicio] was part of the Central American movement and she had the task to recruit clergy for a labor campaign. When she was recruiting she found a great opportunity. Clergy members were responding more than what she was expecting. They were really interested in being involved in this coalition. Then they met and started to develop strategies. Then they [clergy] went back to the community and said we need to make more of an impact. We needed an inter-faith organization because workers and elected officials were from all denominations and backgrounds. (CLUE, personal interview)

CLUE-affiliated clergy visited the homes of immigrant workers and sought to secure their support for the organizing efforts of unions and allied organizations. The organization was also effective in reaching the broader public and pressuring public officials to support union goals (Hondegneu-Sotelo 2006). The new strategy didn't only entail a shift in target populations (immigrants). It reflected a shift in the geography of organizing, making concerted efforts to reach outside of the traditional workplace and extend their reach into immigrant communities and the broader public sphere.

In 1996 Miguel Contreras (former UFW activist, former member of HERE, and husband of Maria Elena Durazo) was elected to the presidency of the powerful Los Angeles County Federation of Labor. The "County Fed," as it is colloquially called, had been dominated by more conservative unions and served as the electoral arm of the local Democratic Party. In assuming leadership, Contreras embraced the new organizing strategy and asserted the organization's autonomy from Democratic Party leaders. Candidates needed to demonstrate their commitment to labor's general goals if they wanted to secure its support. Contreras also worked with other organizations to naturalize immigrants and mobilize them to vote for favorable candidates. This resulted in a powerful political machine to elect politicians who supported the County Fed's policies and campaigns. His efforts transformed the County Federation of Labor into an important counterweight to the anti-immigrant and neoliberal tide of the 1990s. Moreover, the County Fed's voter mobilization efforts changed the balance of power between politicians and the union movement, with the former becoming more dependent on the latter for their survival (*LA Weekly*, May 12, 2005).

New immigrants in Los Angeles, many of whom were undocumented, were certainly workers but they were workers facing a distinctive set of legal circumstances that made them more vulnerable to exploitation than others. Immigrant workers faced discrimination, lived in constant fear of deportation, were threatened by employers' sanctions, worked for unscrupulous employers, had few legal options to lodge complaints, and were denied many protections and social welfare. Organizing immigrants therefore didn't simply involve fighting for workers' rights but also defending the basic rights and protections of immigrant workers irrespective of their legal status. The passage of restrictive immigration measures and laws in the 1990s only made matters worse by further restricting access to public services and enhancing the policing powers of the INS. The more the government rolled back the rights of immigrants, the more union organizers were drawn directly into the fight to extend legal protections and rights to this sector of the working class. In 1997 John Sweeney, the newly elected president of the national labor union (AFL-CIO[5]) and champion of the new organizing strategy, announced the union's rejection of its past anti-immigrant position and its new policy of embracing progressive immigration laws. Following the announcement, the AFL-CIO and several of its affiliates (the SEIU in particular) became dedicated partners in the national campaign for immigration reform. Organizing immigrants in the workplace therefore forced unions to confront restrictive laws and policies, which in turn prompted them to get directly involved in national-level struggles to expand immigrant rights.

Los Angeles-based union innovators did not work in isolation of one another. They socialized, mobilized on each other's behalf, and shared insights on organizing and mobilizing tactics. While past campaigns like those organized by the UFW provided some insight, these new unionists were "learning by doing" and adapting different tactics and methods to this specific organizing environment. By the late 1990s, however, the once-experimental organizing model of Los Angeles (Milkman 2006, 2010) was consolidated and gained national prominence with the election of John Sweeney as president of the AFL-CIO and Miguel Contreras as head of the Los Angeles Country Federation of Labor. Both pushed unions in Los Angeles and across the state and country to embrace the organizing model that had been developed and perfected in this city. By the early 2000s, there were still many unions resisting change but they were now swimming against the tide of innovation (sometimes fiercely).

University intellectuals as activists

Intellectuals have always played a part in social movements (Gramsci 1971; Bourdieu 1984, 1994; Foucault 1984; Mann 1993; King and Szeléyni 2004; Nicholls and Uitermark 2014). As activists, intellectuals have certain levels of cultural and symbolic capital that can be very useful for social movements. Their disciplinary knowledge (law, politics, sociology, geography, planning) can enhance the analytical capacities of a campaign; their methodological skills assist the research capacities of organizations; their linguistic abilities help produce effective mobilizing frames; and their legitimacy helps enhance the credibility of activist claims (Bourdieu 1984, 1994; Foucault 1984).

A cluster of intellectual activists emerged in Los Angeles during the 1980s and 1990s. While faculty and students associated with the University of California, Los Angeles were an important part of this cluster, activist scholars also emerged at the University of Southern California, Occidental College, and Pitzer College. These intellectual activists reflect what Michel Foucault (1984) called "specific intellectuals" – that is, intellectuals who lend their concrete knowledge (urban planning, statistics, mapping, law) and material resources (university buildings, financing, support, access to students) to advance the campaigns of marginalized peoples.

UCLA in the 1980s and 1990s emerged as an important center for fostering these kinds of "specific intellectuals." Activist scholars from the university early on developed close ties to labor and immigrant rights struggles (Nicholls 2003; Milkman 2006; Soja 2010). Scholars in the departments of Geography and Urban Planning[6] used the city as a laboratory to analyze the effects of globalization on the city (Soja 2010; Nicholls 2011b). Their more applied planning colleagues[7] embraced bottom-up traditions of urban planning, inspired by advocacy planners like Paul Davidoff and community organizers like Saul Alinsky. Their interests centered on how planners could play a role in different struggles unfolding in the city. They also developed a tradition of bringing in community and labor activists into the university to participate in seminars and workshops. Goetz Wolff (former PhD student at UCLA, former research director of the County Federation of Labor, current lecturer in Urban Planning) recollected:

> We would bring labor people into the university. Ed [Soja] was willing to use his political economy class to focus on [manufacturing] plant closings … It was a way in which the class and maybe 18 students got involved in the whole thing. There were a greater number of activist types in Urban Planning at that time. From the point of view of academia, there was a very strong environment for applying radical concepts to things that were happening throughout the city. (Personal interview)

Alongside Urban Planning faculty and students, several UCLA scholars began to shape the direction of the Institute for Research on Labor and Employment (IRLE). They wanted the Institute to continue its traditional academic work on labor markets, but they also wanted to work more collaboratively with the city's new generation of union and immigrant leaders. They believed that the Institute could play a decisive role in strengthening the research capacities of Los Angeles unions. The Center for Labor Education and Research ("Labor Center") was a part of the IRLE but its primary function was to work with union and community members to address the problems facing low-wage workers. Under Ruth Milkman's and Kent Wong's (a former SEIU lawyer) leadership, the Labor Center would go on to play a major role in immigrant rights and labor organizing in the city.

Members of Urban Planning and the Labor Center developed a variety of methods to institutionalize ties between the university and the city's activist milieu. They developed curricula and courses to train their students to become skilled organizers. Urban Planning offered courses on

Los Angeles labor markets, taught by Goetz Wolff, while both the Labor Center and Urban Planning offered courses on organizing campaigns in working-class communities. The Labor Center also offered a major in Labor Studies and both the Labor Center and the Department of Urban Planning actively supported internship programs in progressive organizations and unions. These programs trained students to develop and use their skills (economic knowledge, legal and planning analysis, statistics and GIS skills, etc.) to benefit actual mobilizations and activist organizations. Many students went on to join local organizations and unions and played decisive roles in many Los Angeles campaigns. In the case of the Justice for Janitors campaign in the 1990s, Roger Waldinger and his colleagues (1998: 114) observed that "Effective gathering of intelligence requires the appropriate personnel and technology as well as the investment needed to bring these human and capital resources together. Consequently, access to and mobilization of highly skilled, often college-educated organizers and researchers, combined with the ability to command the technological resources that enable them to be effective, were essential to the Justice for Janitors' effectiveness."

UCLA faculty also made a concerted effort to open up the university to activists in the city. Labor, immigrant rights, and social justice activists were invited to participate in conferences, workshops, seminars, and classes addressing activism in the city. These events encouraged activists to come out in a neutral space with other activists, scholars, and students, and discuss the broader meanings of their actions. Such encounters facilitated connections between different people (activists, scholars, students, politicians, public officials) and encouraged them to connect their work to a broader movement for social justice. For instance, the Labor Center sponsored countless workshops over the course of its history. One workshop encouraged scholars to team up with labor and immigrant rights organizations to write the histories of their organizing models. This project resulted in the book *Working for Justice: The L.A. Model of Organizing and Advocacy*.[8] This and similar projects encouraged people and organizations to step outside of their particular worlds and think in reflexive ways about their position in the broader social justice movement.

UCLA also played an important role in supporting and incubating new organizations, projects, and coalitions. Since 1990 the Department of Urban Planning has offered a Community Scholars Program (see Nicholls 2003; Soja 2010). The program invites Los Angeles activists to participate in organizing a year-long course on a specific issue or campaign. The aim of the course is to solidify ties between activists and the university, train students in the practicalities of advocacy work, and provide an opportunity for organizations to prepare and develop campaign strategies. The program played a direct role in creating new "anchor organizations" like Los Angeles Alliance for a New Economy (LAANE) and Strategic Action for a Just Economy (SAJE) (both discussed in the next section) and supporting influential campaigns like Los Angeles Manufacturing Action Project (LAMAP) and the Healthcare Workers Campaign.

Intellectuals at UCLA were interested in developing new methods to contribute their skills and resources to advance the various mobilizations around the city. Gilda Haas, a major actor within this cluster, stressed the importance of these relations:

> Alan [Department of Urban Planning] was part of the rent control movement. The objective of his research was designed to ask questions that could actually investigate the benefits of rent control. Jackie Leavitt [Department of Urban Planning] had worked for many years with communities in New York. When she came to LA, I introduced her to different groups that were doing that kind of work. I was a community organizer before I came to the Department. Kent [Labor Center] used to work with labor unions before he moved to UCLA. *That was the thread binding us together. We were all people who had been directly tied to a movement for people's empowerment.* (Personal interview, emphasis added)

While this "thread" bound them together, their co-location on the same campus helped them to easily connect to one another. Their constant interactions helped break down boundaries and allowed them to see how problems facing people in one issue area (e.g. tenants' rights) overlapped with others (e.g. labor, immigration).

UCLA led the way in forging this activist scholar model, but other universities followed suit. Occidental College created the Urban and Environmental Policy Department. Three activist scholars (Peter Dreier, Manuel Pastor, and Robert Gottlieb) created the department to train students to become effective policy analysts, advocates, and organizers. In the 2000s, Manuel Pastor moved to the University of Southern California and helped create the Program for Environmental and Regional Equity; and the Center for the Study of Immigrant Integration. These centers aimed to develop research that would contribute to environmental justice campaigns (mostly in immigrant communities) and immigrant rights advocacy. USC also became an important institutional site for supporting workshops, seminars, and conferences directly addressing social justice and immigration issues in the city. The group at UCLA had connections to activist scholars at Occidental College and UCLA. Manuel Pastor had strong relations with UCLA Urban Planning faculty and the director of the Labor Center (Kent Wong). Before moving to Occidental College, Robert Gottlieb had been a professor of Urban Planning at UCLA. Other scholars at USC (Laura Pulido) and Occidental College (Martha Matsuoka) were also graduates of UCLA's Urban Planning Department or had been closely affiliated with it.

There were certainly rivalries and disputes between activist scholars, but this cluster reinforced commitments and norms that they should direct university resources to the new activism in central Los Angeles. In 2002 UCLA opened the Downtown Labor Center in the heart of central Los Angeles in an effort to be closer to the innovative immigrant and labor organizations that had clustered in the area. The Downtown Labor Center became a central meeting ground and support structure for this buzzing activist milieu. As a result of these long-term, institutional, and heavy investments, the Los Angeles activist milieu was endowed with extraordinary resources provided by the major universities of the city.

Connecting Clusters, Agglomerating Activism, Forming an Activist Hub

The 1980s and 1990s witnessed the formation of three new and highly innovative activist clusters mobilizing in one way or another to address the rights of working-class immigrants in the city. While activists within the immigrant and labor clusters focused on their specific issue areas, the overlapping nature of their interests encouraged them to step outside their narrow sectors and connect to one another. There were also many "connecting points" (protests, university conferences, workshops, meetings, social affairs) and "brokers" that helped link previously unconnected people, organizations, and groups to one another. The multiplicity of brokers and connecting points, overlapping interests and concerns, and physical proximity helped blur the boundaries between these clusters and enabled activists within them to reach out and work with one another. We suggest that these connections between distinctive activist clusters produced sufficient levels of solidarity, trust, and know-how to make larger and longer-term collective projects possible. These messy relations, in other words, enabled Los Angeles to become more than a geographic location with a dense aggregate of activists. The possibility for complex relational exchanges turned this aggregation of activists into an activist agglomeration.

"Anchor organizations" (see Nicholls 2003) emerged in the late 1980s and early 1990s to support longer-lasting campaigns that cut across traditional class, ethnic, status, and issue boundaries. Eric Mann created the Labor/Community Strategy Center (L/CSC) in the late 1980s. Its first campaign addressed the issue of environmental racism in working-class, immigrant, and African American neighborhoods (Pulido 1996). The organization incubated a broad coalition to stop the location of waste incinerators in minority and low-income neighborhoods. L/CSC also began to address inequalities in the region's public transportation plans (Soja 2000, 2010). It accused the Metropolitan Transit Authority (MTA) of favoring rail projects that benefited middle-class and white suburban residents over bus projects that served working-class and minority commuters in the city center. As part of this campaign, L/CSC created the Bus Riders' Union, assembled a broad coalition to denounce the MTA, and filed a successful lawsuit against the agency.

In the early 1990s, Madeline Janis-Aparicio (CARECEN), Maria Elena Durazo (HERE Local 11), and Gilda Haas (Department of Urban Planning, UCLA) worked together to create an anchor organization of their own: Los Angeles Alliance for a New Economy (LAANE). Gilda Haas suggested using UCLA's Community Scholars Program to develop a comprehensive analysis of the industry and a strategy to improve the wages and conditions of its workers. The outcome of this Community Scholars course was a new organization, the Tourist Industry Development Council (TIDC), in 1993. TIDC's first project targeted the expansion of the Convention Center and the construction of a new stadium (Staples Center) in downtown Los Angeles. TIDC changed its name to LAANE in 1998 and launched a living wage campaign in Los Angeles. It worked closely with allies in labor, the immigrant community, clergy, and the university to push through one of the first living wage ordinances in the country. LAANE went on to organize living wage campaigns across the metropolitan region, but it also embarked on campaigns for environmental justice, opposing the expansion of Wal-Mart, and organizing hotel workers. Each campaign drew upon a similar formula: cultivate alliances between local unions, community organizations, and the clergy in the areas being targeted. While LAANE developed and perfected this strategy in the central city area, it replicated the strategy in localities around the metropolitan region and spurred the formation of cross-sector coalitions in a wide array of localities.

LAANE's sister organization, Strategic Alliance for a Just Economy (SAJE), was created along the same lines. SAJE was originally conceived as an organization that would provide technical assistance to grassroots efforts addressing the economic issues of working-class, mostly immigrant, communities. The founders[9] believed that SAJE could complement LAANE's work and focus more directly on development and housing issues. Its first project addressed the lack of financial services for poor working-class people (immigrants and citizens) who lacked the documents and financial stability needed to open a bank account.

Many people in these neighborhoods depended on "check-cashing" businesses that charged usurious fees to their clients. SAJE worked to create cooperative banks and pursue measures to limit fees in the "check-cashing" business. Following this campaign, it went on to direct its attention to problems associated with urban redevelopment and gentrification. It led a broad coalition (Figueroa Corridor Coalition) to ensure that working-class immigrant communities would benefit from massive redevelopment efforts in downtown Los Angeles. The coalition consisted of anchor organizations (SAJE, LAANE), immigrant associations (CARECEN, *Clínica Oscar Romeo*, CHIRLA), labor unions (HERE, County Federation of Labor, etc.), and activist scholars from UCLA and USC. From this effort, the coalition negotiated one of the country's first Community Benefits Agreements. The agreement guaranteed union jobs, living wages, and affordable housing for area residents.

Working relations between organizers in these different clusters emerged through early coalition work, consolidated through these and other anchor organizations, and reinforced through ongoing collaborations and coalitions. Commenting on these relations in a 2002 interview, Gilda Haas maintained:

> The unions are supporting us [SAJE] and we are supporting the unions. It is just a new level of solidarity and collaboration that was absolutely not available more than 5 years ago. It wasn't there because the relationships were not there. The relationships were established through the historical relationships of leaders ... It came out of organizing, we built upon organizing, we built upon old relationships and new relationships. (Personal interview)

Another observer from the Center for Community Change specifies the attribute that made these relations particularly potent. According to her, a growing sense of trust permitted stronger and more stable collaborations between the partners:

> And if there are not pre-existing relations between activists, then anything can split a group because there is no sense of a context of trust. So that is the most critical thing. But if that context of trust is in place, then people can begin to work out problems ... That has got to be there or it has to be built. People can come together around a crisis or an important opportunity or something they want to do, but some attention has to be paid to the relational side of the thing. (Personal interview)

She went on to note that in the case of Los Angeles, trusting relations had been built up over time between a consistent group of people representing different activist clusters. As trust built up, they learned that the others sitting across the table were reliable partners and could be counted on to contribute their unique resources and know-how to a campaign. Trust, in other words, helped grease the wheels of high-end, high-risk collective action. To this we should add that trust is only as good as a network's ability to sanction bad behavior (Portes and Sensenbrenner 1993). The more these activists worked together and benefited from these and other coalitions, the more they were compelled to fulfill their obligations and maintain their reputations as reliable and standup partners. Their inability to do so would damage their status in the small activist community, raise questions about their reliability, damage reputations, and make it more difficult to draw upon the unique benefits of local activist networks.

Spatial proximity mattered for building strong relations across the different activist clusters. Recurrent face-to-face interactions over an extended period made it possible to build trust, and it helped create tacit understandings and knowledge of how to pool and deploy different resources in effective ways. While trust helped actors make valuable contributions to collective efforts, this tacit know-how allowed them to develop ways to work together and put these contributions to effective political use:

> The harder it is to spend face-to-face time together the harder it is. Clearly trying to build something with some real depth is going to be very hard as people are further away. However, if it is a very clear thing and people can buy in on something that is very clear and you are not being told what to do then I can imagine people doing incredible things at some distance … But I do think that the depth in some ways may be affected … People just wouldn't have the opportunity to have really lengthy conversations and develop a lot of trust. *If there are some precise objectives or very short-terms goals then I can see a long distance coalition working. But if you try to bring people together on a longer thing, they have to get together and it is costly* … (Center for Community Change Los Angeles, personal interview, emphasis added)

According to this respondent, the more complex and longer-term the task, the greater the need for long, face-to-face conversations between the principal actors, especially in the early and more uncertain days of the campaign. Making time to discuss complex issues enables common understandings of what needs to be done and how to do it, and it reinforces trust that the campaign participants will perform according to expectations. The above observer goes on to suggest that shorter-term campaigns with very clear goals permit greater geographical distance between coalition partners. Clear and generic information can be transmitted across great distances without the loss of meaning. There is no need to have "lengthy conversations" to make sense of complex information. This analysis is consistent with the insights of geographer Michael Storper (1997). Complex and innovative tasks encourage geographic clustering, especially at the *front end* of a campaign, the period when leaders are still uncertain about strategies, decisions, and plans.

The robust and productive activist hub in Los Angeles did not simply arise by chance; in response to a single event like the Los Angeles riots; or by the extraordinary will of far-sighted and heroic individuals. It resulted from small steps of meeting together, talking to one another, learning how to work together, and committing more and more valuable resources to larger and larger projects. The members of the activist milieu did not simply decide to undertake big and complex campaigns for the rights of immigrant workers. Going big depended on countless small, trust-building steps between the same activists and organizers over a long period of time. This produced the relational infrastructure that would allow activists to "organize the unorganizable" in increasingly ambitious campaigns. "The way I see it is that the economic and social justice movement in Los Angeles has matured and our ability to build coalitions has developed further. Our relations have become consolidated at the same time that we try to organize the unorganizable. This gives us more power. What we have now is more sophisticated and long term" (activist, formerly CARECEN, currently LAANE, personal interview).

Conclusions

A small, innovative, and well-embedded group of eastside activists in the 1970s moved the issue of immigrant rights to the center of their activist worlds. By the 1980s, the cluster of activists that had succeeded in pushing the issue forward was being eclipsed by changes in the city's social movement environment. The local government introduced a number of subsidy schemes that strongly affected relational dynamics in the eastside. The professionalization of many local organizations led them to turn their attention to the provision of services to "problematic" communities and away from contentious organizing efforts. As most eastside organizations became a part of this new civic monoculture, there was less space for more contentious organizations like CASA. This left them isolated and unable to tap into the local resources needed to mount contentious campaigns for the rights of immigrants. The drying up of public subsidies in the 1980s aggravated the problem by accelerating professionalization of the larger organizations and intensifying competition between smaller organizations. The institutional context therefore contributed to a significant change in relational dynamics among eastside activists, with many organizations distancing themselves from contentious actors and engaging in fiercer competition for a dwindling share of the pie.

In a paradoxical way, the institutional context that contributed to the decline of East Los Angeles's political dynamism also contributed to the rise of new activism in central Los Angeles. While "rollback neoliberalism" accelerated the decline of contentious politics in East Los Angeles, it deprived the city of adequate means to extend its reach into the buzzing politics of central Los Angeles. Just as important, the US government embraced a laissez-faire approach to the political integration of new immigrants. This meant that there were few government instruments introduced during this time to channel and direct the political activities of these communities. Neoliberal urbanism combined with the absence of state-led integration to provide a new generation of activists with a relatively open political space to take root and flourish in central Los Angeles.

Enjoying a certain margin to maneuver, innovative activists from unions, immigrant organizations, and universities emerged alongside one another during the 1980s. They developed new ways to organize marginalized immigrant communities to become potent political voices. While weak political institutions provide them with a degree of autonomy to experiment and organize, their geographic proximity allowed them to engage in frequent interactions with one another over extended periods of time. Nobody at the time knew what he or she was doing and they learned by doing in a series of different actions and campaigns carried out over extended periods of time. These diverse activists imported tactics and methods from various organizations, traditions, histories, and countries; cobbling them together through many campaigns and fights. Proximity and face-to-face contacts facilitated collective learning because it improved communication and interactions between diverse actors, while at the same time allowing them to constantly assess and adjust their assumptions, plans, and actions.

The activism of working-class immigrant communities during this time also shifted from demanding authorization to stay in the country to demanding that immigrant (worker) rights be recognized irrespective of legal status. By 2000, immigrant activists and their allies were fighting for labor rights, the rights of tenants, the right to participate in the development of their cities, the right to live in a safe and healthy environment, and so on. While they certainly continued to fight for legal authorization, the nature of their struggle became more challenging because they were now demanding recognition of equality without formal authorization to reside in the country. They were demanding that their equality as workers be recognized irrespective of their immigration status. As immigrants they were carving out a place in the country by asserting their equality as workers, tenants, and denizens.

The Uneven Reach of the State
The Partial Pacification of Paris

The election of a left government in 1981 marked a positive turning point for the immigrant rights movement in France. Immediately after the elections, the government introduced policies that reflected socialist principles and its commitment to the rights of immigrants. This spirit of openness unleashed a new round of mobilizations by first- and second-generation immigrants. Rather than repressing these mobilizations, the new government welcomed them and tried to understand the underlying conditions that fueled them. It recognized the immigrants' grievances as legitimate and provided them with important levels of political support. This marked what many hoped to be a new golden age of immigrant rights politics in France. By the end of the 1980s, however, the immigrant associations driving these mobilizations had been depoliticized or had disappeared altogether. The extreme right party, the National Front, was ascendant and the French public showed signs of becoming decidedly less tolerant to immigrants. The immigrant associations that had emerged in the 1970s and flourished in the early 1980s were incapable of responding. They issued press releases and started petitions but these efforts were mostly ignored.

While immigrant associations experienced a precipitous decline, other activist clusters faced very different fates. The larger human rights NGOs continued to engage in critical and contentious battles, and they would go on to play a major role in the large-scale mobilizations in the 1990s. Just as important, a new activist cluster emerged on the Parisian

Cities and Social Movements: Immigrant Rights Activism in the United States, France, and the Netherlands, 1970–2015, First Edition. Walter J. Nicholls and Justus Uitermark.
© 2017 John Wiley & Sons, Ltd. Published 2017 by John Wiley & Sons, Ltd.

activist scene: informal collectives of undocumented immigrants (*collectifs des sans papiers*). The *collectifs* made their appearance in the 1980s and were mostly engaged in struggles for decent housing. They would then turn their attention toward the government's immigration policies in the 1980s and 1990s.

What explains this rapid change of positioning in Paris? We suggest that this reflects the uneven deployment of government controls. The 1980s marked the rapid rollout of new institutions and discourses to politically integrate immigrant associations. This presented the immigrant associations with formidable constraints and drove most to drop contentious politics and pursue apolitical service activities. While the government introduced an impressive range of controls during the decade, these were uneven in terms of their targets and reach. The government did not target human rights NGOs and lacked the tools to effectively control the emergence of the unruly *collectifs*.

This chapter begins by describing the mechanisms developed by the Socialist government to politically integrate first- and second-generation immigrants. It stresses that these mechanisms combined to create a rather comprehensive cage, which entangled much of immigrant civil society that had emerged during the early 1980s. We conclude by arguing that political integration was selectively applied, contributing to the relative decline of one cluster while leaving the other clusters relatively unmolested. This particular arrangement would have an important effect on the subsequent trajectory of the immigrant rights movement in France.

Political Integration through Ethnic Management and Territorial Encapsulation

The rapid uptake in immigrant political and associational life presented important opportunities and risks to the government. On the one hand, immigrant associations were seen as vehicles to encourage new immigrants and their children to enter civic life, become active members of their communities, and learn some of the basic norms and values of French political life. On the other hand, this renaissance of political and civic life started to pose considerable risks to the government. The more radical immigrant associations of the 1970s were playing a major role in shaping the social movement. They had been important supporters of wildcat strikes in the 1980s and were providing political training to second-generation youths. While immigrant associations were helping incorporate new immigrant communities, they were also becoming too autonomous, radical, and difficult to control. The promises and risks associated with these emerging immigrant communities prompted the government to embrace a general strategy of political integration through ethnic management and territorial encapsulation.

Integration through ethnic management

By ethnic management we mean government efforts to exert control by targeting risky immigrant and ethnic groups. The government developed methods to monitor and assess political activities, create incentives and disincentives to channel political behavior, and produce clear rules and sanctions to differentiate between acceptable and unacceptable discourse in the public sphere. The objective of this strategy has been to mitigate the risks associated with the population by producing a political subject willing and able to comply with the norms and rules of the political system. This differs from the strategy of "ethnic encapsulation" pursued in the Netherlands, which focused more on demarcating and constructing ethnic groups (Moroccans, Turks, etc.) as objects of disciplinary control. The strategy of "ethnic management" pursued in France had a similar objective (controlling the Other), but the means were different because emphasis was on managing and steering a population that already existed rather than creating ethnic categories and groups as a method to control them. We argue that ethnic management in France, combined with the strategy of territorial encapsulation, was detrimental to the political power of this population. By producing a more pliant subject, the government sapped it of its ability to engage in politically contentious, innovative, disruptive, and constructive acts.

A cornerstone of the government's strategy was to provide subsidies to immigrant associations through the agency charged with immigration affairs, the Social Action Fund for Immigrant Workers and Their Families (FAS). Subsidies were used to steer immigrant associations away from contentious politics and toward cultural and social activities in immigrant neighborhoods, including afterschool programs, sports, and multicultural events. Associations receiving FAS subsidies were barred from engaging in explicitly political activities. In addition to these restrictions, recipients of subsidies were required to meet professional standards and undergo supervision by FAS officials. The directors of immigrant associations were compelled to spend more time building up and professionalizing their organizations and less time engaging in politically disruptive mobilizations.

Oversight of the activities of associations was increased following decentralization reforms in the 1990s. Funding decisions were decentralized from FAS (central state) to department-level prefects who were directly appointed by the Minister of the Interior, the ministry charged with immigration policies. "It became more difficult because the FAS funding came under the domination of the prefect, designated by the Minister of the Interior who we directly opposed" (ATMF, personal interview). For immigrant leaders, FAS and other public institutions tolerated protests but they signaled that overly contentious activities could result in sanctions: "The institutions [public] have never liked protests. For example, when we protested the prefect of Paris [appointed by the Minister of the Interior], we knew that the government would not like this and that it would refuse subsidies when we went to ask for them later. Yes, that has always been a concern" (ATMF, personal interview). The director of another immigrant association agreed with this assessment, stressing that engaging in contentious political activities carried a heightened risk of subsidy cuts: "There haven't been direct controls but the mechanisms of renewing subsidies results in important forms of self-control. That is to say, consciously and unconsciously, associations like ours knew what can determine the renewal or non-renewal of a subsidy" (FTCR, personal interview). Experienced immigrant associations knew that certain acts, claims, or discourses could cross the line and threaten subsidy renewal. This implicit understanding of "acceptable" political conduct steered many immigrant associations away from controversial practices and led many to embrace conventional and tolerated forms of protest. By the end of the 1990s, many immigrant associations received partial or full funding from FAS. ATMF, for example, received 70% of its funding from FAS by 2000. This dependency did not stop immigrant associations from participating in protests and campaigns. However, it increased the risks of engaging in controversial political acts and speech and encouraged them to focus attention on apolitical service provision and other low-risk forms of political action.

In addition to FAS, the Socialist Party developed a strategy that aimed to channel and capture immigrant political dynamics. Party elites introduced initiatives to develop large national associations to recruit second-generation immigrants. The most important of these associations were *SOS Racisme* and *France Plus*. Soon after the huge and successful March for Equality in 1983, party members with close ties to President François Mitterrand (Julien Dray, Laurent Fabius, and Jack Lang) created *SOS Racisme* (Wihtol de Wenden and Leveau 2001). Julien Dray recruited the first president of *SOS Racisme*, the charismatic Harlem Desir, through a friend who was a Paris-based university professor. *France Plus* was the creation of another leading member of the Socialist Party, Lionel Jospin, who would go on to become Minister of Education and Prime Minister.

It was designed to recruit candidates with an immigrant background and develop support for the Socialist Party in immigrant neighborhoods.

These associations were important because they helped create a political channel between second-generation immigrants and the Socialist Party. *SOS Racisme* later created offshoot associations to better address local associational life (Don't Touch my Buddy) and address gender issues (Neither Whores, Nor Submissives).[1] The reach of these associations provided the Socialist Party with the capability to siphon off promising youths from the movement and recruit them into the party. As one part of the youth leadership was channeled into *SOS Racisme* and similar associations, others turned to the highly regulated and monitored world of neighborhood associational politics. For those who moved into *SOS Racisme*, the hopes of moving up the Socialist Party hierarchy were rarely realized. Very few were placed on a leadership path in local sections of the Socialist Party or in the national office (Garbaye 2005).

This association succeeded in becoming a dominant force in second-generation activism. The government lent its symbolic power to support the association and it was able to attract massive media attention. While there were many different associations in the early 1980s working assiduously on anti-racism and immigrant rights issues, *SOS Racisme* became the go-to association for the media and elite. It became the official "voice" of second-generation immigrants in France. For many, *SOS Racisme*'s ability to coopt youth activists and command the media spotlight contributed to the decline of the *Beur* movement (second-generation immigrant).

> I was a part of the *Marche des Beurs* [March of Equality in 1983] when François Mitterrand received the delegation of marchers. I was a student then and a part of this delegation. Then, *SOS Racisme* broke our movement. *SOS Racisme* was an association that was created by the Socialists to contain the authentic *Beur* movement that was emerging from the *cité* [working-class immigrant neighborhoods]. Whereas we had zero francs, *SOS Racisme* had millions and great support from the media. Whereas we were rooted in the neighborhoods, *SOS* had no roots. Because of its abilities to get publicity, of always being in the newspapers and the television, people had the impression that it was a movement of a million people. But concretely, there was nobody from the *banlieue*, the *cité*, just a bunch of Parisian yuppies with friends in the Socialist Party. (FTCR, personal interview)

As a fledgling and independent immigrant rights movement emerged in the early 1980s, *SOS Racisme* was seen as a force that siphoned support, resources, and attention away from the activities of authentic immigrant activists.

SOS Racisme was created by Mitterrand. This association and its offspring were like a steamroller and they took all the space. Their Socialist friends were in all the halls of power … At the level of the regional council [historically dominated by the Socialist Party], most subsidies went to them. If we asked for something, the regional council [of Paris] would direct us to *SOS*. They dominated the network of antiracist and immigrant associations. (ATMF, personal interview)

The prominence of *SOS Racisme* helped it assume a position as a representative of France's "minority voice" while siphoning resources that would have otherwise gone to authentic immigrant associations and activism.

The government used its symbolic power to delineate the rules of acceptable speech and conduct (Bourdieu 1994). For Mustafa Dikeç (2004), the "statements of the state" helped set the rules of "legitimate" discourse and compelled actors to adjust their talk, acts, and organizational practices accordingly. "What the state is and what it does are important," notes Dikeç. "But equally important is what it *says*, what it *states*. The statements of the state have the force of law, power of designation, constitution and regulation; they not only normalise and render 'obvious' certain definitions and designations, but also materialise them" (2004: 196, emphasis in original). During the 1980s, government officials took a more aggressive stand on shaping the boundaries of legitimate political speech: they celebrated speech that cohered with the government's vision of the "good" immigrant and stigmatized speech that disrupted and deviated from this vision.

As immigrant-led strikes wore on at the Talbot-Peugeot automobile plant in northern Paris during the 1980s (see Chapter 4), the Socialist government hardened its line and began to view striking immigrant workers as a disruptive force. This change of position was reflected in new discourses used by the government to frame the mobilization. In 1984 the government began to highlight the strikers' cultural and religious demands[2] while ignoring their material and class-based claims. Prime Minister Mauroy stated: "The main difficulties in this situation come from immigrant workers who are influenced and agitated by *religious groups*. These groups define themselves with criteria that are *disconnected* to social realities in France" (cited in Gay 2010: 12, emphasis added). The Minister of the Interior framed the strikers as "fundamentalists and Shiites." The Minister of Labor, Jean Auroux, remarked: "There is an obvious religious and fundamentalist aspect in those protests which turns it into something that is not exclusively unionist. Some people aim at destabilizing the social and political bases of our country, because we embody too many things as regards freedom and pluralism" (in Gay 2010: 12). Framing the immigrants as religious zealots who were funded by dubious foreign entities served to undermine the legitimacy of the immigrant strikers.

These "statements of the state" demarcated the lines between unacceptable and acceptable speech and practices. The harsh response directed at the Talbot-Peugeot strikers contrasted sharply with the government's response to the *Beur* movement. First-generation strikers and activists were framed as conservative, communitarian, Muslim, and irreducibly foreign. By contrast second-generation activists were framed as progressive, assimilated, *Republican*, and potentially good French. These discursive moves helped introduce divisions between first- and second-generation activists:

> The discourse of the state was, 'Second generation immigrants are really good, they can be integrated into the Republic as long they tear themselves from the archaism of their parents.' Exactly at that time, there was the strike at the Talbot plant that was being driven by immigrant workers and supported by the immigrant associations. This campaign was repressed with the extremely violent discourse of Pierre Mauroy, the Socialist Prime Minister. With one hand, Mitterrand wanted to welcome the marchers [second-generation youths] to l'Élysée and with the other he repressed and strongly stigmatized the striking immigrant workers. (FTCR, personal interview)

By stressing differences between the generations, the government aggravated categorical divisions, while laying down the discursive rules for the political integration of immigrants.

The state later unleashed its discursive powers on second-generation *males* by stressing the attributes that made this subgroup "problematic" and difficult to "integrate." The center-right government (elected in 1993) argued that the permissive and so-called multicultural approach of the Socialists allowed the emergence of a second generation that had stronger ties to their primary ethnic communities than to France. These cultural and social attachments blocked their integration into the country. Second-generation males were said to be particularly susceptible to embracing the "archaic" culture of their parents (i.e. religion, political sympathies, patriarchy, etc.). Young women, by contrast, were framed as the group most capable of assimilating and challenging the cultural and social ties to sending countries. As the Minister of Social Affairs noted in 1993, "Often, why hide it, the demand by young women for a western lifestyle is the cause of serious family conflicts. Because of this, these actors are helping to liberate female immigrants and can be seen as essential actors of integration" (Simone Veil, cited in Schain 1999: 128). A new strategy emerged to provide symbolic and institutional support for immigrant women and their associations. Public agencies – city, region, the FAS – were directed to prioritize associations that supported the autonomy of immigrant women and "the prevention of practices and behavior that victimize too many immigrant women, and are contrary to our values and often to our laws'" (ibid.: 129).

While closing down discursive opportunities for critical associations, a handful of second-generation associations (*SOS Racisme* and its offspring) thrived within this discursive field. They echoed government discourses concerning "good" and "bad" immigrants and employed much of its stigmatizing rhetoric. *SOS Racisme* began to move in this direction in the mid-1990s under the direction of Fodé Sylla, but it became the official discursive strategy under the leadership of Malek Boutih (1999–2003). Boutih gained national prominence for himself and his association by criticizing the culture and behavior of minorities rather than criticizing systemic discrimination. He embraced the idea of Republican assimilation, used the term "barbarians" to describe rioting youths, constantly denounced conservative Muslims as fundamentalists and extremists, called the Muslim intellectual Tariq Ramadan the "Arab Le Pen," and took strong positions against affirmative action because it was "communitarian" (Blandin 2009). Not surprisingly, the resonance of this discourse with broader public norms significantly improved the status of *SOS Racisme* and Boutih in the public sphere. Boutih, in other words, was able to accrue enormous amounts of "symbolic capital" (Bourdieu 1994) by employing dominant discourses to chastise and stigmatize immigrant populations while simultaneously differentiating himself and his association from it. Boutih's friend and colleague, Fadela Amara, employed the same strategy in the 2000s. In 2003, Amara – in close collaboration with *SOS Racisme* – created a new association, Neither Whores, Nor Submissives (NPNS), to address the conditions of women in low-income, high-immigrant neighborhoods (*banlieues*). Amara's association criticized the treatment of young women in the *banlieues* by their fathers and brothers. She often used violent, highly mediatized, and cherry-picked examples of patriarchal violence to do this: "How can we tolerate in the 21st century that Sohane and Chahrazad are burned alive by a man in the heart of the neighborhood? How can we accept that Gohfrane is stoned to death in Marseille?" (www.niputesnisoumises.com). The association argued that the culture of minorities produced behavior that threatened the lives and prosperity of young minority *banlieue* women. Young minority women could only achieve freedom by breaking with this culture, rejecting cultural relativism, and assimilating into the values of the French Republic (Amara and Zappi 2006). French insistence on cultural homogeneity was not the problem for the second generation but the solution.

During the 1980s and 1990s, the window of acceptable discourse and conduct became increasingly narrow for immigrants. Many of the expressions and actions that had been celebrated in the early 1980s were considered deviant and dangerous in the 1990s. Only those immigrant activists who publicly eschewed the "archaic" and "communitarian" cultures of their parents, criticized immigrant movements as anti-Republican, and embraced an assimilationist vision of citizenship gained much traction in the public sphere. Already swimming against the tide of public opinion, the discursive rules of the game narrowed the path of immigrant political integration and made it extremely difficult for any critical voices to gain a broader audience. If young activists didn't want to be banished to the sidelines ("noises"), they had to couch their claims in ways that resonated with French Republican discourse. Some prominent associations (SOS, NPNS, etc.) embraced the rules of the game, embraced Republicanism, and denounced the "archaic" ways of immigrant communities. As a result, their status and power increased at a time when anti-immigrant sentiment in the public flourished (Berezin 2009). Other immigrant associations have simply steered away from claims that would draw unhelpful attention to them and lead to their being labeled as anti-Republican, communitarian, or Islamic fundamentalists. Immigrant associations (first- and second-generation) had to constantly reassert their conformity with national norms and their distance from deviants (communitarians, Muslims) or risk marginalization. As their loyalty and belonging to France came under permanent suspicion, expressing loyalty to the country became a normal practice even when they were not prompted do so.

Integration through territorial encapsulation

The French government also aimed to integrate immigrant communities through "territorial encapsulation." Territorial encapsulation refers to government policies that identify high-risk areas (in our case, urban); develop methods to monitor and assess threat levels in these areas and factors responsible for the threats; develop techniques to reach into the grassroots and steer the actors and associations operating within them; and produce new norms and discourses that bring the worldviews of inhabitants and local associations in line with the expectations of the government. Territorial interventions are different from the ethnic interventions described above because they act on the specific *territories* that enable and sustain risky groups. Both ethnic and territorial methods combined to serve as twin pillars of France's political integration strategy during this period.

The new government in 1981 rolled out a new urban policy program (*politique de la ville*) in response to the large-scale urban riots (Estèbe 1999; Estèbe and Donzelot 1999; Estèbe and Jaillet 1999; Estèbe and Le Galès 2003; Garbaye 2005; Nicholls 2006; Dikeç 2007). The program was envisioned as a form of territorial affirmative action for low-income neighborhoods. "Priority neighborhoods" were provided with the additional public resources to foster local development. Such resources included educational funds for failing schools; increased public services like transit connections to the city center, pools, libraries, jobs services, and financial services; and incentives to attract private sector investors to these areas. In the early years, the "bottom-up" wing of the Socialist Party[3] inspired the major tenets of urban policy. This faction believed that the state should empower residents and local associations to take an active role in redeveloping their neighborhoods. Local associations were viewed as a lynchpin to neighborhood development because they possessed a certain level of flexibility and innovation that government institutions lacked. They were also seen as vehicles for reviving urban citizenship by connecting residents to concrete government actions (Estèbe and Donzelot 1999; Nicholls 2006). In exchange for their participation, local associations received a subsidy distributed to them by the city and prefect.

During the 1980s and 1990s, urban policy expanded rapidly. By 1984 24 "priority neighborhoods" came under the jurisdiction of this program. The number of neighborhoods quickly expanded to 148 in 1988, 546 in 1993, and more than 1,300 in 1998. In 1990 the government also devised a formal measure to identify deprived neighborhoods, the "Synthetic Index of Exclusion" (ISE) (Dikeç 2007). The criteria used for the ISE included the proportion of immigrants in a neighborhood, long-term unemployment, and level of education. The concentration of immigrants was one of the most important criteria for an area to be designated a "priority neighborhood." Consequently, hundreds of urban neighborhoods with high concentrations of immigrants (first- and second-generation) came under the scope of this policy. The hundreds of new local associations emerging during the 1980s would come directly under the auspices of this particular policy.

In moving from a small experimental program in 1981 to a large national one in the early 1990s, the government introduced formal measures to coordinate tasks among all the different stakeholders (national, local officials; public officials, private associations) involved in the increasingly complex policy. These measures also ensured that the goals of the central government were uniformly transmitted and implemented in localities across the country. At the national level, the National Commission of Neighborhood Social Developments (CNDSQ) developed the general goals of urban development and outlined expectations for local actors involved in projects (Donzelot and Estèbe 1993; Estèbe 1999). At the local level, commissions were created for "priority neighborhoods." Each neighborhood commission was accountable to the mayor and the department prefect. The commissions developed the concrete strategies for achieving government goals and coordinating the activities of stakeholders (public officials, agencies, and associations). The project manager (*chef de projet*) was responsible for overseeing day-to-day projects carried out in "priority neighborhoods," monitoring neighborhood associations, and reporting back to the commission.

The capacity of the state to reach deep into immigrant neighborhoods limited what local associations in "priority neighborhoods" could do and say politically. While associations in "priority neighborhoods" were framed as partners in urban policy, they were subordinate partners and expected to fulfill specific services on behalf of the local government. Most local immigrant and minority associations were given one-year, project-based contracts to fulfill specified tasks for the city (sports, afterschool care, elderly support, cultural events). They were encouraged to dedicate their time to service and they competed with other neighborhood associations for small amounts of funding. Project managers in each of these neighborhoods were charged with supervising associations and ensuring they fulfill government expectations. The physical proximity between project managers and associations, and the power of project managers to monitor and report on the conduct of associations presented important constraints on what associations said and did. Most long-time members of immigrant associations believed that subsidies stemming from urban policy programs presented more constraints than those provided by national funding agencies like FAS. "The weight of constraints varies according to the degree of controls. I think that locally, the constraints from urban policy (*politique de la ville*) are much heavier" (FTCR, personal interview). City officials were partly responsible for making funding decisions, but the department prefect had ultimate authority in these matters. This presented another constraint on associations. "There were contracts linked to urban policy. The majority of these passed through the prefect. However, because we were an association that confronted the prefect, it became complicated to ask the prefect for funding" (ACORT, personal interview). Urban policy made important resources available to immigrant associations in deprived neighborhoods, but these subsidies came at the cost of placing recipients under the watchful eye of the local government.

Enhanced government oversight and control affected immigrant associations unevenly. For better-connected and more established associations, their prominence and access to multiple streams of revenue helped mitigate the effects of government controls. The immigrant associations operating in low-income neighborhoods, however, were mostly small and lacked the resources to counterbalance government control. Their constant struggle to obtain and hold on to government subsidies and the government's heightened surveillance and control capacities favored compliance over transgression. The more urban policy expanded the institutional net, the more it created a system of expectations, oversights, and controls that reached deep into the associational milieu of immigrant neighborhoods and imposed sharp limits on contentious speech and action.

Depoliticizing immigrant associations

Many prominent immigrant associations (ATMF, AMF, ACORT, FTCR, etc.) continued to be located in immigrant-rich northeast Paris. These associations had a long history of working with one another in spite of some divergences over tactics and ideologies. Since their emergence in the 1970s, they continued to maintain friendly and professional ties to one another. These associations have collaborated in political projects but such projects have not been particularly contentious. Such projects include candidate forums, information gathering, the common production of pamphlets, and the circulation of petitions. When contentious campaigns have arisen, the immigrant associations provide nominal levels of support (sign petitions, show up at demonstrations, etc.) for campaigns largely led by the human rights NGOs.

Various French governments successfully exploited generational tensions by stressing differences between first- and second-generation associations. This aggravated cleavages between them and weakened cooperation. "Yes we worked with them but there was a generational conflict. The immigrant associations are older people that are interested more in their ties with their country of origin than the situation in France. So emotionally they support us but they do nothing in reality" (MIB, personal interview). The most prominent second-generation associations (*SOS Racisme* and its sister organizations) have been dismissed by first-generation immigrant activists entirely because of their tight relations with the Socialist Party and their embrace of government and dominant cultural discourses. "There is contempt for them not only by us and the other immigrant associations but also by the whole associative movement" (ATMF, personal interview).

The smaller neighborhood associations (first- and second-generation) have mostly opted out of politics. Subsidy programs introduced by urban policy schemes provided the state with extraordinary means to survey the associational landscape of cities, monitor and intervene in the activities of individual associations, train associations to pursue service-oriented functions, and, in the last instance, threaten funding cuts in the event that their acts and words threatened the public order. This institutional setting encouraged professionalization as associations began to respond to funding expectations and move away from protest politics. "To have money you have to fill out these grant applications. To fill out grant applications you have to have somebody who knows something about them. The small associations can no longer survive if they don't have professionals, people who can fill out the applications, know accounting, know how the funding system works" (*Association Hasure*, personal interview). For most associations in immigrant neighborhoods, this precipitated a change in what they did (more service provision than contentious advocacy) and who did it (more professional and paid workers than militants). As professional and service-oriented associations proliferated in deprived neighborhoods, the older and more political associations faded. One longtime activist reflected on this process of associational succession: "When the public sector started financing them in the 1980s, there began to be fewer volunteers and more paid workers and then, as a result, more need of money. Therefore, one *normalized* the associative tissue and in the process, much of the militantism that existed before was lost" (*Génération Solidaires*, personal interview). Many of the smaller neighborhood-level associations in France have therefore stopped thinking of contentious politics as part of their competencies and have instead focused on the provision of services to narrowly targeted subgroups (youth, unemployed, the elderly, etc.). In her ethnography of neighborhood associations in the Paris suburbs, Hamidi concludes that local "associations … tend to make people avoid politics and politicization. They cannot be considered as places of politicization but on the contrary as places of evaporation of politics" (Hamidi 2003: 327).

Government subsidy schemes associated with urban policy (*politique de la ville*) have also eaten into the quality of relations between associations. Project-based funding schemes required local immigrant associations to focus on providing specific types of services (afterschool, tutoring, recreation, security, etc.) to specific categories of people (youths, women, boys, at-risk groups, the elderly, unemployed, etc.) in specific geographical areas (street, housing block, neighborhood, etc.). As neighborhood associations became focused on narrow populations and activities in low-income neighborhoods, they had no compelling reason to work with associations outside their narrow areas of interest. Competition for subsidies further reduced motivation to work with others in similar issue areas out of fear of being betrayed by partner associations. "Competition, insecurities, and the games they [public officials] play result in each association preferring to stay in its own corner. If you work closely with another association, you might be forced to say things, reveal things. This type of insecurity means that we talk to one another but only on very superficial matters" (*Association Vivre Ensemble*, personal interview). This low-trust environment results in a preference to work alone and avoid most forms of collective action, political or not. Associations might have agreed to work with others on low-risk projects but were likely to eschew longer-term, higher-risk ventures because they simply did not trust most others in their environment. The institutional context favored narrow tasks and roles by associations and strong competition for limited public resources. Such conditions weakened the relations and ties between associations, contributing to the atomization of the neighborhood associational milieu.

These constraints did not completely eclipse the desire to engage in contentious politics in immigrant neighborhoods. They just eroded the relational and organizational conditions that support contentious politics in neighborhoods. During the 2000s, for instance, a handful of second-generation youths in Paris launched a new coalition, Movement of Immigrants and *Banlieues* (MIB),[4] to revive a tradition of contentious politics in these areas of the city. MIB fashioned itself as France's version of the Black Panther Party. The association's entry into the public sphere produced a buzz because of its controversial image and confrontational discourse. Rather than embrace the discourse of Republican assimilation (as *SOS Racisme* had done), MIB stressed that the marginalization of first- and second-generation immigrants was a function of systemic racism and police repression. MIB found itself isolated in the neighborhoods where it was seeking to organize and was unable to build a sustainable support base. "The problem was that in 90% of the neighborhoods in the Paris region, there are no more associations. I am not talking about the social centers, sports clubs, and things like that. I am talking about neighborhood associations that are seeking to improve things through political struggle. Before, in the 1980s, they were everywhere" (MIB, personal interview). The lack of local bases of support in Paris prompted MIB to develop alliances with like-minded activists in the distant cities of Toulouse and Lyon, but geographic distance crippled their ability to begin basic campaigns. "Distance was a big handicap ... because you can contact them by telephone or internet but you don't know what they are really doing, concretely. You are not there; you cannot see things. You can agree to do things but nobody really knows if anything is getting done" (MIB, personal interview). In spite of its efforts to spur contentious mobilizations, MIB failed because of the impossibility of drawing support from others in

Paris's immigrant neighborhoods. The environment that would have supported its insurgency had effectively been drained by government controls (a similar situation to the one faced by CASA in Los Angeles during the late 1970s).

As organized forms of contention have been closed off, some (especially second-generation youths) have opted to use riots as a vehicle to express grievances and deep frustrations. There were five large-scale riots between 1982 and 1989 in France, all concentrated in low-income, immigrant neighborhoods. The rate of riots increased dramatically during the 1990s, with 48 large-scale riots over the decade. In addition to these, there were 250 smaller riots, referred to by law enforcement agencies as "mini-riots" (Dikeç 2004: 203). The rate of rioting accelerated during a period in which associations underwent rapid depoliticization. The claims of rioting youths had largely remained the same since the early 1980s. Most were directed at systemic police brutality and territorial marginalization (Dikeç 2007). In spite of consistency in the claims of the rioters, government officials and the media framed them very differently from the decade before. The same kinds of riots were now framed as "acts of violence rather than claims for justice" (Dikeç 2004: 193). Thus, as aggrieved second-generation youths pursued alternative methods (riots) to express discontent, these acts and utterances unfolded within a more restrictive discursive and political context. Negative representations transformed urban struggles into acts of senseless barbarism instead of legitimate expressions of anger concerning the systemic wrongs facing the population.

There remains in northeastern Paris an important cluster of immigrant associations but this cluster is an *aggregation* of organizations rather than an *agglomeration*. Government controls have encouraged them to focus on the provision of services to narrow publics (women, youth, the elderly, delinquents) in specific neighborhoods. This has narrowed their scope of thinking and action. Government controls have also contributed to aggravating tensions and distrust between associations. First- and second-generation associations rarely collaborate on projects and smaller neighborhood associations seem to display high levels of distrust as they engage in ferocious competition for subsidies. We witness many associations in immigrant neighborhoods but associations with weak relations between one another. There are therefore aggregations of associations, but they lack the relational links needed to produce thriving activist clusters that can serve as driving forces of political change.

The early 1980s was marked by a proliferation of political activities in France's immigrant civil society. The number of immigrant associations grew rapidly and many of these associations took important roles in high-profile mobilizations during the early years of the decade. Government measures in 1981 (legalization of associations, freedom of speech, etc.) facilitated this rapid politicization of first- and second-generation immigrants. Officials quickly understood that they had little control over the movement and their political integration into the country. This spurred a major effort to introduce a range of techniques to steer their political integration. These techniques overlapped and reinforced one another, infiltrating the political life worlds of immigrants. The collective effect of these techniques was a comprehensive discursive and institutional cage that discouraged contentious political activities and eventually drained politics as a reason for associational life. In such a context, the possibilities of *being political* were narrowed to those acts and discourses that government officials found "reasonable."

The Limits of Control: Autonomous NGOs and Unruly *Collectifs*

Government efforts to "integrate" immigrants into politics during the 1980s and 1990s ultimately placed important controls on first- and second-generation associations at national and local levels. Government controls were by no means total or complete. They primarily targeted formal immigrant associations by creating an institutional and discursive cage that was difficult to escape. By contrast, the government presented human rights NGOs with fewer constraints. Just as important, a new cluster of informal undocumented immigrant rights groups (*collectifs des sans papiers*) emerged beyond the government's reach. Public officials had not anticipated this latter cluster and lacked effective tools to coopt and incorporate it within the political order. We therefore stress that political integration as a strategy of government control was unevenly executed and produced varying effects on activist networks in Paris: it caged first- and second-generation immigrant associations, permitted the political activities of human rights NGOs, and overlooked the *collectifs des sans papiers*. Government control did not neutralize all immigrant rights struggles but rearranged the playing field by providing different opportunities and constraints for the principal clusters involved.

Relative autonomy for human rights NGOs

Human rights NGOs (LDH, MRAP, FASTI, GISTI) working with immigrant communities received important subsidies from FAS. They also faced constraints concerning their political activities. However, their size, prestige, and high degree of institutionalization helped mitigate the effects of government controls:

There is a question of age; also a question of institutional relations. When we accept a subsidy from the state for a project, we accept the obligation of that project. But we don't want to be under the obligation of the state all the time. Up to the present the state has not sought to control us, at least it has never said, 'You don't have the right to say those things.' It also hasn't told us that, 'You don't have the right to help undocumented immigrants.' We still do these things in an indirect way, which is dangerous not just for MRAP but all the associations working for human rights. (MRAP, personal interview)

Others from human rights NGOs expressed similar views about their relations to the government: while human rights NGOs were vigilant about what they said and did, most directors of these associations believed that their size, importance, and prestige provided them with enough clout to mitigate the sanctioning powers of the state.

National associations also had greater freedom than *local* associations to protest immigration policies. These associations received their funding primarily from national agencies or from dues-paying members. This revenue structure protected them from the threat of subsidy cuts from irate local prefects and mayors. Local and grassroots associations (the vast majority of immigrant associations), by contrast, depended largely on subsidies administered by mayors and prefects, making them more vulnerable to cuts associated with political activities (Garbaye 2005). Paris contained the most prominent human rights NGOs in the country and their prominence and national scope allowed them to avoid some local political and institutional constraints.

In spite of their relative security, some did experience subsidy cuts in response to political activities. For instance, in 1995 the Minister of the Interior ordered a cut of 500,000 francs to FASTI, a well-established human rights NGO. The subsidy cut was made in response to a satirical cartoon that lampooned the minister. In a meeting with other Paris-based NGOs, the director of MRAP conveyed a message from the minister to his colleagues: "Eric Raoult [Minister of Integration] said that what happened to FASTI would not be generalized. It was done to sanction FASTI because it went too far ... He is ready to meet FASTI and the 500,000 francs could be redistributed to the ASTIs [local branches] but not to the central federation" (FASTI minutes, September 16, 1995). The minister was willing to reinstate the subsidy to the local branches of the national federation. This was consistent with the government's general efforts to enhance control by localizing subsidies (vis-à-vis department prefects and mayors). The minister subsequently sent FASTI and the other big human rights NGOs a letter stating that the "public sector will no longer subsidize associations of counter-power [*contre pouvoir*]" (FASTI minutes, March 3, 1996). Through this public and punitive sanction, the minister intended to send a signal to the other human rights NGOs that had moved beyond humanitarianism and into the world of contentious politics.

Paris-based human rights NGOs with history, prestige, national scope, and elite backers were able to mitigate controls better than local and national immigrant associations. But mitigation was not the same thing as immunity. The government at times displayed its willingness to make a spectacular example of an association (FASTI) that had gone "too far." It placed this association on the scaffold and denied it the resources needed to survive. This spectacular exertion of punitive power was different from the more totalizing controls developed to discipline the speech, conduct, and thoughts of immigrant associations. Whereas the margins for autonomous speech and action decreased precipitously for immigrant associations, human rights NGOs continued to enjoy a degree of autonomy needed to participate and lead contentious mobilizations in the 1990s and 2000s.

Unruly collectifs de sans papiers

The 1980s and early 1990s witnessed the eruption of a new cluster on the Parisian political scene. Undocumented immigrants, primarily of West African origin, began to organize themselves into *collectifs des sans papiers* to fight for legal status. The *collectifs* were typically made up of family and friendship networks. They sometimes adopted names but lacked any formal organizational structure and resources. They were often created in response to very specific grievances and would disappear as fast as they were created. Local and national government officials did not anticipate them and had great difficulty exercising control over them. The *collectifs* were informal and self-organized, which made them ineligible for government subsidies and oversight. Only the cruder methods of control were available to the state: threats, repression, and divide-and-rule.

The *collectifs* emerged across the country, but they were most strongly concentrated in the Paris region. Paris had established itself as the most important gateway city for sub-Sahara African immigrants, with 60% settling in the metropolitan area by the end of the 1990s (Boëldieu and Borrel 2000). Many West African immigrants were drawn from compact regions in Mali and Senegal (Siméant 1998; Péchu 1999, 2004). The close family and friendship ties were used to reconstruct solidarity networks from sending regions in Paris and its close suburbs. These interpersonal networks combined with emerging ethnic associations to form the foundations of a robust organizational infrastructure for the

West African community. In her extensive research on this community, Cécile Péchu (1999, 2004) observed that this infrastructure played a key role in providing important information to community members, including information concerning immigration policies, decisions made by the prefect and mayor, and various advocacy and support groups and associations.

These networks served as an important resource for survival, but they also helped translate grievances into contentious forms of collective action because of strong kin and friendship relations. Early mobilizations targeted the housing policies of the mayor. Family reunification visas required a certificate of "decent housing" issued by the mayor's office. This meant that "For immigrants, housing takes on a dimension that it simply does not have for French families. It affects the right to live as a family and to obtain papers for the family which are in order" (Péchu 1999: 734). Many immigrants who would normally have qualified for a family reunification visa were denied one because of the difficulty in obtaining housing certificates (Péchu 1999). Thousands of families subsequently entered the country without authorization and settled in dilapidated hotels or squatted in unoccupied buildings. This made it more difficult to obtain housing certificates and spawned the growth of slum dwellings in the center of Paris.

The mayor in the mid-1980s, Jacques Chirac, responded through mass evictions from squats, hotels, and other dwellings. A group of West African families in one squatted building resisted the mayor's efforts. They formed one of the first *collectifs* and called on the mayor to relocate them in social housing and provide them with a certificate of decent housing. These efforts attracted the immediate support of the association Housing First (ULA),[5] a squatting and housing organization with ties to Paris's radical activist networks. Immigrant and radical housing activists inhabited and interacted with one another in the same building for several months (Péchu 2004: 305). In 1990, 10 of the West African squatters initiated a hunger strike and activists with the ULA used their networks to expand political, associational, and media support for the action (ibid.). The coalition eventually succeeded in pressuring the mayor to offer the immigrant families social housing and provide its members with housing certificates.

In 1993, another group of West African families squatted in a building on the rue de Dragon and they drew on the immediate support from activists who had been engaged in the earlier campaign. Their experience permitted them to quickly turn this new action into a high-profile event. Commenting on their heightened level of expertise, a West African organizer noted:

So we became more and more *efficient, we knew how to do things.* We were very capable at having dialogues, pressuring for changes in housing policy. We also avoided being beaten up by the police and when that did happen, we were sure that a crew of photographers and media were present. The rare cases in which we were beaten up, we had three television chains and 25 photographers on location, all outside and inside the squat. (Cited in Péchu 2004: 89, emphasis added)

This statement illustrates the heightened capacities of this particular cluster. They were indeed becoming more "efficient" in learning "how to do things" because of their ongoing collective engagement in hard-pitched battles. The primary tools to exercise government control were limited to repression, but the activists had developed the knowhow to respond and use government repression to their advantage.

As the 1993 campaign unfolded, immigrant and French activists sought to expand the scale of the struggle and make clearer connections between this housing struggle and the unjust exclusion of immigrants. The French activists involved in the action formed a new association, *Droits Devants*, which would go on to play a key role in later immigrant rights mobilizations (Siméant 1998; Péchu 2004).

In spite of the rollout of new methods of political control during the 1980s, these methods were by no means all-encompassing. Certain clusters were deeply affected by them (immigrant associations), others were less unaffected (human rights NGOs), and still others operated beyond the reach of state control (*collectifs des sans papiers*). Rather than these controls destroying Paris's social movement milieu, they contributed to rearranging the clusters and readjusting opportunities for contentious political activities. Paris moved into the 1990s with a dense assortment of organizations and clusters dedicated to the fight for immigrant rights. Activists would go on to play a leading role in large-scale mobilizations later in the decade and into the 2000s.

Conclusions

The mid-1980s marked a change in the government's strategy regarding immigrant associations. In contrast to how they were viewed in the 1970s, immigrants were no longer considered strictly as "lepers" (Foucault 2004) that needed to be expelled beyond national boundaries. Some restrictions stayed in place and continued to exclude unwanted immigrants from the country. However, the new government in the 1980s also began to view this as a population that posed important yet manageable risks. Rather than banish the whole population, the governments of the 1980s and 1990s sought to monitor, discipline, and channel the large population of authorized immigrants settled in the country. The government carved out a place for them within the well-policed political order. As most immigrant associations (first- and second-generation) were integrated into a proper place within the order of things (Rancière 1993; Dikeç 2006), they lost their capacity to act and speak in ways that would disrupt the order.

While the state controlled immigrant associations by steering their integration into the French Republican order, it did no such thing for the human rights NGOs. These associations were run by middle-class, mostly white French, mostly male, and highly professionalized advocates. They did not need to be "integrated" into the Republican order because they were a part of the order. They were dissidents but they were dissidents within the French tradition of activism. They tapped into a history and cultural repertoires of criticism that were well known to the public and to the government officials they targeted. They were therefore critics but critics that had a strong and valued place within the Republican tradition. Immigrants, on the other hand, had no place. Their resistance posed a unique threat because their actions, demands, and values could not be anticipated or clearly understood. This required the state to take a more assertive stance and ensure their integration into the Republic. Just as important, the human right NGOs had prestige, resources, and many more elite supporters than the immigrant associations. This helped to mitigate the extent to which the government could extend its reach into their worlds. The government could occasionally make a spectacular repressive gesture, but these were rare events that failed to produce substantial changes in their behavior and thoughts.

Lastly, the *collectifs des sans papiers* emerged as a new and robust force on the political scene. They emerged in response to a very specific grievance: the need for "decent" housing as a condition for permanent residency status. The government did not and could not anticipate their formation. Its normal tools of control (surveillance, subsidies, monitoring, contracts, symbolic violence, etc.) were ill-adapted to the informal and ephemeral character of the *collectifs*. The government lacked the capacity and flexibility to adapt the existing tools of control to respond to this new and unanticipated risk. The only tool at the government's disposal was straight repression, but clever immigrant activists used displays of government violence to gain more support and sympathy for their efforts.

Government controls were therefore important but they were unevenly applied and somewhat inflexible when presented with new and unanticipated risks. When they were well developed, they depoliticized and normalized their targets (e.g. immigrant associations).

However, they left openings for other actors (e.g. human rights NGOs) and failed to anticipate and respond to new insurgents (*collectifs des sans papiers*) that emerged beyond the well-governed order of things. The government – even in a strong state system like France's – produced important technologies of control but these technologies were prone to inflexibility and blind spots that permitted the emergence of new forces of dissent. What the French government controlled, it controlled well but it showed a certain level of inadaptability, which impeded its ability to reach out and respond to new political risks that it had not anticipated in the past.

8

The Cooptative State
The Pacification of Contentious Immigrant Politics in Amsterdam

Nihat Karaman had come to the Netherlands in the 1970s to escape from the Turkish government's backlash against communists. It was natural for Karaman to continue his political activism after he arrived in the Netherlands and settled in Amsterdam East. Together with his wife and comrades, he helped to establish the communist organization HTIB and various offshoots, creating a cluster of radical immigrants from Turkey within Amsterdam's social movement milieu. Karaman wrote for the magazine of the Foundation for the Welfare of Foreign Workers (SWBW) on the necessity of a proletarian revolution and engaged in community organizing in an information center for foreigners in Amsterdam East. As leftists like Karaman were catapulted into the center of Amsterdam's movement milieu, they used their newly gained power to sabotage their political opponents, including the so-called Grey Wolves – that is, supporters of the extremely nationalist MHP party in Turkey. Whenever Grey Wolves opened up a meeting place or applied for subsidies, Karaman and his organization stepped in and campaigned until the government withdrew its support. The support from native Dutch anti-fascists and the government allowed Karaman and HTIB to marginalize more conservative currents within the Turkish community. After the political conflicts in Turkey had peaked in 1980 and Amsterdam's social movements lost steam, Karaman came to adopt a very different role. He lost his radical edge and profiled himself as a bridge builder connecting the various political strands within the

Cities and Social Movements: Immigrant Rights Activism in the United States, France, and the Netherlands, 1970–2015, First Edition. Walter J. Nicholls and Justus Uitermark.
© 2017 John Wiley & Sons, Ltd. Published 2017 by John Wiley & Sons, Ltd.

Turkish community to one another and to Dutch government agencies and civil society associations. When Karaman was killed in 1988 (under circumstances that remain opaque to this day), he was not celebrated as a radical vanguard igniting the proletarian revolution but as a skillful broker uniting the Turkish community (Vermeulen 2006).

There are many reasons why someone like Karaman would transform from being an agitator to become a keeper of social peace, but the extensiveness and structure of Amsterdam's governance configurations certainly played a role. Karaman's development quite closely reflects broader political developments in Amsterdam. Amsterdam's politics had been exceptionally contentious in the 1960s, 1970s, and early 1980s. A select group of leftist immigrants could flourish in this climate and achieve central positions within Amsterdam's movement space as they took up leading roles in the struggle against injustices in the housing market, in the labor market, and in politics. But the late 1980s, 1990s, and 2000s presented a completely different picture. Governance became much calmer. Many of the social problems that had elicited sympathy, solidarity, and outrage among guest workers as well as their native Dutch supporters had been largely resolved: the hundreds of guest worker hostels had closed down as immigrants had moved into the social housing sector; immigrants were still in the bottom ranks of the labor market but for the vast majority of them conditions of indentured servitude had ended; and many former guest workers had received permanent residence or acquired Dutch nationality, allowing them access to the Dutch welfare state and to take part in elections. While confrontations in the form of street fights or heated debates had been a hallmark of Amsterdam's politics before the mid-1980s, after that point politics became more controlled.

This chapter focuses on the pacification of immigrant rights politics in Amsterdam. It first examines how the vanguards that had spearheaded the immigrant rights movement were gradually absorbed into governance networks and lost their inclination and capacity for organizing broad and powerful mobilizations. It then examines how the Amsterdam government responded to a new kind of challenge, that of Islamic radicals. How were the governance structures created in response to contention and anxieties of the 1980s and 1990s transformed in the 2000s to get a grip on these new challengers? By addressing this issue, we stress the Dutch state's capacity to flexibly adapt and respond to points of rebellion that it had not anticipated. Whereas the French state has had difficulty anticipating and adapting to new risks like *collectifs*, urban riots, and (increasingly) Islamic radicals, the Dutch government has shown itself to be capable in extending its control. The flexible and adaptable character of this state has enabled it to extend the circuits of government deep into immigrant civil society. The differences from

France are apparent enough, but those from the United States are stark. The laissez-faire approach to governance in Los Angeles during the late 1980s and 1990s contributed to a veritable collapse of the state in low-income immigrant neighborhoods. By thick and adaptable meshes of government, control in the Netherlands did not completely close off all possibilities of contention but certainly placed constraints on how seeds of conflict and resistance could evolve over time and space.

Political Integration through Ethnic and Territorial Encapsulation

By the early 1980s, radical grassroots organizations had consolidated. In particular, Amsterdam's historical center and the adjacent neighborhoods had become hotbeds of social movement activity. In these neighborhoods different clusters of activists were active on a day-to-day basis and occasionally linked up during large-scale mobilizations. These linkages within and across neighborhoods and clusters were established through a series of mobilizations in different fields, ranging from protests for the regularization of immigrants to demonstrations against nuclear weapons. During such mobilizations, linkages among organizations and clusters were established based on ideological affinity or shared interests. We might say that these social movement organizations were self-organized: neither the government nor any other central authority orchestrated the process of coalition formation. However, the government did seek to create order within Amsterdam's civil society and offered recognition and resources to organizations willing to cooperate. The radical immigrants could translate their centrality within movement networks into centrality within governance structures: they tapped into subsidies, received professional support, and were recognized as the legitimate voice of their community. However, the organizations that had now been formally recognized and integrated experienced soon enough that they were not just closer to the government but that the government was closer to them. While the radical left used resources and influence to extend their organizational reach and promote their radical agenda, the government provided these subsidies in the expectation that the organizations would align with its agenda of promoting minority integration. The government demanded not only that subsidized immigrant and community organizations address certain issues but also required that they spoke in specific ways and, even more significantly, created specific types of networks. As a result, leftist organizations were increasingly encapsulated in a governance logic that was not of their own making and constrained their capacity and inclination to mobilize based on ideological affinity or shared interests. This section discusses two mechanisms of political integration: ethnic encapsulation and territorial encapsulation.

Integration through ethnic encapsulation

By ethnic encapsulation, we mean the process through which organizations are compelled to organize and speak as ethnic groups. Amsterdam's governance structures of the 1980s and 1990s represented a prime example of such encapsulation. To understand the origins and effects of these structures, it is essential to understand the history of the so-called minorities policy, a policy that provided ample resources to minority groups in the hope and expectation that representatives of these groups would assist the government in reducing ethnic conflict. Although contemporary analyses often assume that politicians and administrators in the Netherlands only recently became aware of socio-cultural tensions, policies toward immigrants have long been informed by fears of cultural strife. Such fears reached new heights in the 1970s as a result of conflicts involving the Moluccan community. Moluccans hailed from Indonesia, where they collaborated intensively with the Dutch colonial powers. Several thousand Moloccans who had served in the Dutch army were demobilized after Indonesia's decolonization and shipped to the Netherlands. They received a cold welcome in the country they had served with patriotic passion. They were accommodated in substandard housing and even in former concentration camps that had been disused since the Second World War. The older generation of Moluccans became increasingly frustrated with the Dutch government as it refused to advocate for an independent Moluccan state. A new generation of Moluccans became disillusioned with the Netherlands as they felt their loyal parents had been shortchanged and betrayed. They resorted to violent means, including taking hostages during occupations of government buildings and the hijacking of trains. During two train hijacks, in 1975 and 1977, several people – hostages as well as hijackers – were killed (Bartels 1986). These events reflected a very peculiar immigration trajectory of a very particular community. The argument that immigration results in tensions because of cultural conflicts had no prima facie validity for the Moluccans: they were Christians, they were patriots, and they revered the Dutch royal family. And still the hijackings and occupations fueled fears of immigration, as they were considered to be frightful examples of what might happen when immigrants group together and form parallel communities (Essed and Nimako 2006). The Moluccan tragedies intensified policy makers' efforts to get a grip on tensions arising from immigration: immigrant groups were extensively monitored (cf. Penninx 1979), advice was requested (cf. WRR 1979), and funds were made available. In 1983, the so-called "minorities policy" was established. The policy aimed to incorporate immigrants by facilitating their organizations and involving them in decision making. Since the minorities policies recognized and accommodated groups defined according to their ethnicity, it could be said that the policy was multicultural, but it was multiculturalism with a twist: the policy did not celebrate cultural diversity *tout court*, but was founded on a fear of cultural tensions and specifically targeted *deprived* minority groups in the hope of preventing the formation of parallel communities.

This policy played out in different ways in different parts of the country. In Amsterdam, left-wing immigrant organizations reaped most of the benefits. While literature on multiculturalism often suggests that the institutionalization of ethnic differences results in the reification and conservation of culture, this is not at all what happened in Amsterdam, at least not at first: Turks and Moroccans were not represented by religious leaders, tribesmen or other leaders with ethnic nostalgia but by a revolutionary vanguard firmly committed to the international struggle for equal rights. Dissidents who were on the fringe in their home countries had become central in Amsterdam. They received subsidies and took up dominant positions in the ethnic advisory councils. While leftist immigrant organizations had been established and flourished with the help of social movements, they now also could call on the state for support and they were generally recognized as representing their ethnic communities. This governance arrangement remained in place in the 1980s, but it was vulnerable as it was based on selective amplification and silencing: the voice of radical leftists was amplified by native Dutch sympathizers, while the voice of other (more conservative) elements within ethnic communities was ignored or actively silenced. The governance arrangement began to crack as rivals and the government questioned the leadership of the leftist organizations. As conservative and religious organizations were established and grew more assertive, it became increasingly apparent that the minority policy's structure suffered from the fundamental problem that representatives of organizations should speak as *ethnic* groups that were deeply divided politically. To convincingly argue that they were legitimate representatives, the leftist immigrants were now forced to liaise with other organizations within their ethnic group, even if they had different or conflicting beliefs. The effects of the minorities policy on the networking patterns among immigrant organizations are especially well documented for the Turkish community thanks to the efforts of Floris Vermeulen (Vermeulen 2006; see also Fennema and Tillie 1999). Vermeulen's analysis shows that in the (early) 1980s no collaboration existed among left-wing and right-wing Turkish organizations. There were various reasons for this. The conflict between Turkish nationalists, Kurdish separatists, religious fundamentalists, and socialist radicals was at its height in Turkey and (consequently) in the Netherlands. In addition, the leftist immigrant organizations had few incentives to collaborate. At this point they had privileged access to the state's resources and could call upon a wide network of sympathizers. This situation started to change in the course of the 1980s. Conflicts in Turkey had de-escalated somewhat, reducing tensions in the streets of Amsterdam. But the opportunity structure provided by the Dutch and Amsterdam governments also played an important role in reducing tensions and altering the relational dispositions of organizations. Organizations like HTIB had thrived on strong ties with Dutch sympathizers who provided them with practical support and information, but such ties lost their value and were severed once the organizations could use subsidies to recruit their own professionals (HTIB archives at the Institute for Social History, article 135). The networking strategies of HTIB's leadership were also influenced by the minorities policy. As mentioned in this chapter's introduction, Nihat Karaman, the chairman of HTIB, had been an ardent communist and radical organizer during the 1970s, but he slowly but surely began to profile himself as a spokesperson for the Turkish community under the influence of the minorities policies. HTIB was established by members of Turkey's Communist Party and its leadership was, and remained, steeped in a radical leftist and unionist ideology, but this ideology was bracketed in favor of a more pragmatic and consensual approach as the Dutch government incentivized organizations from Turkey to organize as ethnic (rather than political or religious) organizations. To establish the national platform for consultation of Turkish affairs (*Inspraak Orgaan Turken*), Karaman steadfastly networked with organizations of all ideological stripes. Karaman was someone who could, according to Vermeulen (2006: 103), "uniquely overcome the ideological differences that characterize Turkish organizational populations." Karaman "curbed the more extreme elements in his own organizations" and developed into "a strong supporter of collaboration between different Turkish political groups and Dutch organizations" (ibid.: 103). Karaman's case shows how individual dispositions, political opportunities, and networking strategies interacted in Amsterdam: ethnic encapsulation incentivized radicals from all sides to collaborate and thus helped to mute tensions and pacify relations within ethnic communities. This contrasts with a city like Berlin, where there were fewer connections among organizations from Turkey and especially among ideological competitors (Vermeulen 2006).

The linkages among Amsterdam's organizations were mostly established for pragmatic and opportunistic reasons. The Turkish community managed to resolve internal conflicts but it did not achieve the ideological and social cohesion necessary to effectively organize. Rather than mobilizing around issues of general interest in broad coalitions, the organizations participating in the minorities policy's institutions were embroiled in petty conflicts as the leftist immigrants lost ground. In particular, the mosque federation Milli Görüş moved from a marginal to a central position as the organization established ties with Dutch organizations and government agencies. The chairman of Milli Görüş, Haci Karacaer, recollected in an interview that the Turkish council became an ethnic bastion, "closed and narrow-minded. That's where I see fundamentalism, at the church of leftist Turks" (personal interview). Karacaer would become chair of the Turkish council but warmly welcomed its dissolution, which would ultimately take place in 2003, long after the council had started its demise.

Similar pacification mechanisms were in play in the Moroccan community. Just before and just after the minorities policy was formally established, leftist immigrants, especially KMAN, had no inclination or incentive to collaborate with their ideological opponents. KMAN's leader, Abdou Menebhi, had been a sworn enemy of organizations loyal to Morocco's regime; the fight against the loyalists of the *Amicales* brought him to the Netherlands in the first place and his animosity toward the Moroccan regime was the driving force behind his and his comrades' activism. However, like Nihat Karaman of HTIB, Menebhi evolved from being an antagonist to a broker in the course of the 1980s as he took it upon himself to unite the Moroccan community in the Netherlands. Developments in the home country were partly responsible for this; King Hassan's regime loosened its grip and the memory of major outbursts of state violence faded somewhat.

The minorities policy also played an important role. Menebhi became the chair of the City Moroccan Council (SMR)[1] and as such had to speak for all Moroccans. Feuds between different factions remained (and remain to this day) but eruptions of violence and open conflict became rarer. In the 1990s, the radicals of KMAN and the conservatives of the mosque federation UMMON even formed a coalition and shared the leadership and associated benefits of the City Moroccan Council. Previously KMAN had accused UMMON of being part of the repressive apparatus of Morocco's regime but now Menebhi voiced a very different opinion:

> The progressive movement has made a historical mistake. We considered religion as opium for the people. We did not see that Islam is an integral part of our people's culture. The regimes were therefore able to play out Islam against socialist movements … Now the Left hardly plays any role of significance, both because of its own mistakes and international

developments. Islam is playing the lead role. The progressive movement is now learning its lessons ... What mosques are doing in North-Africa now, the Left was doing in the 1970s: social activities, education, organizing, and food for the poor. (Menebhi, cited in Haleber and De Meijer 1993: n.p.)

The alliance with UMMON allowed KMAN to represent and reach much larger groups. This was especially important considering that the government had come to believe that mosques, not secular civil society organizations, could serve as a bridge to at-risk groups (delinquents, school drop-outs, illiterates, etc.) yet were out of policy makers' reach. The City Moroccan Council also continued its political protests and participated in demonstrations against racism, for Palestine, and against police violence.

However, the Moroccan Council, too, suffered from internal strife. The veterans of KMAN and UMMON came into conflict with Moroccans of the second generation who wanted to wrest themselves from the tutelage and patronage of the first generation. For instance, representatives of the youth center Argan, established to reach out to Moroccan youths, complained bitterly about attempts by veteran members of KMAN and the mosque federation UMMON to gain control of the center. The chairwoman of the center, Fatima Belkasmi, said that they were not interested in "Quran lessons, card games or demonstrations" but wanted to have Moroccan youths develop their own ideas (*Trouw* 2000). The municipal government had never been pleased with the City Moroccan Council,[2] but it nevertheless felt that its demise had created a void that had to be filled given the anxiety about Islamic radicalism and delinquency within the Moroccan community. In 2003, the municipal government asked the group around Argan to reinvigorate the initiative of uniting the Moroccan community. Argan agreed, but it was hard to get different groups to participate in the project, as one of the people at Argan explained during an interview:

We tried to involve the older generation. We did not succeed. And then we drew the conclusion that there is a huge gap between the young and the old. The older generation is very activist ... The young generation too but there are some conflicts where we can just turn the switch and think without emotions. We want to enter into a conversation with everyone to create a solution to the problem. The older generation does not have that idea. (Personal interview)

Attempts to bridge divisions within the Moroccan community and recreate a platform for Moroccan organizations were made for years but ultimately proved to be in vain.

Ethnic encapsulation fits in the long tradition of pillarization and served to pacify conflictual relations within ethnic communities. One might say that the Netherlands's consensual political culture was successfully extended to minority groups, just as the minorities policy had intended. This culture is not simply a collection of norms and values but carried through a set of institutions and procedures that changed the operational logical of formerly antagonistic organizations. Ethnic encapsulation forced organizations that already had lost much of their momentum into a straitjacket by assigning them certain policy-defined roles and allocating them policy-defined tasks. While the organizations involved profited in the short term from subsidies and recognition associated with their formal status as community representatives, in the longer term the consequence was that meeting government requirements became more important than finding new causes and constituents in a period of movement decline. The councils' fundamental problem – the predicament that representing ethnic communities forces radicals to liaise with groups they have no ideological affinity with – was exacerbated when previously marginalized and stigmatized groups (religious groups or the younger generation) challenged the dominance of left-wing organizations. The ethnic councils and their member organizations consequently developed into relics of the past and became sites of petty feuds between different policy stakeholders. In spite of these disputes, the ethnicity-based structures of the minorities policy were remarkably tenacious: the ethnic councils existed until 2003 and the government continued to organize dialogues with the "Moroccan community" or the "Turkish community" in response to alarming statistics or mediatized incidents.

Integrating through territorial encapsulation

In addition to ethnic encapsulation, the government adopted a range of strategies to get a grip on minority groups. These included the development of spatially sensitive policies and the attempt to foster the political integration of immigrants at the neighborhood level. Instead of having parallel policy fields and separate groups, the newly established "integration policy" (established in 1994 but anticipated for almost a decade before official adoption) was supposed to promote "integral" forms of policy making. Integration policy was merged with territorial policies; a development starting with the adoption of the social renewal policy in 1990 and reaching its climax with the appointment of a Minister of Big Cities and Integration in 1998 (Uitermark 2003). By bringing together various parties and groups at the neighborhood level, "social cohesion" was to be achieved.

In Amsterdam, this typically happened at the level of the neighborhood district. These urban jurisdictions – usually between 25,000 and 100,000 residents, with an elected government – were gradually established over the course of the 1980s. Though neighborhood councils have limited discretion to make policies of their own, their purported aim was to bring government closer to the people. They did so among other ways by bringing together a variety of neighborhood groups into inter-associational platforms run by civil servants. In some cases these platforms consisted exclusively of minority associations, in other cases they included voluntary associations of various kinds, but in all cases they drastically increased the intensity of strongly formalized interactions among associations and neighborhood councils. Since they were not uniting on their own initiative or on the basis of ideological affinity, the platforms were chronically occupied with bridging differences between the various participants. The platforms were strongly self-referential: the goals invariably were to bring different groups together, promote neighborhood cooperation, and streamline interactions between the associations and the government. To keep the platforms going and commit the volunteers, associations received small subsidies and extensive political and administrative attention. Some associations highly appreciated the recognition and resources, others were deeply frustrated about what they perceived as tokens – either way, the enthusiasm and the frustration were put in a territorial straitjacket and contained within the neighborhood. While many organizations were originally established as off-shoots of organizations operating at the city, national, and international levels, they were encouraged to reconceive themselves as *neighborhood* organizations.

These shifts in the geographical focus and socio-spatial networking coincided with a growing emphasis on *governing* and *policing*. While in the past community groups had emerged out of resistance to urban renewal, now policy actors actively mobilized residents and formed communities of stakeholders as part of efforts to smooth the process of urban restructuring; the formation of communities now became something that was achieved through governmental programs directed at neighborhood communities rather than civil action directed at governments. After a period of strong resident activism in the 1980s, states co-opted antagonistic neighborhood organizations (Mayer 2007) and created new coalitions in which select groups of residents and associations were incorporated as "partners" (Nicholls 2006). Thus, the neighborhood emerged as a site where the promotion of cohesion aided attempts of governing actors to constitute and mobilize communities to assist in governing unruly territories (Uitermark 2014; De Wilde 2015).

This shift also impacted the organizations that had fueled the wave of contention of the 1980s, including neighborhood-based activists and minority associations. Now that they were regarded as "partners" and represented "the neighborhood," minority associations were increasingly called upon to connect the government to groups that were out of reach, such as illiterates, youths at risk, and women who are kept at home by their husbands. Employed, assertive, responsible, well-connected, and literate people were emphatically *not* considered as target groups. While they may have been assets for associations, they were not problematic enough to warrant policy attention – the government rewarded associations for reaching out to exactly those groups that it could not handle itself. The people within the associations' reach were transformed from constituents united according to reciprocity and ideological affinity into target groups composed of problematic cases within a particular neighborhood. Countless initiatives were taken, ranging from house visits by social workers and "street coaches" to boot camps and martial arts courses. Naturally, the remaining associations could count on little support from prospective constituents and supporters – after all, they were no longer organized to represent or serve constituents but to reach out to problematic target groups.

The depoliticization of immigrant rights politics

In the 1990s the activism that had characterized Amsterdam evaporated. The nineteenth-century neighborhoods that the government had failed to raze in its earlier modernizing zeal were now more cautiously "restructured": social housing was demolished or renovated and replaced by owner-occupied housing on a block-by-block basis. Gentrifiers were moving into these neighborhoods while deviant and defiant groups like squatters were moved out. There was still opposition to the government but it was reduced to manageable proportions, in part because of the government's intense efforts to institutionalize interest representation. While before residents and communities had asserted themselves, now the government was increasingly seeking out partners in civil society. The power of these cooptative governmental technologies was further reinforced by the establishment of neighborhood districts focusing on the micro-management of urban space.

The erosion of social movement networks and the extension of government policy into organizations and the grassroots shifted power relations in favor of the government. The government now dealt with numerous unconnected, small, and uncritical associations instead of a handful of connected, large, and critical ones. While minority organizations were increasingly required to operate in tight ethnic and territorial straitjackets, the municipal government used its increased discretionary powers to conceive of minority integration that focused less on anti-racism and social justice. In the policy document *The Power of a Diverse City*[3] the local government states it "not only wants to address problems" but also "aims to create opportunities" (Gemeente Amsterdam 1999: 3). The minorities policy allegedly worked in the opposite direction by imposing categories on people and by associating them with negative stereotypes. The new aim was to break down the artificial barriers between groups and to portray diversity in a positive light. This new discourse on diversity also suggested new ways of organizing civil society. While before policies had especially aimed to support organizations for marginalized groups, policies now aimed to fund only carefully circumscribed projects. In practice this meant that, in particular, consultancy agencies and highly professionalized associations were funded, as these actors produced the sort of upbeat and constructive discourses that the government was looking for.

Around the turn of the century, contention within minority groups appeared to have been neutralized. The municipal government had adopted an optimistic discourse of diversity and had established strong relations with a new generation of civil and commercial entrepreneurs, while numerous small organizations functioned as subcontractors in a market where the municipal government exercised almost monopolistic control. The organizations that were central in the social movement networks of the 1980s had lost their momentum and were strapped into a straitjacket through territorial and ethnic encapsulation. Associations seeking to address injustices through broad mobilizations had withered away or become anachronistic by the year 2000.

Unanticipated Contention and the Flexible Adaptation of the Dutch State

New seeds of contention on the margins

Although the government reached deep into the grassroots and pacified groups and territories that had been contentious in the 1980s, it also lost control over areas of the city and civil society. Especially in the garden cities in the western part of Amsterdam, referred to as "New West," the government experienced a loss of control. New West cities had been built in the 1950s and 1960s with the purpose of creating spatial and social harmony. Families escaping the overcrowded inner-city areas had found in New West new spacious homes in a green environment. The political turmoil of the 1960s, 1970s, and 1980s largely by passed New West. But in the course of the 1980s New West increasingly lost its status as a solidly middle-class and "respectable" environment as native Dutch families moved to more remote suburbs. By the early 1990s New West had the country's largest concentration of immigrants of Moroccan and Turkish descent, many of whom occupied low positions within the labor market and school system. The extent of deprivation and stigmatization of the area and its population was perhaps limited in comparison to that of American ghettos (see Wacquant 1993, 2008), but New West nevertheless came to be seen as a frontline of the multicultural society. News media over the years have produced a steady stream of vivid accounts of Moroccan teenagers harassing women, provoking police or teachers, intimidating neighborhood residents, and engaging in petty, as well as organized, crime. Policy makers were very alarmed and feared that New West was about to get caught in a spiral of decline.

In response, the government unfolded a drastic strategy of urban and social renewal: the housing stock was upgraded and partly privatized, while a range of supportive and punitive measures were taken to ensure that residents of New West would integrate into the Dutch mainstream. Although many residents criticized the policies, no resident movement of significance emerged: residents were deeply divided and lacked community organizations speaking on their behalf (see Mepschen 2012, 2013). Ethnic tensions among residents and a general feeling that New West faced urgent problems undoubtedly contributed to the lack of resistance, but in addition state institutions exercised much more control over the grassroots than they had done in the 1970s and 1980s. Housing corporations and welfare organizations carefully directed participation trajectories and ensured that resistance was nipped in the bud through tailored interventions (Huisman 2014).

Although the fine-grained web of control that was spun around deprived groups and their habitats pre-empted large-scale resistance, it did not contain contention altogether. After the attacks of 9/11 in 2001 and especially the assassination of Theo van Gogh in 2004, the anxieties about New West were further aggravated by fears of radical Islamists. Theo van Gogh had made a movie with Ayaan Hirsi Ali, a noted Muslim apostate who had been under police protection because of threats to her life. The Muslim extremist Mohammed Bouyeri shot Van Gogh and then stabbed a note with a death threat to Hirsi Ali into his chest. Bouyeri had killed Van Gogh in the East of Amsterdam but attention quickly focused on Amsterdam West where Bouyeri had grown up and become embroiled in networks of Muslim radicals. Reports in the media and from the intelligence services reinforced concerns about radicalism among certain segments of the Muslim population. In spite of intense state involvement, discontent had been brewing. The case of Mohamed Bouyeri, Van Gogh's killer, is illustrative of both the intensity and fragility of the state's micro-management. Bouyeri had a long history of involvement in youth and community projects. He was a "positive" and "promising" kid who eagerly agreed to run computer lessons and social events in a community center (Buruma 2006: 197). But he grew frustrated as he saw how his father was losing his grip over the household and failed – in Bouyeri's view – to protect the family's honor as his younger sister got into a relationship. Bouyeri had run-ins with the police because of the vendetta against his sister's boyfriend, he mistrusted the social workers coming to his family's house as part of an urban renewal project, and he grew angry and frustrated as community workers did not support his plans for community initiatives. In a careful reconstruction, Ian Buruma concludes that Bouyeri felt that officials of the Dutch welfare state "had all let him down, out of impotence or treachery, or possibly even hatred of Islam" (ibid.: 210). Bouyeri found confirmation and purpose in the ideas of a radical Islamist preaching in covert meetings in stores and private houses. "Here, finally, was the real thing: a wise man from the East, who would give meaning to his life, and justification to his resentments" (ibid.).

Although the large majority of Moroccan youths did not take a studious interest in religion, Bouyeri was not the only troubled teenager to develop into an Islamic radical. Across cities in Europe radical Islam proved attractive to a small yet consequential minority among immigrant youths. While these networks operate internationally through itinerant activists and the internet, they find points of support in urban clusters that provide the cover, trust, and the critical mass necessary to sustain radical discourses in hostile environments. Bouyeri was part of such a cluster of young Muslims who congregated in informal meeting places like garages or living rooms, firing up each other's emotions, debating interpretations, and engaging in rituals like watching videos of Western-led atrocities in the Middle East and *mujahidin* mutilating putative enemies of Islam. Bouyeri's group was part of an emergent counterpublic that did not take the legitimacy of the Dutch state for granted and debated radical alternatives, even if most fundamentalist Muslims felt that Bouyeri had misinterpreted Islam. Bouyeri's group was extreme but not unique. Slootman et al. (2009) and Buijs et al. (2006) researched different groups of orthodox (*salafi*) Muslims whose sympathies and religious interpretations had been cultivated in informal networks forming at the fringes of mosque communities, within groups of friends, and around charismatic leaders.

Recalibrating control through religious encapsulation

The murder of Van Gogh and the subsequent revelation that diffuse groups of Muslim radicals had been organizing under the radar showed that the fine-grained infrastructure of state institutions did not incorporate all potential challengers. The mechanisms of controlling the grassroots discussed in this chapter – ethnic encapsulation and territorial encapsulation – had not extended the state's reach to the informal settings where international religious radicalism found local support. Religion had been largely ignored. Initially, left-wing opposition to conservative organizations had prevented the government from engaging immigrant groups who identified first and foremost as Muslims and later the stress on diversity as a factor of success had steered attention away from deprived and stigmatized groups and areas. This did not mean that the state was absent. To the contrary, as Bouyeri's biography showed, the state was very much present in areas like New West: the strong presence of police officials, social workers, and community centers is illustrative of the density and reach of governance networks. The managing of the minutiae of the social life of marginalized groups makes it highly unlikely that mass revolts à la France would erupt. But the state's constant wiring and rewiring of the circuits of community control did also not fully quell contention, as the very structures designed to achieve control also produced friction and tension because "a young Moroccan male [in Dutch society] might find it easier to receive subsidies than respect" (Buruma 2006: 207).

In response to the failure to win the hearts and minds of the groups that were so close to the state yet out its reach, the Amsterdam government recalibrated its governmental rationalities and technologies, making Islam a central concern. After the turn of the century, the government, and especially the mayor, Job Cohen, developed a discourse that revolved around the idea that all groups within society had an obligation to defend civil unity. It was the task of administrators to stand above and connect the different groups – an approach that developed under the slogan "keeping things together" (*de boel bij elkaar houden*). On several high-profile occasions, Cohen argued for mutual understanding and expressed his concern over the backlash against Muslims after 9/11. Whereas national politicians like Frits Bolkestein, Pim Fortuyn, and Ayaan Hirsi Ali often portrayed Muslims as intruders, Cohen argued that religious institutions, including Islamic institutions, could facilitate integration. One might say that – after ethnic and territorial encapsulation – the government now opted for religious encapsulation, but its goal was not to bring all Muslims together or to speak to the Muslim community. The government instead observed differences within the Muslim population and adopted a differentiated policy approach to different clusters of Muslims: the municipality formed coalitions with those who embraced liberal democracy and fought extremism; provided spaces, subsidies, and opportunities to induce the disaffected; and isolated and prosecuted radical and disruptive elements within this broader community (Uitermark et al. 2014).

In this differentiated policy approach, a special place was reserved for a group of prominent Muslim members of the Labor Party. Key figures like Ahmed Aboutaleb, Haci Karacaer, and Ahmed Marcouch combined their membership of the Labor Party with an Islamic background. These social democrats had in various capacities called upon Muslim communities to show more civil commitment and the government was eager to provide them with support. When Haci Karacaer, as the director of the local wing of the international Turkish religious federation Milli Görüş, got into a struggle with conservative opponents within his organization, the Amsterdam government agreed to (covertly) help with an indirect subsidy of €2 million for the construction of a mosque (see Uitermark and Gielen 2010). Karacaer was later recruited to help establish a debating center for Muslims conceived by Ahmed Aboutaleb (the deputy mayor for diversity) and Job Cohen. Both these plans ultimately did not materialize but they show how the Amsterdam government attempted to strengthen the position of liberal and social-democratic Muslims relative to more conservative and orthodox groups. In addition to supporting liberal elites, the government reached out to the grassroots and attempted to rewire relations among devout Muslim youths. One example is Muslim Youth Amsterdam,[4] which brought together youths from different ethnic backgrounds and mosques. The Amsterdam government also supported cultural centers like Mozaïek and Argan, to stage public debates. These debates attracted large numbers of people from groups that have been notoriously difficult for the media and administrators to reach, such as orthodox Muslims and Moroccan youths.

To discipline the most defiant groups, the government also increasingly turned to Muslim authorities and Muslim associations. This development, which took place throughout Amsterdam, was especially evident in Slotervaart, the neighborhood in New West where Bouyeri had grown up. Media scrutiny and political interest in this neighborhood further intensified when Labor Party member Ahmed Marcouch ran for and became chair of the neighborhood council in 2006 – the first Moroccan to achieve this position in the Netherlands. The policy document in which Slotervaart's neighborhood government laid out its strategy against radicalization states that it would counter "dichotomous worldviews" with "religious prescriptions" and that it would convince parents that "their wish to give their children an Islamic identity does not entail a clash with Dutch norms and values" (Stadsdeel Slotervaart 2007: 8–9). At a time when many secular and neighborhood associations in Amsterdam were losing government subsidies and accommodations, associations catering to groups close to potential radicals or delinquents acquired or consolidated their roles as intermediaries. For instance, the Slotervaart government provided assistance for recruiting participants in child-rearing courses through Islamic associations. It also organized debates within mosques and provided support to mosques wishing to represent and explain themselves in the media or engage in dialogues with other groups. In her evaluation of a course for Moroccan parents offered as part of the anti-radicalization policy, Amy-Jane Gielen (2008) shows that religious precepts were used to delegitimize cultural beliefs or practices that supposedly inhibited success in Dutch society. These mothers felt that their ethnic culture held women back and that greater knowledge of Islam would lead to a re-evaluation of the mother's role. As one mother put it: "I do not find traditions and being Moroccan very important, because I think we mostly have bad traditions. The fact is that a girl is kept down, while a boy is allowed to do anything he likes. Islam is against this" (cited in Gielen 2008: 15).

In sum, the state attempted to employ the governing tools at its disposal to reconfigure relations within civil society to prevent radical and extremist groups from proliferating. To do so it established relations with Muslims and Muslim associations favoring religious interpretations in line with the Dutch mainstream. We thus see that the government differentiated the Muslim population and crafted different policy responses for different segments. This created tensions between the different organizations, as some were embraced as liberal partners whereas others were declassified. But in all cases, the local government unfolded a dense web of institutions and engaged different organizations and authorities in its efforts to secure the sociopolitical order.[5]

Conclusions

Amsterdam's vibrant social movement milieu of the 1980s contracted in the 1990s, almost to the extent of evaporating altogether. In the 1980s leftist organizations within civil society had been able to use state resources to act as a counterforce to the government. In the 1990s the government increasingly tightened its grip on civil society. By circumscribing what organizations did and where they did it, *the government rewired organizational circuits and transformed civil society from a relatively autonomous space for antagonistic organizing into an extension of the government.* The overall result of these various developments was that by the year 2000 contention over immigrant rights had become a thing of the past. However, while the government had incorporated and aligned large parts of civil society and regained control over previously contentious neighborhoods, unanticipated feelings of discontent were simmering in previously orderly areas.

The government responded to contention by incorporating challengers and expanding its reach into contentious groups and places but these efforts at achieving control left other groups and places untouched. Unanticipated discontent came to the surface when Theo van Gogh was killed. In response, the government reconsidered its integration discourse and intervened in the grassroots and even the minutiae of people's lives to nip radicalism and extremism in the bud, demonstrating how the extensive state infrastructure can be adopted for new purposes and adjusted to new circumstances.

Although its control is clearly not complete, the degree to which the government subjugated immigrant civil society in the 1990s and 2000s is noteworthy, especially when compared to the contentious 1980s. Such control does not preclude rebellious groups but it makes it very difficult for these groups to consolidate themselves into potent challengers capable of mounting strong campaigns. Amsterdam may be widely known as a city of vice or portrayed as "the most liberal city in the world" (Shorto 2013), but it has also become an astoundingly orderly city largely devoid of rebellious sentiments, impulses, and discourses.

Part III

New Geographies of Immigrant Rights Movements

The last part of the book charts the "new geographies" of immigrant rights activism that emerged in response to increased restrictions during the 1990s and 2000s. The restrictive and local nature of immigration policies sparked conflicts across these countries, in small towns and large cities alike. While the seeds of conflict spread to all places where these restrictions have been enacted, certain cities (Los Angeles, Paris, Amsterdam) have provided contexts of mobilization that have helped sustain, nourish, and grow small seeds of conflicts into sizable struggles.

The strength of the movements in the respective countries is in part explained by the differences in the extent to which immigrant organizations had come under government control. Activist organizations in Los Angeles had not been enlisted in governmental programs and were able to use the city's robust activist infrastructure to become a driving force of the national immigrant rights movement. Rather than Washington-based NGOs setting the agenda, associations with a grassroots history and spirit in Los Angeles have taken up a leadership role in setting the targets and strategy of recent campaigns. The peripheral tail of the movement is now wagging the national dog.

Paris emerged in the 1990s with strong clusters of human rights NGOs and *collectifs des sans papiers*. While the two clusters gravitated toward one another in a fight against restrictive measures during the 1990s, increased stress and conflicts emerged between them as they competed

Cities and Social Movements: Immigrant Rights Activism in the United States, France, and the Netherlands, 1970–2015, First Edition. Walter J. Nicholls and Justus Uitermark. © 2017 John Wiley & Sons, Ltd. Published 2017 by John Wiley & Sons, Ltd.

over legitimacy. The concentration of strategic cultural, legal, and symbolic resources by human rights NGOs put them at the forefront of these struggles. They assumed a role as representatives of undocumented immigrants. For many immigrant activists, this was seen as a threat to their own legitimacy to speak and make political demands in the public sphere. Competition over legitimacy eventually evolved into open conflicts between these clusters, impeding their ability to effectively work together during subsequent mobilizations in the 2000s. Paris in the 2010s has continued to enjoy a central position within national networks but it has become a center without the power to exert direction and leadership over the many peripheries. The "new geographies" of the immigrant rights movement in France are characterized by small struggles throughout the country with a center (Paris) that is too weak to impose a durable and lasting order over the countless resistances.

Amsterdam is contending with a different legacy characterized by the almost complete dismantling of the social movement infrastructure. The city continues to concentrate financial, organizational, and cultural resources. This makes it a favorable environment to support various resistances against restrictive policies. However, because organizations have been channeled away from contentious politics, new resistances have difficulty gaining heavy organizational support from trained and experienced advocates. Instead, they rely on individuals responding to humanitarian impulses and individual radicals motivated by transformative ideologies and goals. Formal organizations that get involved either mask their participation or strongly oppose contentious tactics, ultimately blocking an important flow of resources to support and sustain budding resistances. Potent resistances have arisen across the Netherlands in response to restrictive immigration measures and Amsterdam continues to provide the most fertile ground for these activities. The depoliticization of immigrant associations and NGOs, and the evisceration of Amsterdam's activist networks, have resulted in a scattershot geography of immigrant rights mobilizations characterized by multiple and individualized resistances, but no real network structure to channel these resistances into a movement for political change.

Our cases show that anti-immigration measures continue to generate grievances and resistances, and that such resistances have actually been effective in modifying how these measures are enacted. Rather than governments making the issue of immigration go away, restrictive policies have spurred and fortified countless mobilizations for the various rights of immigrants in these countries. In spite of the ubiquity of small and large struggles, we also stress that these have taken very different forms and possess different levels of power to exert themselves in the national political field. The US case clearly stands out as the most potent mobilization, with its string of local, state, and national victories imperiling the country's deportation regime. In Europe, advocates and activists continue to make demands for some immigrants deemed "deserving" of special exceptions but usually at the expense of accepting increased repression of those left out of these agreements. Thus, where there are border restrictions, there is certainly resistance, but the power of resistance varies dramatically from city to city and country to country. Our aim now is to map out and explain differences in the new geographies of immigrant rights resistance.

9

Los Angeles as a Center of the National Immigrant Rights Movement

In spring 2013, the US Senate passed the Border Security, Economic Opportunity, and Immigration Modernization Act (S. 744) with resounding bipartisan backing. The Senate bill was given wide support by the major *national* NGOs advocating immigrant rights, including the National Council of La Raza, America's Voice, and Center for Community Change. According to estimates, the bill would have provided half to two thirds of the total undocumented population – circa 11 million people – with a path to legal status and eventual citizenship. However, this also meant that many other undocumented immigrants would not qualify for the measure. Moreover, new immigrants would face a surge in border enforcement as the bill allocated $46.3 billion in additional funding for border control measures.[1] The bill also included a "trigger." Legalization of eligible immigrants would only begin *after* a special commission had verified that the border had been sealed. The legalization of many therefore depended on reinforcing the illegality of many others. Most *national* NGOs accepted these restrictions as an unfortunate compromise needed to secure Republican support. However, many *local* grassroots organizations and activists balked. They understood that this measure would institutionalize the divide between "deserving" and "undeserving" immigrants, and that those in the latter category would face intensified repression.

Though critical of the proposed immigration bill, the Los Angeles-based organization National Day Laborer Organizing Network

Cities and Social Movements: Immigrant Rights Activism in the United States, France, and the Netherlands, 1970–2015, First Edition. Walter J. Nicholls and Justus Uitermark.
© 2017 John Wiley & Sons, Ltd. Published 2017 by John Wiley & Sons, Ltd.

(NDLON) held a neutral position during spring 2013. This organization grew directly out of the immigrant activist cluster in central Los Angeles. It was born as a project of the Center for Humane Immigrant Rights of Los Angeles (CHIRLA) and went on to become the principal advocacy organization for day laborers in the country. By summer 2013, NDLON was playing a leading role in fighting enforcement measures, criticizing the restrictive aspects of the Senate bill, starting a campaign (Not One More) to suspend deportations, and branding President Obama "Deporter in Chief." NDLON teamed up with undocumented youth activists (often known as DREAMers). In Los Angeles, CHIRLA started Wise Up in 2001 to socialize and organize undocumented immigrant youths (Seif 2004; Terriquez 2014). The youths gained their political knowhow through collaborations with seasoned rights activists in the Los Angeles area. They also participated in many campaigns throughout the decade, which culminated in a massive effort to pass the DREAM Act (Development, Relief, and Education for Alien Minors) in 2010 (failed) and Deferred Action for Childhood Arrivals in 2012 (successful). The DREAMers mobilized for measures that favored undocumented youth but they also extended their activities to support more general campaigns, including the Not One More campaign in 2013–2014.

The alliance between undocumented day workers and youths played an important role in turning the tide of the national immigrant rights movement. Much richer national NGOs followed their lead by easing their support for the comprehensive bill and throwing their weight behind executive action to provide millions of undocumented people with relief from deportation. By March 2014, Janet Murguía, the executive director of National Council of La Raza and a long-time ally of the Obama administration, came out and denounced the president as the "Deporter in Chief" (adopting NDLON's tagline). Other national organizations and unions followed and pressed the administration to ease its enforcement and deportation policies. On April 4, 2014, the president of the AFL-CIO, Richard Trumka, backed the Not One More campaign in a formal press release.[2] President Obama originally rejected calls for executive action on the grounds that this would be unconstitutional, but by November 20, 2014 he yielded and promised to provide relief to approximately 5 million undocumented immigrants.[3]

This chapter examines how a network of grassroots activists – with a major leadership hub in Los Angeles – assumed such a central role in the country's immigrant rights movement. The grassroots outmaneuvered the much larger and much richer national NGOs located mostly in Washington, DC and successfully pushed for this and other important measures (state and federal). The chapter begins with a description of the proliferation of anti-immigration policies, laws, and measures at both the federal and local levels. Following this, the chapter examines how the localization of repression contributed to encouraging the greater participation of immigrant organizations that had become enmeshed in local politics. Finally, the chapter examines how Los Angeles provided a favorable context to transform grievances and localized resistances into a national campaign. In particular, it shows how the relational opportunities afforded by Los Angeles enabled organizations with specific constituents (like day laborers and students) to transcend their differences and become a leading force in the national struggle for immigrant rights.

Localizing Immigrant Repression and the New Landscapes of Grievances

The 1990s marked the introduction of a string of new policies to restrict the rights of immigrants and accelerate deportations. Newer and more restrictive policies were introduced during the 2000s to patch up the remaining "holes" in the system. The expansion and localization of restrictive measures would go on to spark new grievances among immigrant communities and their organizations, drawing them directly into the struggles against restrictive immigration policies.

The 1990s marked an important uptick in legislation and executive measures to enhance the country's bordering capacities. In 1996, the Clinton administration supported the passage of the Illegal Immigration Reform and Immigrant Responsibility Act (IIRIRA). IIRIRA allocated more resources to enforcement, expedited deportation procedures, lowered the threshold of deportable offenses, severely restricted judicial discretion during removal proceedings, and reduced the possibility for appeals (Durand and Massey 2003; Varsanyi 2008). The "War on Terror" in the 2000s reinforced these restrictive tendencies. In addition to passing five restrictive laws during the 2000s, the Department of Homeland Security introduced 12 measures to strengthen borders and facilitate the deportation of undocumented immigrants (Massey and Pren 2012: 10–11). These initiatives combined to accelerate deportation rates from 30,039 immigrants per year in 1990 to 358,886 in 2008 and to 392,000 in 2011 (Johnson 2012; Lopez and Gonzalez-Barrera 2013).[4]

IIRIRA also introduced a Memorandum of Understanding agreement between the federal Department of Justice local law enforcement agencies. These 287(g) agreements deputized state and local law enforcement officials in the area of immigration and provided participating police officers with training and authorization to identify and detain undocumented immigrants. This program was expanded into the Secure Communities program in 2008. Secure Communities required state and local police to cross-check fingerprints of arrestees against Homeland Security's databases. For those flagged for possible immigration violations, Immigration and Customs Enforcement agents could request local enforcement officials to hold the person for federal immigration agents.

The devolution of enforcement powers to localities encouraged state and local governments to develop their own independent policies to restrict irregular immigrants (Coleman 2007; Varsanyi 2008; Walker and Leitner 2011; Strunk and Leitner 2013). These local measures included restrictions on the solicitation of jobs by immigrant day laborers, penalties on employers for hiring undocumented workers, prohibitions on renting property to immigrants, the strict enforcement of housing codes, bans on street-vending activities, and mandates on the use of English for city business. Some 270 restrictive local measures were introduced between 2005 and 2010 (Walker and Leitner 2011). These varied from the comprehensive measures to smaller restrictions on undocumented immigrants and the activities associated with immigrant populations. Between 2010 and 2011, states enacted 164 anti-immigration laws, addressing everything from restrictions on driver's license eligibility to the mandatory use of the federal government's electronic employment verification system (E-Verify).[5] Several states also bundled anti-immigrant measures together into comprehensive legislation aimed at restricting services and enhancing local policing capacities. Arizona passed such a law in 2010 (S.B. 1070), with five states passing similar laws soon thereafter.

The 2000s can certainly be considered the "golden age" of local anti-immigrant policies but California anticipated these aggressive policy moves by decades. As early as 1970, Assembly member Dixon Arnett introduced a bill to impose criminal sanctions on employers for hiring undocumented immigrants. While the bill was deemed unconstitutional by the state Supreme Court, the employers sanction part of the bill provided a template for restrictive federal bills in the 1970s and 1980s, eventually becoming incorporated into IRCA in 1986 (Acuña 1996). Voters in California also passed Proposition 63 in 1986, which made English the official language. Most importantly, Governor Pete Wilson in 1994 bolstered his flagging reelection campaign by supporting the most aggressive anti-immigration state proposition in the country, Proposition 187. The measure aimed to deter immigration to the state by closing access to health care, public education, and other life-enabling services. While Proposition 187 was approved by a strong majority of California voters (59%), a federal appeals court deemed it unconstitutional on the grounds that it exceeded the state's authority in the area of immigration. Several years later, voters supported Proposition 209 (a ban on affirmative action) and Proposition 227 (a ban on bilingual education). California municipalities also introduced measures to restrict the rights and protections of immigrants. Ordinances were passed in several municipalities requiring that business signs be posted in English. Day laborers also became a particular source of public ire, with many cities and counties passing legislation to restrict the public solicitation of work. Between 1989 and 2005, 60 California municipalities enacted restrictive ordinances and 38 of those municipalities were located in the four counties making up the greater Los Angeles region (Los Angeles, Orange, Riverside, San Bernardino) (Gonzalez 2011).

While many California municipalities passed single-issue measures (bans on foreign language, day labor work, etc.), the city of San Bernardino introduced a comprehensive anti-immigration measure, called the Illegal Immigration Relief Act, in 2005 (Varsanyi 2011). The measure aimed to restrict the use of public funding to "operate, construct, maintain, or fund any day labor agencies"; restrict individuals from soliciting and hiring day laborers; penalize employers for hiring "illegal aliens" by denying or rescinding the employer's business license for five years; prohibit "illegal aliens" from renting property, and landlords from renting to "illegal immigrants" within city limits; and mandate that all city business be conducted in English (Varsanyi 2011: 303). The majority of city councilors initially supported the bill but the controversy associated with it led to its rapid defeat. The legal wing of the Federation of American Immigration Reform (FAIR) – the country's premier anti-immigrant organization – used the San Bernardino measure to create generic legislation that could be used by local affiliates across the country.

By the 2010s, these copycat measures had spread throughout the country, but California remained ground zero for many of these experimental policies. This meant that immigrant rights activists and advocates developed early expertise in responding to local repressive policies, and later in spreading their knowledge and strategies to other battles across the country through networks of local, grassroots immigrant organizations.

Incubating Grassroots Resistances

Localizing immigration policy through local initiatives, state laws, or federal programs like Secure Communities sparked acts of resistance across the country. Some of these were expressed in litigation, others in small protests, and still others in efforts to create new ordinances to provide sanctuary and protection to undocumented immigrants. While the extension of enforcement contributed to the spread of immigration-related conflicts in localities across the country, certain *contexts* provided more fertile soil for resistances to take root and grow into larger mobilizations. Los Angeles provided a supportive context because it furnished relational opportunities to provide new groups of activists with support and resources to grow their struggles.

Incubating day labor struggles

Los Angeles provided a unique context of mobilization to incubate resistances in the 1990s and 2000s because of its fast-evolving and dense social movement infrastructure (see Chapter 7). Greater pressure on employers to monitor the legal status of their immigrant employees contributed to workplace discrimination and exploitation. Restrictions on certain kinds of work (day labor, street vending) presented immigrants with constraints on their livelihoods. Many of the immigrant organizations in Los Angeles responded to these restrictions by expanding their service and advocacy work in the area of workers' rights (Milkman et al. 2010; Patler 2010). Several immigrant rights organizations (CHIRLA, CARECEN, IDEPSCA, El Rescate, etc.) mounted and participated in long-term and mostly local campaigns to protect the rights of immigrant workers.

One of the earliest and most prominent campaigns concerned the fight against day labor bans throughout Southern California. CHIRLA advocated the creation of day labor hiring cities ("worker centers") in the city of Los Angeles. The centers would provide a safe space to sell labor, set a wage floor for competing workers, and provide legal protections against wage theft (Patler 2010: 77). Many of the worker centers operated in the following way: workers met in the morning at a building or trailer on a hiring site. Workers were assigned jobs on the basis of skills needed for a particular job and placed on the wait list. The lead organizer at the center mediated relations between potential employers and workers. In the event that employers violated the rights of workers (wage theft was and continues to be extremely common), the organizer and worker would proceed to pressure the employer for restitution. The worker centers also provided food, beverages, workshops, and courses for day laborers waiting for a job. The centers became places for socializing as much as for finding a job.

CHIRLA ramped up its efforts in 1995 when it hired a permanent organizer (Pablo Alvarado) and obtained a contract from the city of Los Angeles to manage two worker centers. As this was one of the first programs operating at a larger scale in the country, the city provided the organizers of CHIRLA with extensive autonomy in how to develop and implement the centers. Public funding from the city was not accompanied by onerous oversight and control mechanisms. CHIRLA collaborated with the Southern California Institute of Popular Education (IDEPSCA), El Rescate, and CARECEN to manage these and subsequent centers (Dziembowska 2010). They learned how to work with one another to improve the rights and conditions of day laborers. IDEPSCA had long established itself as an organization with great skill and expertise in "popular education." Alvarado, who was also a member of IDEPSCA, embraced Paulo Freire's "population education" method and made it a central part of the day labor campaign. The aim was to make workers into politicized leaders who were capable of managing and running their own campaigns and worker centers. This required intensive "consciousness raising" with day laborers through meetings, leadership workshops, newsletters, popular theater, musical events, and soccer matches, among other things. "We were providing them with the means to express what they [the workers] already knew to be something very wrong" (IDEPSCA, personal interview). These activities helped build solidarity for the workers as a group while providing them with critical discursive frames to interpret their particular situations. In addition to employing popular education methods, they spent considerable time and resources on "leadership training" for undocumented immigrants. In discussing these activities at an embryonic worker center in 1996, Alvarado remarked to a reporter that "There is an executive committee that deals with the issues here. The guys have organized a soccer team and a musical band. And the guys write their own *corridos* [folk songs]" (Pablo Alvarado, cited in *Los Angeles Times*, September 7, 1996). CHIRLA and the other organizations recognized that the worker centers should provide important services to marginalized workers, but they also believed that these centers should be frontline instruments to politically empower the most marginalized immigrant workers in the city (Patler 2010).

The day laborer campaign provided opportunities for new relations to develop between various organizations. The Mexican American Legal and Educational Defense Fund (MALDEF) had initiated a lawsuit against the County of Los Angeles for its ban on the public solicitation of work in areas under its jurisdiction. The lawsuit brought MALDEF and another legal advocacy organization (Legal Aid of Los Angeles) into regular contact with CHIRLA and CARECEN (Narro 2010). Collaborations with legal organizations provided local immigrant rights organizations with access to extremely important legal resources. Activists also worked closely with their legal team to make lawsuits into mobilization tools that were coupled with demonstrations and media campaigns. These events were designed to send a powerful signal to local officials contemplating similar restrictions in their own cities. They were also intended to inform day laborers that they had constitutionally protected rights to seek work in public places. Thus, the ability of immigrant organizations to develop strong working relations with important legal advocacy organizations made important resources available to them while allowing them to integrate litigation into their normal mobilizing repertoire.

The success of the day labor campaign encouraged the leading immigrant organizations to create a countywide day labor union in 1997, the Day Labor Association of Los Angeles (Dziembowska 2010). The Association sought to coordinate the activities of new worker centers throughout Southern California, politicize immigrant workers, and train some workers to assume leadership roles of the centers. The Association also provided an important opportunity for workers to leave their particular corners and areas of the city and interact with others like themselves. "At CHIRLA we met with other workers from other cities to talk about our common problems and to create a union. I didn't know anybody there except for Marlom [IDEPSCA] and Pablo [CHIRLA]. After that we selected officers. I was named the treasurer of the union. At that time, we had meetings every eight days at CHIRLA and I represented Pasadena" (Pasadena Day Labor Association, personal interview).

The Association failed to take off but it served as a model for the National Day Labor Organizing Network (NDLON), which was created in 2001 (Dziembowska 2010). Through their work on day laborer issues in Los Angeles, local organizers came into contact with other immigrant organizers working on similar issues throughout the country. NDLON was seen as a way to pool information and resources concerning their particular struggles. It was also viewed as a vehicle to advocate for day laborers in regional and national political fields. NDLON's director remembers that "The idea was that we were going to build this organization so that it can add value and we can bring more power to the local level, that we could increase the capacity of local organizations to create worker centers and fight against anti-solicitation laws through litigation and big campaigns" (NDLON, personal interview).

NDLON was originally under the fiscal sponsorship of CHIRLA and was housed in its central Los Angeles office. It moved to a new office provided by UCLA's Downtown Labor Center in 2006 and stayed under CHIRLA's sponsorship until 2008. The Labor Center was a major connecting point for immigrant and labor organizers in the city. The Labor Center's director brokered relations between NDLON and Los Angeles labor leaders, the Laborers' International Union of North America, and the AFL-CIO. In 2006, the AFL-CIO and NDLON announced a landmark partnership between them, with the president of the union stating:

> By combining our resources in communities and states, we hope to translate the substantial gains achieved by Worker Centers into the lasting improvement of working conditions. Worker Centers will benefit from the labor movement's extensive involvement and experience in policy and legislative initiatives on the local, state and national levels. This partnership will also benefit AFL-CIO unions and local labor bodies by establishing channels to formally connect with local Worker Centers in order to expose abuses and improve workplace standards in various industries to the benefit of all workers.[6]

This alliance provided NDLON with *major* institutional support and legitimacy for its local and national efforts.

NDLON and its allies (local and national) believed that the emerging immigrant rights movement had to turn its attention to increasingly repressive federal and local policies unleashed during the 2000s (Walker and Leitner 2011; Steil and Vasi 2014). Federal policies like 287(g) and Secure Communities introduced partnerships between federal and local law enforcement agencies (Varsanyi 2008; Walker and Leitner 2011). During the mid-2000s, NDLON and other organizers had made important gains in creating worker centers and litigating against local hiring bans. However, new enforcement measures reversed this progress. "I think we've filed about fifteen challenges against these [anti-solicitation] bans nationwide, and we've won most of them. These efforts linked litigation with organizing. So we've made great progress. But, these wins were irrelevant when you had police officers with the power to ask workers for papers" (NDLON, personal interview). These federal and local measures rendered the most "public" immigrants (day laborers) most vulnerable to government repression.

Thus, local resistances to local anti-day labor measures were facilitated by Los Angeles's rich social movement milieu. Locally embedded organizations like CHIRLA, CARECEN, El Rescate, and IDEPSCA worked with one another to create an innovative and empowering day laborer campaign. Their efforts opened opportunities for productive collaborations with locally based legal advocacy organizations (Legal Aid, MALDEF, ACLU) interested in these matters. As the campaign grew in size and sophistication, activists from Los Angeles came into contact with other immigrant activists in cities around the country, resulting in the creation of NDLON. This "national" organization sustained itself through its ties with local organizations: its main organizers and supporters came from Los Angeles immigrant organizations, it was under the fiscal sponsorship of CHIRLA, it drew important levels of legal support from local legal organizations, and it made the UCLA Labor Center its permanent home. Moreover, local brokers (in particular, the Labor Center) helped connect NDLON to important national labor leaders, which bolstered its presence and power in the national political field. The Los Angeles milieu was therefore particularly well suited for nurturing early seeds of resistance and facilitating their growth into potent struggles and organizations with regional and national reach.

Incubating student and youth resistance

Undocumented youths who arrived in the United States as children faced a situation that was rather unique. Their lack of authorization to reside in the country rendered them "illegal" like their parents and other adults. Such a status made them susceptible to discrimination, the threat of deportation, and damaging stigma (Gonzalez 2011). However, unlike the adults, undocumented children were granted the right to a public education, as a result of a Supreme Court ruling in 1982 (*Plyler v. Doe*). Schools served as relatively safe spaces where these children were allowed to undergo processes of acculturation and assimilation (Gonzalez 2011; Nicholls 2013). This disjuncture between becoming American and the lack of legal residency posed serious problems as undocumented children transitioned into adulthood (Gonzalez 2011). They would have to confront the fact that they could not access a driver's license, could not travel, could not work outside the migrant economy, could not have access to welfare support, and faced huge barriers to higher education. They were youths who were raised in the United States but who were considered "illegal" and therefore ineligible to a normal life in their country.

By the 2000s there were approximately 1 million undocumented youths in the United States. Their concentrations were highest in areas with large undocumented populations like Los Angeles. Greater restrictions resulting from IIRIRA made it more difficult to regularize the status of children with precarious legal status even when family members possessed permanent residency status or citizenship. This contributed to the growth of this population and mixed-status families (Pallares and Flores González 2011; Dreby 2015). In 2000, CHIRLA became involved in a broad campaign to pass a California law that would provide undocumented students at public universities with in-state tuition (A.B. 540). The campaign sparked an outpouring of youth support. Some youths were the children of CHIRLA, IDEPSCA, CARECEN, and other local activists, but many others connected to the campaign through word of mouth, informal friendship networks, and the media. Recognizing the potential of youth, CHIRLA created Wise Up to organize and socialize the immigrant youth. Wise Up was designed to organize a potent youth wing of CHIRLA but it was also supposed to serve as a safe space where youths could come out and share the trials and tribulations of being raised undocumented.

After the passage of A.B. 540, substantial numbers of youths enrolled in Los Angeles universities like CSU Los Angeles, Long Beach, Fullerton, Northridge, UCLA, and various community colleges. Once enrollment grew in these area universities, they had sufficient numbers to create on-campus support organizations, or A.B. 540 clubs. These clubs helped pool information about college life, inform students about grants and educational support, and provide access to food and other essential resources. These support groups also provided a space in which the students were able to come out of their private worlds and talk to others about their status. CHIRLA received a grant in 2006 to connect A.B. 540 groups throughout California. CHIRLA hired two youth activists from Wise Up to organize the A.B. 540 groups into the California Dream Network (CDN). CDN leaders connected A.B. 540 clubs and provided assistance to support these clubs. Just as important, they employed the organizing methods developed by CHIRLA over the years to organize and empower undocumented students on university campuses. While CDN was supposed to be a California-wide effort, it was rooted in Los Angeles area universities where Wise Up and CHIRLA activists built upon their own personal networks. The first director of CDN describes the early days:

> There were maybe a solid seven local organizations around the area of Southern California and maybe three far away. For me, during that time, it was just working with those ten through personal relations. So, it was like "Hey do you know other students?" and "Hey I do! And it's at this college, blah blah blah." So, I mean, this was exciting, electrifying work. The word spread like wildfire, so everybody wanted to tell somebody, like: "Hey, go, participate, do this!" The outreach was really word of mouth. And once we got those solid contacts through word of mouth in this [geographical] area, then we continued with emails and follow-up calls to folks farther from here. (California Dream Network, personal interview)

At the same time, the UCLA Labor Center provided support for UCLA's A.B. 540 group after 2006, which would go on to become the most important organization within the statewide network. The UCLA Labor Center provided internships for some youths, which made it possible for them to dedicate time to building up their organization. Thus, while youths were forming support organizations on individual campuses across the state, two important Los Angeles-based organizations (CHIRLA and the Labor Center) provided crucial levels of support to strengthen individual capacity-building efforts and connecting campus organizations in regional and statewide networks. This helped form an important component of the undocumented youth movement (DREAMers), and the Los Angeles region stood out as a hub of activities.

As the California Dream Network was taking off, national NGOs with a stake in immigrant rights (Center for Community Change, National Immigration Law Center in particular) sponsored a national-level undocumented youth organization, United We Dream (UWD). The CDN would play an important part in the national effort because it was the most developed and far-reaching organizational network of its kind in the country. The incorporation of the CDN into this national infrastructure helped spur communication and organizing training. It also drew grassroots youth organizing more intimately into national campaigns and made the strategies of locals more dependent on national leaders. CHIRLA played an in-between role at this juncture, trying to guard its own localized network against national cooptation but also viewing the CDN as a potentially important tool in the national struggle for immigrant rights. These tensions between undocumented youth activists with grassroots proclivities and national NGOs increasingly came to a head in 2010 (Nicholls 2013).

The 2000s marked an important turn in localized immigrant rights organizing. On the one hand, organizations working with the most marginalized immigrant workers had grown in sophistication and scale. They were not only developing better techniques to organize this population, they were also reaching out to one another and forming strong regional and national networks. The culmination of these efforts was NDLON, which was a national organization that was strongly rooted in local organizing networks. On the other hand, organizations working with the more privileged elements of the undocumented population (privileged in terms of cultural acculturation and access to educational institutions and capital) also emerged onto the local political scene. While local DREAMers merged with national NGOs, their early efforts were strongly rooted in local grassroots efforts in the city of Los Angeles. Youth activists certainly emerged as a potent force in other cities as well (Chicago in particular), but Los Angeles became one of the strongest nodes in national networks because of the organizational supports found in the city. These two sides of the "new" immigrant rights movement were intimately bound to one another; having shared offices (at CHIRLA), participated in the same social circles, and engaged in similar campaigns over long periods of time. These personal ties made it easier for an organization like NLDON to come out in support of the DREAMers when they later sought to assert their autonomy from national NGOs.

Nationalizing and Centralizing the Immigrant Rights Movement

Immigrant rights mobilizations in the 1990s and 2000s remained local, or they focused on narrow issues concerning agricultural workers and asylum seekers from El Salvador, Guatemala, and Haiti (Coutin 2000; Nicholls 2013). The years 2006 and 2007 presented new challenges and openings that accelerated efforts by large immigrant rights NGOs (Center for Community Change, America's Voice, and National Council of La Raza) to centralize and nationalize these efforts. The House of Representatives passed the Border Protection, Anti-terrorism, and Illegal Immigration Control Act of 2005 (the so-called "Sensenbrenner bill"), which essentially aimed to criminalize undocumented status. The Senate, by contrast, passed the Comprehensive Immigration Reform Act of 2006, which introduced a guest workers program, a path to legalize millions of undocumented immigrants, and new resources to enhance border enforcement. This particular combination of threats and opportunities spurred an intense round of mobilizations in 2006, with hundreds of thousands pouring into the streets of cities like Los Angeles and Chicago during spring 2006 (Chavez 2008; Voss and Bloemraad 2011).

Both bills failed to become law, but they encouraged national organizations and their funders to create a more unified and centralized front in the fight for immigration reform. Leading national organizations and private foundations agreed that there was a need for greater unity across the countless immigrant rights organizations, coalitions, and groups. Many believed that the political power of the immigrant rights community was limited by its radical heterogeneity. This restricted its ability to pool resources, focus on a common target, and speak with a common voice. The solution would be to centralize and unify the national movement. The leading associations believed that the efforts of all stakeholders in the immigrant rights movement should focus on winning the 279 Congressional votes and one presidential signature needed to pass the Comprehensive Immigration Reform Act. This reflected a major and conscious effort to nationalize and centralize the social movement space from a network that was made up mostly of local organizations.

National funders played a pivotal role in enabling this strategic move. After repeated failures to win comprehensive immigration reform, foundations like the Atlantic Philanthropies and the Advocacy Fund sponsored efforts for national organizations to regroup and start a new coalition.

> After that setback, Atlantic provided funds for the key advocacy groups we support – including the Center for Community Change, National Council of La Raza, National Immigration Forum and Asian American Justice

Center – to regroup and come back with a proposal for strengthening their efforts next time. The result was Reform Immigration for America (RIFA), a strong coalition with resources provided by Atlantic ... and other funders that have enabled the movement to field an unprecedented campaign.[7]

Atlantic invested $16 million in national organizations addressing immigration issues.[8] Funds by Atlantic and Advocacy strongly favored national NGOs (America's Voice, National Immigration Forum, National Council of La Raza, Center for Community Change) and their coalitions (Reform Immigration for America [RIFA] among several others). The self-appointed leadership of the immigrant rights movement was made up of national and highly professionalized organizations located in Washington, DC and without membership or ties to the immigrant communities they were representing. According to the Atlantic Philanthropies's database, no substantial funds were made available to the smaller, local, and membership-based organizations which made up the bulk of the immigrant rights movement in the United States.

The election of Barack Obama in 2008 provided many rights advocates and activists with a unique political opportunity. A self-described progressive had been elected to the presidency. Substantial Democratic majorities controlled both chambers of Congress. Many believed that maintaining a unified front in the face of this unique opportunity would help ensure the passage of favorable legislation. The administration and Congressional Democrats prioritized other issues over immigration (economic stimulus, financial regulation, and healthcare reform). They suggested that 2010 would be the year for comprehensive immigration reform. To pressure the White House and Congress, the Atlantic-sponsored coalition Reform Immigration for America (RIFA) mounted a large demonstration in Washington, DC in March 2010. The organizers of the demonstration stressed that after the passage of the Affordable Care Act, immigration should be the first issue on the administration's legislative agenda. A representative from the Center for American Progress noted: "We are trying to send a strong message that when health care is past us, this is the issue that needs to be up at bat." She went on to note that demonstrating the power of the immigrant rights movement was essential to moving the legislation forward. "We've been in the bullpen for a long time, and now we want to show the strength of the team and the power of the issue" (Angela Maria Kelley, cited in *New York Times*, March 20, 2010). RIFA and their partners invested millions of dollars and mobilized more than 100,000 people to the event. In spite of the impressive show of force, the event was overshadowed in the media by the passage of the Affordable Care Act, which was passed on the same day as the demonstration. The rights demonstration garnered little media coverage and national politicians ignored it. Moderate Republicans who had supported reform in the past went on to argue that the passage of the healthcare bill would spell defeat for immigration reform. "If the health care bill goes through this weekend, that will, in my view, pretty much kill any chance of immigration reform passing the Senate this year" (Lindsey Graham, cited in *New York Times*, March 20, 2010).

The demonstration and subsequent campaign resulted in tepid commitments by the White House and national politicians. A representative from the Atlantic Philanthropies suggested that a one-hour meeting between President Obama and national advocacy organizations justified their massive financial investment: "The value of this investment was starkly demonstrated last week when President Obama ... met at the White House for an hour and fifteen minutes with campaign advocates, including seven of RIFA's steering committee members."[9] The multimillion-dollar campaign won *access* to the president but RIFA was still unable to translate *access* into favorable immigration legislation. This outcome led many grassroots organizations to seriously question the strategy of national centralization which benefited large and professional NGOs over small and grassroots organizations. Many of these grassroots organizations went along with RIFA's strategy early on but RIFA's inability to achieve any wins under the most optimal political and funding conditions opened important cracks in this consensus.

Realigning the Movement from the Grassroots Up

Several organizations played a pivotal role in turning away from RIFA's centralized strategy. NDLON and dissident DREAMers initiated campaigns that departed sharply from RIFA's strategies and goals. NDLON began to argue that comprehensive immigration reform was important but focusing too much on this left immigrants vulnerable to attack on other fronts. All the resources of the movement were being poured into passing comprehensive reform with nothing substantial (except for occasional access) to show for it. These fruitless efforts were occurring at a time when the federal government's deportation rates were reaching record levels and states and localities were passing increasingly restrictive policies. NDLON and the DREAMers argued that the movement needed to shift its strategic priority of passing comprehensive immigration reform in Congress because it was too costly, it sapped all the energy of the movement, and it resulted in deeply problematic compromises with right-wing forces. Moreover, and just as importantly, they argued in favor of a movement that was rooted in the grassroots and expressed the authentic concerns of undocumented immigrants.

Downscaling the struggle: Day laborers take the fight to Arizona

NDLON began organizing in Arizona in the mid-2000s. The Sheriff of Maricopa County, Joseph Arpaio, obtained a 287(g) contract with the federal government, which granted him the authority to detain undocumented immigrants and transfer them to Immigration and Customs Enforcement for deportation. The sheriff's massive neighborhood sweeps, discriminatory stops of Latino residents, and poor treatment of detained immigrants triggered various resistances among local associations, churches, and citizens. NDLON viewed Sheriff Arpaio's belligerent behavior as a way to draw national attention to the problems of the 287(g) program and to discourage other local law enforcement agencies from following in his footsteps: "Arpaio got involved in 287(g) early on and began doing all the shit that he was doing. That's when we drew him into the fight, because we knew that what he was doing was paving the way for other police chiefs and sheriffs in the country ... We knew that he was going to be a determinate factor ... And we knew that the country was going to go in that direction. So that's why we decided to invest significant resources in Arizona" (NDLON, personal interview).

One of the first campaigns was a series of weekly protests against police harassment of day laborers in front of a local furniture store (*New York Times*, July 21, 2012). NDLON had already developed good relations with the local organizer of this campaign, Salvador Reza, through his work with day laborers. NDLON worked with Reza to create Puente in 2007. This organization embraced what it called a "closed hand, opened hand" strategy. The closed hand was conceived as a fist and "represents fighting against enforcement. Fighting is conceptualized as fighting against anti-migratory policies through direct action, civic engagement, public awareness, protest, and civil disobedience." By contrast, the open hand "represents Puente's mission to serve the immigrant community by welcoming immigrants and providing a space for immigrants to co-exist as a community."[10] In addition to providing crucial services like English as a Second Language courses and workshops to help immigrants legalize their status, Puente offered community defense courses that aimed to provide immigrant communities with methods to exercise their rights when confronted by the local police. They sought to provide services to besieged immigrant communities while empowering them in the struggle for basic rights.

The campaign in Arizona escalated in response to the passage of the highly restrictive law S.B. 1070, passed in 2010. NDLON worked with Puente to create a new organization: Alto Arizona. The ensuing campaign was impressive because of its breadth and complexity. Puente and their local allies had already established a strong coalition and built up neighborhood-level infrastructure to support and mobilize immigrants. This local infrastructure provided activists with a vehicle to pool their different resources for various anti-enforcement campaigns and it provided organizers with access to the everyday worlds of thousands of immigrants. The local infrastructure allowed Alto Arizona to create Barrio Defense Committees (BDCs), which combined the self-defense tactics of the Black Panther Party with the "base community" model of the Latin American left.

> BDCs are organizing strategies adapted from our ancestors and from the Social Movements in Latin America. Our African-American brothers adopted these forms of organizing during the civil rights movement to defeat racist policies and treatment of their communities ... The BDCs, the name they arose out of the political reality that the members found themselves in, are nothing more than grassroots organizations.[11]

NDLON assisted in connecting the local activist cluster in Phoenix, Arizona with other organizations, advocacy groups, and funders beyond this specific place. In addition to building up a community of empowered immigrants, NDLON worked with legal advocacy groups like MALDEF and the ACLU to pressure the federal Justice Department to initiate a lawsuit against Arizona on the grounds that S.B. 1070 superseded its authority to legislate in the area of immigration. MALDEF would also initiate its own lawsuit on the grounds that S.B. 1070 discriminated against Latinos.

While pursuing a legal strategy, Alto Arizona also launched a large-scale boycott. Their connections to media and entertainment personalities allowed them to bring the case of Arizona to national attention. National and local politicians, businesses, entertainers, academics, and many others became directly involved in the Arizona campaign through their direct participation in the boycott. In drawing a parallel to the Civil Rights Movement, the Reverend Jesse Jackson came out in strong support of the Arizona boycott: "I encourage a boycott of Arizona, the law will encourage racial profiling. Arizona has become today's Selma" (Jesse Jackson, cited in *New York Times*, May 1, 2010). The boycott impacted Arizona's economy and reputation, negatively affecting the state's powerful tourist industry. The boycott aggravated existing grievances with the state's Republican leadership, drawing the tourist industry directly into the campaign against S.B. 1070 and other enforcement measures. In a letter to the state legislature in March 2011, 60 business leaders demanded that the state stop enacting repressive immigration measures. The letter "'blamed last year's bill [S.B. 1070] for boycotts, canceled contracts, declining sales and other economic setbacks" (*New York Times*, March 18, 2011).

While the campaign did not convince the Arizona legislature and governor to repeal S.B. 1070, the Supreme Court eventually took up the Justice Department's lawsuit and struck down three of four provisions. The Justice Department went on to indict the Sheriff of Maricopa County for Civil Rights violations. Alto Arizona also contributed to ousting state Senate Majority Leader Russell Pearce (the principal sponsor of S.B. 1070) in a special runoff election. The campaign produced a general sense of what one Republican state senator called "immigration fatigue" (John McComish, cited in *New York Times*, March 18, 2011). This was precisely the intent of the campaign: to raise the costs of restrictive measures and stop other states from pursuing similar measures. Tom Saenz, the director of MALDEF, expressed the Supreme Court victory in these terms: "[T]he decision sends a strong warning to any states or localities that have enacted or that may be considering enacting their own immigration regulation schemes. In short, the Court's decision should bring to a grinding halt the machinery of intolerance and racism that has promoted these laws."[12]

The Arizona campaign was a multi-front battle that centered on building up community mobilization capacities, litigating restrictive measures in federal courts, a massive public relations campaign and boycott, and a legislative strategy to punish the main architects of S.B. 1070. By transforming Arizona into ground zero of the immigrant rights struggle, it sought to increase pressure on the federal government to roll back restrictive measures while also sending a strong signal to other state and local officials interested in passing similar measures. NDLON and its allies turned a local affair in Arizona into a national civil rights scandal. This was a conscious adaptation of the Southern Christian Leadership Conference's strategy to draw national attention to southern injustices by highlighting the abuses of Alabama's Eugene "Bull" Connors (see McAdam 1982). NDLON and Arizona activists transformed the state into the Alabama of the 2000s. While one eye was focused on nationalizing this local dispute, the other eye sought to build up and empower the immigrant grassroots through the creation of Barrio Defense Committees. They needed to provide the people most affected by these laws with information concerning their rights and the tools to exercise those rights in the face of police repression. Involving and politicizing people was not a secondary concern. It was viewed as one of the central goals of the struggle and a central condition for its success.

NDLON and its allies moved toward this more territorialized and bottom-up strategy, but the coalition of national NGOS (RIFA) insisted that all important immigrant rights organizations should pursue the strategy of national centralization. The national NGOs talked to NDLON's director about the risks of fragmenting the movement and taking away from its core message. The director of NDLON responded to these entreaties:

> We said, 'We're very sorry for that, but the thing is we're not going to use the fight in Arizona and the suffering of people to help this [CIR – comprehensive reform] *failed effort* ...We're going to fight because we need to bring justice to the people of Arizona –no question about it. There is nothing to discuss here.' ... So that's it. We couldn't come to terms with them. (NDLON, personal interview)

Making the struggle piecemeal: The fight to legalize DREAMers

NDLON was not the only organization to find itself at odds with national NGOs and their strategy. A growing faction of dissident DREAMers believed that comprehensive reform would not pass in the 2010 Congress and that efforts should be made to pass what was feasible: the DREAM Act. Rather than aim for the "whole enchilada," as grassroots activists called comprehensive reform, the DREAMers (along with NDLON) proposed an alternative strategy of pushing against restrictive policies and for favorable measures wherever they could. Each favorable measure passed in one arena (like the DREAM Act) would provide a legal, political, and normative stepping stone for other measures. Each measure would open a new crack in the wall, with mounting pressure from the movement forcing each of these cracks to grow, overlap, and eventually bring down the wall. Transformative incrementalism, as it began to be imagined, would eat into the immigration state, provide more openings for different kinds of immigrants, and ultimately undermine the state's capacities to retain its bordering powers.

The youths who started to think along these lines began to openly argue this position in 2009. Becoming frustrated with national NGOs, some dissident youths began to strike out on their own. One group initiated a four-month walk from Miami to Washington, DC (the "Trail of Dreams"). Dissident DREAMers across the country were inspired and began to embrace confrontational tactics long eschewed by risk-averse national leaders. DREAMers in Los Angeles, Chicago, San Francisco, New York, and Phoenix formed Dream is Coming. This loose network of like-minded grassroots activists initiated a round of direct actions to pass the DREAM Act. While some members of the dissident network retained their affiliation with United We Dream (the national DREAMer organization), UWD was tied to national NGOs and faced great pressure not to veer from the party line. It was only after the dissidents successfully captured the spirit and momentum of the movement that UWD came out in full support of dissident efforts (Nicholls 2013).

On May 17, 2010 four undocumented students occupied the office of Senator John McCain in Arizona. The occupation of high-profile political figures by undocumented immigrants was up to that time rare. It reflected a major break in the tactical repertoire of immigrant rights activists. It moved away from large, carefully staged demonstrations coupled with lobbying to hard-hitting direct action coupled with forceful demands. The occupation of Senator McCain's office unleashed a wave of hunger strikes, marches, and other occupations throughout the country. The aim was to escalate, disrupt the normal state of political affairs, and demand the passage of the DREAM Act. The DREAM Act failed to pass the Senate in December 2010 by a narrow margin, but the campaign provided the youth activists with an enormous sense of empowerment and a robust social and organizational infrastructure.

Though the DREAMers were fighting anti-immigrant adversaries in Congress and civil society, they were also confronting the national leadership of the movement. The national NGOs dismissed their efforts, treated them in a patronizing fashion, and employed some strong-arm tactics to keep them in the fold. The youths rebelled and argued that the national leadership had no legitimacy to become the "voice" of undocumented people and choose their strategies. The youths argued that the movement should not simply be about winning the legal right to stay in the country, but it should also be about the right for undocumented immigrants to gain recognition as equal, self-representing, and public beings. In a foundational statement authored by dissident Los Angeles DREAMers, they argued that "if we accept and embrace the current undocumented student movement, it means the social justice elite loses its power – its power to influence politicians, media and the public debate. The power is taken back by its rightful holders."[13]

As the dissident DREAMers initiated this break with the leadership, CHIRLA took an ambiguous position. It had allied itself to the national effort to pass comprehensive immigration reform but it also continued its engagement in local- and state-level campaigns. It attempted to keep dissident DREAMers in the fold, which triggered a major rupture in the California Dream Network. Dissident DREAMers went on to form their own organization: Dream Team Los Angeles (DTLA). Other organizations in Los Angeles supported the dissidents. NDLON, the UCLA

Labor Center, IDEPSCA, and MALDEF provided them with important levels of political, material, and legal support. Well-established personal relations enabled dissidents to reach out to the leaders of these other organizations. A leader of the Dream is Coming and DTLA stressed the importance of these relations in the early efforts: "I knew Pablo [NDLON], Raul [IDEPSCA], and Victor [UCLA Labor Center] since I was a child. We were close enough to have a genuine conversation. I could trust and confide in them to not share, but also to ask them for help – because we were going to need that help from these organizations" (Dream is Coming, DTLA, personal interview).

NDLON played a particularly crucial role. Its leaders had long-time personal connections to many of the dissident DREAMers. Many of them shared offices at CHIRLA in the mid-2000s and then later at the UCLA Labor Center. In addition to personal reasons to support the youths, they agreed strongly with their piecemeal and incremental strategy and saw the youths as opening doors for day laborers further down the road. A project leader at UCLA Center and a close ally of NDLON remarked, "They [NDLON] realized that promoting day laborers in ... the public is not biting. But if they [NDLON] supported the students and got the DREAM Act, then it helped them [the day laborers] in the medium to long term, because this opened the door for other reforms" (UCLA Labor Center, personal interview). NDLON leaders admired the youthful energy and the radical impulses of the youth and believed that they were the future of the immigrant rights movement.

After 2010, DREAMers in Los Angeles and across the country (including UWD) embarked on a series of campaigns (state and national) to push their youth-specific agenda. After a series of actions in 2012, they pressured the Obama administration to introduce Deferred Action for Childhood Arrivals (DACA). This measure provided approximately 553,000 undocumented youths with temporary relief (two years) from deportation (Gonzalez and Chavez 2014). DACA was an important victory in its own right, but it also provided the legal and political precedent to push for a broader measure to cover all undocumented immigrants ("DACA for all"). DACA was a precedent-setting measure because it provided the legal and political legitimacy for activists to push for broader legalization measures. When the White House argued that it lacked the constitutional authority to provide temporary legal status to other undocumented immigrants, activists pointed to DACA and argued that the same legal logic could apply but just on a broader scale. Without the first step of DACA, subsequent legalization efforts would have been much more difficult.

While the DREAMers pursued youth-specific campaigns (like DACA and in-state tuition), they also participated in NDLON's new campaigns to fight the Obama administration's Secure Communities initiative. They believed in the cause but they were also aware that many of their detractors in the movement had painted them as "selfish," interested in youth-specific issues, and aggravating the divide between "deserving" and "undeserving" immigrants. Participating in the Secure Communities campaign was a way to demonstrate their commitment to the broader struggle for *all* immigrants, and not just the most "deserving" immigrants in the community. NDLON and others in Los Angeles had provided them with important levels of support in 2010. It was important for them to reciprocate and assert their reputation as standup members of the broader immigrant rights milieu.

The early years of the 2010s marked a strategic realignment in the immigrant rights movement. As the national NGOS were centralizing and nationalizing the movement, grassroots activists (from day laborers to the youths) were devising their own infrastructures, tactics and strategies, and mobilizing frames. This move away from the centralizing leadership unleashed important disputes between national NGOs and more localized activists while laying down the infrastructure and relations (alliances between laborers and youths) that would prove important in the years that followed.

Harnessing grassroots power: Territory and networks

The period from the late 2000s to 2013 marked an effort to develop a strategy that contrasted with RIFA's strategy of national centralization. The different branches of the federal government (executive, legislative, judicial) all played major roles in producing and executing immigration policy and these different arenas needed to be targeted. However, rather than only target the national government, they began to argue that localities (cities, regions, states) could be used as bases through which claims on the national government could be made. Wins in local arenas could, under the right conditions, produce leverage for extracting wins from different branches of the federal government.

The strategy that emerged in the 2010s rested on two pillars: creating territorial strongholds and channeling flexible networks. First, localized campaigns required building strong clusters among local activist organizations, extending relations to diverse allies in these places and elsewhere, and recruiting and politicizing undocumented immigrants. Building territorial strongholds therefore enhanced leveraging capacities with the federal government while also creating bases of support for immigration issues. Second, NDLON and the DREAMers always operated as a network made up of local organizations and activists embedded in different communities across the country. They understood how these networks could be used to harness scattered grassroots efforts. They went on to use their networking knowledge to develop a campaign to fight to stop the deportation of *all* undocumented immigrants. The strategy that emerged therefore rested on building *territorial* strong-holds made up of thick and committed activist relations, and connecting these localized activist hubs to one another through complex relational and organizational *networks*. This strategy contrasted markedly with the strategy of national centralization developed by Washington, DC-based NGOs.

Empowered territories: Making California into the anti-Arizona

In late 2010 and early 2011 NDLON's target shifted from Arizona back to California. While NDLON's base was in Los Angeles, California, it invested heavily in the neighboring state of Arizona because it had become the national epicenter of repressive immigration measures. However, now that the Arizona campaign had picked up its own momentum, NDLON and its allies were ready to pivot back to their home state. Activists believed that political opportunities in the state (a newly elected and friendly Democratic governor, and a super-majority of progressive Democrats in the state legislature) would facilitate efforts to pass progressive immigration laws. By enacting these laws, they would make California into a national model for progressive, state-level immigration reforms, in contrast to Arizona. California, in other words, would become the "anti-Arizona." At a meeting of DREAMers in December 2010, the director of MALDEF sketched out this strategy and California's role in it:

> California is going to become the anti-Arizona ... [W]e will make California the good model in contrast to Arizona. California can then put pressure on the Federal government ... We have to recognize the oppor-tunity we have in California. We need to make the life of all people in the state easier, regardless of their status. Together we will make this a dream state on our way to making it a dream nation. (Field notes, December 21, 2010)

The statement is telling because it identifies several components of the territorial strategy: making states into models of good and bad immigra-tion policies; using states to exert pressure on the federal government; and using the momentum built up from state-level wins to push for national-level reforms ("from dream state to a dream nation"). NDLON, DREAMers, MALDEF, CARECEN, CHIRLA, and other immigrant rights activists in Los Angeles launched several campaigns to expand the rights and privileges of immigrants in California. These included campaigns to grant undocumented immigrants access to driver's licenses, provide DREAMers with access to financial aid for universities, and limit California's participation in the federal Secure Communities program. By transforming California into a model state of immigrant rights (the "anti-Arizona"), activists aimed to create legal and political momentum to increase their leverage in the federal arena.

In 2011 DREAMers mounted a campaign to provide students with access to in-state grants and financial aid for university (California Dream Act, A.B. 130 and A.B. 131). The bill's author (Assemblyman Gil Cedillo[14]) worked closely with the DREAMers, NDLON, MALDEF, and CHIRLA to mobilize support for the measure. The DREAMers organized public actions and media events, and sent delegations to the state capitol to lobby for the bill. Labor unions associated with the UCLA Labor Center also contributed to the push by lobbying the Senate, Assembly, and governor. While this was a statewide effort, the activist networks driving the campaign were firmly rooted in Los Angeles.

Alongside this campaign, NDLON mounted another campaign in 2011 to pass a state law to restrict police participation in the Secure Communities program. This measure was called the Transparency and Responsibility Using State Tools (TRUST) Act. The TRUST Act aimed to block local law enforcement agencies from holding detainees for federal immigration agents, except in cases when the detainees were accused of certain felonies. The coalition developed a strong network of institutional allies in the Los Angeles area, including the County Federation of Labor, Los Angeles's Mayor Antonio Villaraigosa, the city council, the Catholic Archdiocese of Los Angeles, and influential members of the state Assembly and Senate. Local DREAMers assumed a major frontline role in many acts of civil disobedience. Several DREAMers were also hired by NDLON to serve as permanent organizers of this and other campaigns. This broad coalition succeeded in pushing Governor Jerry Brown to sign the TRUST Act into law on October 5, 2013. Being in the largest state in the country to have passed this law, immigrant rights advocates were able to improve protections for undocumented immigrants in California while ratcheting up pressure on the Obama administration to ease its deportation efforts. Deportation rates in Los Angeles declined from 8,727 in 2012 (before the TRUST Act) to slightly less than 5,000 in 2014, with federal agents expecting steep reductions in 2015. This reflects efforts to make California and Los Angeles into territories of refuge for undocumented populations.

Between 2011 and 2014, NDLON and DREAMers collaborated in various Los Angeles coalitions aimed at passing state laws to stop Secure Communities, provide undocumented youths with more access to state universities, and obtain driver's licenses for undocumented people. In addition to these important pieces of legislation, the governor of California signed into law a number of smaller laws aimed at expanding the rights and privileges of immigrants. While these measures made the state into a safer and more secure place for undocumented immigrants, they also put increased pressure on the Obama administration to change federal policies through the use of its executive authority.

Networking empowered places and activists

In addition to building up grassroots capacities, NDLON helped launch the Not One More campaign in early 2013. The campaign called upon the Obama administration to use its executive authority to extend deportation relief to undocumented immigrants eligible for legalization under the current version of comprehensive immigration reform. The campaign employed a new and more decentralized strategy to scale out from the Los Angeles region. There are approximately six people from various organizations (NDLON and United We Dream being the most important) who serve on the steering committee. A paid NDLON organizer has served as a director of the network. No formal affiliation is required to become a member of the network and organizations often connect through Twitter and Facebook accounts. The steering committee is charged with developing protest actions and mobilizing frames and these are transmitted to affiliates across the country.

The leaders of the campaign do not command and control the political acts and language of their distant allies. Instead, they work with one another on different kinds of actions (press conferences, hunger strikes, civil disobedience, etc.), develop messaging and mobilization frames, and disseminate information about actions and to network members across the country. The rather loose nature of the campaign has led some NDLON leaders to call it an "open source" campaign. In spite of the rather loose character of this strategy, its continued focus on its goal, the scope and intensity of its actions, and its nimble and flexible framing tactics have allowed the campaign to become a major force in shaping the direction of the general immigrant rights movement. While conservatives and progressives alike initially dismissed the campaign as an unhelpful distraction with an impossible goal (i.e. not one more deportation), several of the large national organizations (National Council of La Raza, AFL-CIO, etc.) came out in open support of it. As momentum built in their direction, their influence and reputation grew. There were certainly coordination problems that arose with such a loose network but it enabled NDLON and the DREAMers to extend their national influence over the immigration debate with remarkably few resources (only one full-time organizer dedicated to the entirety of the national campaign). On November 20, 2014 President Obama responded to this campaign and announced the introduction of a new executive order to provide temporary relief for undocumented youths who did not qualify for DACA and to parents of legal citizens. While falling short of providing permanent residency status, the measure nevertheless provided relief to an expected 5 million people.

The network strategy was based on the premise that immigration enforcement depended on many different institutional points rather than a single point (i.e. Congress) in the center of power. This has resulted in unleashing various campaigns to pressure those points that can produce tremors across the whole system. While NDLON and its allies continue to keep an eye on Congress, they also target towns, counties, states, the Department of Homeland Security, and the president. By supporting and sponsoring battles in these multiple terrains, they have aimed to undermine the legal, institutional, and ideological foundations of the national immigration regime. While the strategic and geographic characteristics of the movement have become more complex than before, the movement has by no means become chaotic. Most advocates of the new strategy have embraced a common vision that rests on building mobilization capacities in communities and cities (i.e. local capacity building), mobilizing through whatever windows of opportunity are available to them at whatever level of government, employing concrete wins in these political arenas as leverage for making broader demands, and working in complex networks to bring about changes in the immigration system. This particular phase of the immigrant rights movement has a geography and strategy that contrasts sharply with the top-down and centralized strategy of the past. The immigrant rights movement is "scaling out," which has meant that immigrant rights activists have moved horizontally from strong territories (Los Angeles, California) to weaker territories (Arizona, Georgia, etc.) and developed the capacity to steer loose networks of local organizations and activists across the country.

Conclusions

This chapter began with a simple question: how were locally based grassroots activists able to assert themselves as the leading force of the immigrant rights movement? We stress that the power to achieve national stature resulted from relational opportunities found in specific local contexts. Those areas with thicker agglomerations of rights advocates and activists have been better able to respond to the localization of law enforcement, prompting them to undertake a wide range of actions to push back on repressive measures. Los Angeles became an intensive and often unruly laboratory of strategic thinking and practices, with activists embedded in the city jointly learning how best to organize immigrants and make rights claims. CHIRLA, NDLON, IDEPSCA, CARECEN, DREAMers, and others developed their strategic repertoire by working with one another in the local trenches. This cluster focused on organizing and politicizing immigrants, deploying rooted activists, targeting local restrictions, and using wins in one geopolitical arena to maximize leverage in others. They also learned how to scale up and out from their Los Angeles base, coordinating activities and diffusing information, ideas, and frames to their comrades across the country. The chapter thus shows how relations that developed in urban hubs like Los Angeles can help grassroots activists to become potent forces in national-level struggles for rights and recognition.

The result was the creation of a grassroots strategy that contrasted sharply with the centralizing strategy of national NGOs. In terms of assessing the merits of the two strategies, Congress has failed to respond to the RIFA strategy. It did not produce a significant piece of reform legislation between 2006 and 2014. By contrast, with fewer resources, NDLON, the DREAMers, and their allies have made important inroads into municipalities and states across the country. They have also eaten into the federal government's enforcement policies, first with the passage of DACA and then with the passage of administrative relief in 2014. Thus, in terms of assessing these strategies on the basis of concrete outcomes, the strategy of the grassroots has proved to be far more effective than RIFA's in expanding the rights and protections of undocumented immigrants.

10

Paris as Head of Splintering Resistances

On May 1, 2004, the heads of France's leading human rights NGOs held a press conference denouncing the anti-immigration policies proposed by the Minister of the Interior, Nicolas Sarkozy. The coalition and campaign were called United Against Disposable Immigration (CIJ).[1] CIJ was made up of a broad range of human rights NGOs, smaller associations, and unions across France. The leaders exuded a sense of confidence, talking and joking with one another freely on the platform above the press. They had known each other for years and had gained extraordinary experience through many hard-fought campaigns. One thing stood out about this meeting: the absence of actual immigrants from the coalition's leadership. During the same period, undocumented immigrant activists were engaged in battles that were proliferating in localities across the country. *Collectifs des sans papiers* engaged in numerous small, almost imperceptible, struggles with department prefects. Through their direct actions (hunger strikes, occupations, protests), the *collectifs* demanded that department prefects reopen their cases and legalize their status.

The silence of actual immigrants at the press conference was indicative of the broader power arrangements of France's immigrant rights movement. The immigrant rights movement continued into the 2000s but in a splintered form: between a cohesive, elitist (mostly white, male, professional), and *national* center; and a fragmented, marginalized (undocumented immigrants with few resources), and *locally* entrapped

Cities and Social Movements: Immigrant Rights Activism in the United States, France, and the Netherlands, 1970–2015, First Edition. Walter J. Nicholls and Justus Uitermark.
© 2017 John Wiley & Sons, Ltd. Published 2017 by John Wiley & Sons, Ltd.

grassroots. While there was a center, it had a limited capacity to steer the multiple localized peripheries that emerged and propelled the struggle forward. This geopolitical configuration stood in contrast to the strong and productive collaborations between the human rights NGOs and *collectifs* during the 1990s. During that time, the *collectifs* and the human rights NGOs in Paris formed strong enough ties to coordinate one of the most potent immigrant mobilizations in the postwar period.

What accounts for the splintering of the Paris activist landscape in such a short period of time? And how has this affected the capacity of activists and advocates to achieve favorable reforms? This chapter addresses these questions by examining power relations that emerged between human rights NGOs and *collectifs* during the second half of the 1990s. The chapter begins by examining the passage of the highly restrictive Pasqua Law. It then explores how these laws spurred *collectifs* into a series of pitched battles with local prefects. These small and localized battles grew into large and national mobilizations that drew important levels of support from the Paris-based human rights NGOs. Together, immigrants and human rights NGOs went on to successfully push for the legalization of 80,000 undocumented immigrants. Soon after this important win, the movement splintered because immigrant activists denounced the human rights NGOs for monopolizing power. This chapter therefore explains the splintering process by highlighting the hierarchies that developed between the principal partners (rights NGOs and *collectifs*) of the movement.

Bad blood between these past partners festered in Paris, making it difficult for them to reconcile differences and collaborate when new threats surfaced in the 2000s. These different actors certainly mobilized in response to threats but they did so apart from one another. This resulted in mobilizations that were either overly national (national NGOs had little capacity to reach the grassroots) or overly local (*collectifs* had little capacity to reach beyond cities and departments). The local and grassroots immigrant activists also faced enormous competition and conflicts, which undermined their ability to build an alternative power base in the national immigrant rights movement (as they were able to do in the United States). Radical splintering left the movement ill-equipped to confront the growing popularity and legitimacy of anti-immigrant forces.

Landscapes of Grievances and Localizing State Repression

France pursued restrictive immigration measures in the 1990s. As was the case in the United States and the Netherlands, these restrictions were aimed at sharpening the line between "legal" residents and "illegal aliens." And, as in those two other countries, these restrictive measures triggered resistances that sought to push back, circumvent, and eat away at this line. The Minister of the Interior in 1993, Charles Pasqua, authored legislation to restrict legal migration (Hayward and Wright 2002; Berezin 2009). Politicians were responding to the belief that supposedly uncontrolled immigration presented a material and existential threat to the country. They asserted that immigrants had become adept at exploiting the two avenues of legal status: marriage and asylum. In the context of the recent Schengen agreements, government officials became worried that lax controls on asylum and marriage would make France a major target of cunning immigrants. According to the Minister of the Interior, "Recent changes in Europe make it that our country cannot continue to constitute a sort of paradise or oasis in which others wish to settle" (Charles Pasqua, Minister of the Interior, cited in *Le Monde*, June 2, 1993). The Minister of Justice echoed this concern and stressed that even the slightest openings made the country vulnerable to a flood of undocumented immigrants: "The obligation to admit the interested parties, *even provisionally*, to stay on our territory risks to create an uncontrollable avenue of clandestine immigration" (Pierre Méhaignerie, Minister of Justice, cited in *Le Monde*, October 29, 1993, emphasis added).

In spite of these concerns, government officials recognized international obligations concerning the rights of asylum seekers and families. The policy emphasis centered on introducing measures that could weed out immigrants who "deserved" to stay in the country from those "undeserving" immigrants who needed to be deported. "All those who are persecuted in their countries have the right to be welcomed on our territory: it's a French tradition. But for the others, it's no" (Charles Pasqua, Minister of the Interior, cited in *Le Monde*, June 2, 1993). The Pasqua Law of 1993 eliminated the right of automatic citizenship for those children of immigrants born on French soil. It raised the criteria needed to qualify for legal residency through family reunification and asylum and introduced new restrictions on welfare and medical services to undocumented immigrants. It enhanced the housing conditions needed to qualify for legal residency and required French residents to register foreign visitors to their homes. Lastly, the law sanctioned identity checks of suspected unauthorized immigrants by local law enforcement agencies. The government expanded "holding centers" at airports, ports, and cities to detain undocumented migrants and facilitated identity checks and detentions by local law enforcement agencies (Hayward and Wright 2002).

The law was executed by the national government, but it required the participation of countless local officials, service workers, and organizations that encountered suspect immigrants. Welfare workers, local police agents, medical practitioners, airline workers, mayors, housing agents, employers, and so on were called upon to participate in the process of detecting, detaining, and deporting targeted populations. Each of these actors became local "relays" (Rose and Miller 1992) of the immigration regime. They now had an obligation to play a role in enforcing the line between "deserving" immigrants and true "illegals." Department-level prefects were the local representatives of the Minister of Interior and had already assumed a frontline role in monitoring and assessing the applications of immigrants (Hayward and Wright 2002; De Barros 2004; Péchu 2004).

The roles of city mayors were also enhanced as a result of these measures. As early as 1977, French law required family immigrants to obtain certificates of "decent housing" from mayors, which gave mayors an inordinate amount of power in the migration process. The Pasqua Law reinforced this role while also giving mayors the authority to register and monitor foreign visitors to their jurisdictions. Mayors were required to report suspected "fake" marriages to state authorities. The denial of most welfare services to undocumented immigrants required local service providers to inquire and verify the legal status of their clients. Lastly, as detentions and deportations accelerated, workers in transport and security industries as well as nonprofit care providers were now called upon to participate in monitoring and reporting undocumented immigrants. The passage of the Pasqua Law therefore contributed to growing state intervention in the area of immigration, and this intervention depended on thousands of local officials and service providers to play aggressive border-enforcing roles.

The Social Movement Space: Paris as a Centralizing Hub

Proliferating resistances and mobilizations

Less than a year after the Pasqua Law's passage, one mobilization arose in a western suburb of Paris. Complying with the new law, the mayor of the suburban municipality suspected a couple of marriage fraud and forwarded their case to the department prefect. He went on to deny the marriage license and the legal visa that would have come with it. The French groom (Gilles Verger) was morally outraged because he believed that the government had violated his fundamental right to marry and start a family with whomever he pleased, irrespective of national origin. "I am a French citizen and my country is blocking me from living with the woman I have chosen … Even in South Africa, mixed marriages are possible!" (Gilles Verger, cited in *Le Monde*, February 7, 1994). He went on to express his grievance to an association working on family rights in his city. This association in turn contacted the National Union of Family Associations for further assistance. While the latter association typically did not involve itself in immigration issues, this specific restriction was viewed as an egregious violation of family rights, prompting the organization to come out in support of Mr Verger's case. "The exercise of the right to marry, to live with the conjoint of one's choice with their children, is an inalienable right; this right cannot be subordinated to restrictive policies targeting immigrants" (National Union of Family Associations, cited in *Le Monde*, February 7, 1994). The case went to court and the tribunal ruled in favor of the plaintiff, agreeing that his fundamental rights to live with the family of his choice had been violated. Citing this and similar cases, the National Human Rights Commission stated that "The foreign conjoint is confronted with multiple obstacles to obtain legal residency which would permit them to stay in France legally. The Pasqua Law is a grave reversal of essential human rights" (cited in *Le Monde*, March 22, 1994). Gilles Verger's case illustrates how restrictions aimed at so-called cheating immigrants spilled over and violated the "inalienable" rights of immigrants and citizens alike, prompting a political chain reaction that spread the conflict beyond its point of origin.

In a similar fashion, the Pasqua Law's enhanced restrictions on access to healthcare drew medical professionals directly into the area of immigration as they were now obliged to deny people coverage on the basis of legal status. Some healthcare providers balked at this requirement and expressed their grievances to their unions. These grievances overlapped with those of immigrants denied access to healthcare, giving rise to a small campaign in Paris (Action for the Rights of Sick Foreigners). The campaign eventually gained the attention of the prominent LGBT association Act-Up, since some members of the gay community were being denied healthcare because of their immigration status. While this association had not been an active participant in immigrant rights struggles before, the Pasqua Law drew it into the battle because it denied some within the LGBT community life-supporting care. "We underline the increased difficulty to obtain even a short reprieve for sick people … To exclude these people of basic healthcare is to render more dramatic the human costs of the Pasqua Law" (Act Up, cited in *Le Monde*, June 4, 1994). The Pasqua Law denied needed services to immigrants, placed medical providers in the difficult position of assessing the distribution of care on the basis of legal status, and denied essential services to immigrants suffering HIV and AIDS. Facing growing pressure from this unexpected alliance of healthcare, LGBT, and immigrant rights advocates, the government eventually granted seriously ailing immigrants a special reprieve on the grounds of "humanitarian reason" (Fassin 2012).

Government efforts to enact greater restrictions therefore resulted in the unintended consequence of intensifying grievances of immigrants and spreading grievances to populations not directly targeted by these measures. These struggles were responses to specific restrictions enacted in hospitals, city halls, department administrations, and transportation facilities throughout the country. While many struggles stayed small and local, others grew and garnered the support of organizations and people with an expansive reach. Some became broad enough to make it into national newspapers like *Le Monde* but most did not make it onto the pages of the national press. They stayed small, local, and finite disruptions in the circuits of governmental power.

Paris as a center of the struggle

In spite of the breadth of these small immigrant rights resistances, Paris continued to provide a favorable context of mobilization because of its high concentration of resources and supportive networks. The *collectifs des sans papiers* became a major force of resistance from the mid-1990s onwards. Ties to, and support from, Paris-based human rights NGOs bolstered their early efforts. The alliance between older and richer clusters (the human rights NGOs) and newer and more dynamic ones (the *collectifs*) re-energized the immigrant rights movement following the slump of the late 1980s and early 1990s.

In response to the Pasqua Law, some immigrants created new *collectifs* to demand legal residency for their members. One of the first *collectifs* that emerged at this time was the Foreign Parents of French Children (PEEF).[2] Their initial target and demands were limited: they targeted the department prefect (charged with processing visa applications) and demanded a 10-year residency visa for the members of their particular *collectifs*. They did not target the Ministry or the parliament and they did not call for the abrogation of the Pasqua Law (Siméant 1998; Blin 2005). Initially, the *collectif* employed traditional social movement tactics such as rallies and petitions to pressure the department prefect. Most of the participants saw the *collectif* as a collective means to adjust the precarious legal status of their families and friends. The precarious positioning of these and other undocumented immigrants meant that they prioritized the short-term and immediate goal of legalizing their status over the longer-term and more uncertain goal of changing French immigration policy. A former member of the *collectif* remarked, "For the people, their principal objective was getting their papers, getting a decent job, and finding housing. Some were interested in politics but politics was not their principal preoccupation, getting their papers was" (*Collectif de Montreuil,* personal interview). Though this *collectif* organized demonstrations in 1994, the *collectif* did not gain the support of key human rights NGOs in the city and the prefect ignored them.

The PEEF *collectif* escalated its efforts in spring 1995 by embracing more aggressive tactics. It occupied a public building, initiated a hunger strike, and shifted the target from the department prefect to national government officials. The presidential campaign in 1995 provided the *collectif* with an opportunity to draw national attention to its situation, thereby forcing the department prefect to respond to its demands for legalization:

> We had hoped that the prefect of Paris would have accepted to engage us in a negotiation to find a positive solution for the hundred families of our *collectif*. Facing the intransigence from the prefect, eight among us have decided to start a hunger strike. This is not blackmail. The hunger strike is a cry; the last cry we make to the Prime Minister of the Government. (archives, PEEF, April 18, 1995)

Growing media and political attention for this action prompted the human rights NGOs to connect with the *collectif* and provide it with legal and political support. The prefect responded by reopening the cases of the members of the *collectif*, granting only a handful with the strongest claims (parents of citizens, long-time residents) a residency permit.

In 1996, a second *collectif* exploded onto the Parisian social movement scene. Approximately 300 undocumented African immigrants occupied the St Ambroise church in northern Paris. The size and intensity of the initial action at the church drew immediate attention from across the Paris activist milieu. Some of the undocumented activists had developed relations with several more radical activist groups in the city through their participation in earlier squatting actions (see Chapter 7). *Droits Devant*, for instance, was an association that had emerged in the 1990s to support the squatting actions of undocumented immigrants. Its director, Jean-Paul Amara, had established good relations with certain members of undocumented immigrant activists in the new *collectif*. He also had good relations with some of the most important human rights NGOs (FASTI and MRAP in particular) in Paris. Relations to both clusters (the informal *collectifs* and the big associations) enabled him to broker relations between them. He made in-person requests to the human rights NGOs for support of the action at St Ambroise church (minutes, FASTI, March 30, 1996). His efforts helped convince the four prominent associations (LDH, GISTI, FASTI, and MRAP) to support this action.

Several weeks after the occupation of St Ambroise, the police force-fully removed the undocumented activists from the church. The human rights NGOs employed their contacts to find an alternative place for the activists to stay: a theater (*la Cartoucherie de Vincennes*) on the eastern outskirts of the city. The theater director was a veteran supporter of various prominent causes, dating back to Michel Foucault's prison reform campaigns and the SONACOTRA struggles in the 1970s. The move to the theater unleashed another important round of networking. The human rights NGOs each assumed a brokering role and began circulating information about the struggle to their own networks. Through constant outreach, the associations were able to connect to two activist clusters. The cluster of older and increasingly marginalized immigrant associations (ATMF, ATF, FTCR, ACORT) entered the network through these channels. The human rights NGOs also recruited a group of prestigious personalities (intellectuals, media personalities, humanitarians) who went on to form the College of Mediators.[3] The principal function of the College was to use the cultural and symbolic capital of its members to represent the demands of the *collectif* to the government and the national media.

It soon became clear that the small theater lacked the capacity to house the hundreds of undocumented immigrants and supporters. The human rights NGOs then contacted allies within the rail workers union[4] in Paris for assistance. The union provided a warehouse and basic communication infrastructure. The union's involvement encouraged greater interest from other Paris-based unions.[5] This support was important because unions were relatively rich organizations and provided funding and equipment to the campaign. These resources were used to provide the *collectif* with the basic materials (i.e. office space, paper, copier machine, telephone, etc.) needed to create an organization of its own. Members of one union (CGT) also worked closely with several undocumented leaders to create the National Coordination of Sans Papiers (CNSP),[6] the first national organization to coordinate the actions of *collectifs* emerging throughout the country.

On June 28, 1996 the *collectif* occupied the church of St Bernard in northeastern Paris and eight of them went on a hunger strike. St Bernard became a major focal point of the campaign. As word of the campaign spread, undocumented immigrants throughout Paris descended on the site in an effort to have their own individual cases reviewed by the authorities. St Bernard also became an important focal point by drawing the support of prominent Parisian entertainers and intellectuals. Entertainers like Emmanuel Béart and intellectuals like Pierre Bourdieu and Emmanuel Terray became fixtures at the site. The symbolic capital of these personalities drew in more media and enhanced the moral weight and legitimacy of the immigrants' claim.

St Bernard also intensified working relations between the human rights NGOs. Their increased role in the struggle prompted them to increase the frequency of their meetings to three or four times a week. By this point in the campaign, meetings intensified to one or two a day (MRAP, personal interview). In addition to deepening ties between the human rights NGOs, these interactions improved their ability to work with one another under conditions of extreme political uncertainty. The president of the Human Rights League (LDH) remembered that "St. Bernard became a giant village where we all converged to provide support for the undocumented immigrants (*sans papiers*). Working like this, working under these conditions, helped transform the relations between our different groups because we really learned to work together" (LDH, personal interview). The initial action at St Ambroise had picked up momentum and snowballed into a major mobilization that culminated at the St Bernard church. The relations built up through urban space and time allowed this campaign to concentrate an extraordinary amount of resources and energy in this particular part of the city.

Just as important, the concentration of activist networks allowed the mobilization to spill out beyond the city's limits. Union supporters of this struggle pressed their national organizations to block Air France from using charter flights to deport immigrants. Union employees servicing these flights had already expressed their grievances to Air France officials. This was now an opportunity for them to express their solidarity with the struggle at St Bernard while also expressing their disapproval of participating in the deportation regime. In an announcement from their union, these workers stated, "The Minister of the Interior has solicited Air Charter, a company of Air France, to deport foreigners. We have expressed our concerns to the director of Air France and to refuse that planes and personnel of Air France be used for these police operations" (CFDT, cited in *Le Monde*, August 29, 1996). Jean-Paul Amara of *Droits Devant* also encouraged the human rights NGO to call upon their branches to support mobilizations of *collectifs* in their localities. Reporting on Amara's personal visit to FASTI, one observer reported, "After having evoked the dangers and difficulties of the struggle, the nervous and physical exhaustion of the refugees, and the repressive attitude of the government, Amara called on FASTI to relay the struggle to its sections across the country" (minutes, FASTI, March 20, 1996).

Some of the national associations responded favorably by encouraging them to support the efforts of local *collectifs* and provide them with information and mobilization frames developed from the central campaign in Paris. "It seems to us very natural to rapidly circulate information and material we acquire to the branches. This material strengthens their abilities to support the *collectifs* in their respective cities" (minutes, FASTI, April 27, 1996). Information included legal information analyzed by expert lawyers from LDH and GISTI as well as analyses concerning the shifting positions of the government. In addition to specialized information, the national offices of the associations provided branch sections with mobilizing frames and demands. "You can, if you wish, employ the texts emanating from the intellectuals and writers that affirm, 'The procedures of expulsion are unjust and render hardworking families into clandestine criminals ...' You can even take up the pen to write something along these lines" (minutes, FASTI, April 27, 1996).

The campaign in 1996 intensified networking in and beyond Paris. Direct connections were established between several clusters in the city, including trade unions, prominent intellectuals, immigrant associations, and media personalities. Face-to-face brokering by well-connected activists (Amara among others) played an essential role in connecting different clusters of actors and extending the struggle beyond the original point of conflict. Each new connection resulted in different contributions to the struggle, including money, legal expertise, facilities, strategic expertise, and cultural and symbolic capital. The relational momentum that had gathered in Paris snowballed into a potent and destabilizing mobilization. The growing complexity of ties and the buzzing energy that emanated from the events, occupations, and hunger strikes allowed the campaign to extend far beyond the city. Union workers at airports refused to collaborate with deportations and local branches of national associations began to lend support to *collectifs* in provincial cities. The power generated in Paris allowed the mobilization to scale up and achieve national scope.

Strengthening the Center, Multiplying the Peripheries

The intense campaigning in 1996 gave shape to a social movement space with a distinctive center that steered mobilizations in several peripheral areas. This particular configuration would enable these actors to achieve important goals (like a far-reaching legalization in 1997), but it also planted seeds of conflict in the network. These conflicts would have lasting effects on activist relations in this and subsequent campaigns.

The mobilization helped contribute to the consolidation of a central leadership group. Once some of the human rights NGOs began to get involved (GISTI and FASTI), the others quickly followed suit. The director of MRAP remembers, "That day in March 1996, all the organizations came out to support the *sans papiers*. For one year, we followed them constantly and we developed a habit of constantly meeting. Little by little we developed a strong network among us to oppose the new policies of the government" (MRAP, personal interview). These associations went on to form a leadership group called the Group of 10, which was made up of the principal supporting associations in Paris. Their intimate work with one another reinforced their commitment to the struggle and strengthened their relations to one another. The network configuration was therefore made up of an emerging leadership consisting of human rights NGOs, the activists of the *collectifs* who assumed a frontline role in this battle, and a varied network of supporters in Paris and across the country who contributed different resources to the mobilization.

The concentration of cultural, legal, and political resources by the Group of 10 transformed the human rights NGOs from supporters of undocumented immigrant activists into leaders of the campaign. They became the representational brokers of the movement, giving voice to undocumented immigrants and using their networks to diffuse this voice across multiple publics (media, civil society, public officials). The human rights NGOs (especially GISTI and LDH) carefully analyzed the underpinnings of government policies and found legal inconsistencies. This work provided the larger movement with the legal rationale to push their argument for legalization forward. They also crafted representations and mobilization frames that resonated with the broader French public. The associations possessed the political networks to connect to the government and a broad range of associations and unions in Paris. They had established ties to a range of intellectuals and media personalities in the region. Few other actors had the resources and contacts needed to assume a position in leading and sustaining this campaign in the face of an increasingly revanchist and conservative government.

Commenting on the leadership position during the campaign, the director of a smaller association remarked, "There were people who put themselves in front like LDH, GISTI, and MRAP. These were associations that addressed these questions for a long time. It gave them the feeling that it was legitimate that they manage the campaign … I think there were associations that put themselves in front because they had been the pillars of this struggle for years" (Autremonde, personal interview). The strong reputation of the human rights NGOs also convinced some immigrant associations (especially those with a more militant history) to participate in this campaign in spite of the risks. "It's a common history of participating in different struggles. They helped us. We discussed with them. They understood our problems and actions. Ties existed. More than anything it was the long period that we established this trust in them. These were affective ties … There was a feeling. We knew how these associations thought. That inspires confidence" (ATMF, personal interview).

Because the leading associations could instill confidence in the milieu, they were in a unique position to motivate many other actors and organizations to join and participate in this campaign. This resulted in a network structure of concentric circles, with the human rights NGOs in the center and their allies (immigrant associations and unions) playing supportive or secondary roles.

The *collectifs* played crucial but increasingly peripheral roles as the campaign grew in scale and momentum. At the outset of the campaign, the human rights NGOs conceived of themselves as mere "supporters" of undocumented immigrant activists. As the campaign expanded in scale, growing complications required the human rights NGOs to assume a leading position in analyzing legal texts and arguments, crafting resonant discourses, negotiating with the police and politicians in and out of the government, and so on. The *collectifs* had important mobilization capacities that were derived from their strong-tie networks, but they lacked the kinds of resources needed to sustain an intense national campaign. Scaling up to a national-level campaign therefore contributed to the marginalization of the undocumented activists who actually initiated it and took the most serious risks (arrest, deportation, health problems arising from hunger strikes).

The human rights NGOs made a concerted effort to include undocumented activists in decision-making processes and negotiations with the government, but many undocumented activists believed that they were incorporated as tokens in a campaign that had ceased being their own. The marginalization of undocumented activists planted seeds of distrust between the human rights NGOs and the undocumented activists involved in the campaign. Many believed that the human rights NGOs had usurped the campaign and used it as an instrument to advance their own political goals rather than the goals of the actual immigrants involved in the *collectif*. One of the undocumented leaders noted that "The people who are at the head of these associations used the *sans papiers* movement to advance their careers. They were only interested in themselves. All that stuff didn't interest us; we were created only to help our brothers and sisters. We just wanted to get them their papers" (CNSP, personal interview). She went on to stress the patronizing attitudes displayed by the heads of the professional human rights NGOs: "In France, the associations would say 'our' *sans papiers* as if we they owned us. They treated us like children" (CNSP, personal interview). A long-time undocumented activist adds, "The supporters [i.e. national human rights NGOs] manipulate the undocumented immigrants, so they are not supporters. Or, they support the people like a rope supports a hanged person" (*Ouvrier Sans Papiers*, personal interview).

The cleavages between the undocumented activists and the human rights NGOs affected how the undocumented activists interpreted the outcome of the campaign. A new center-left government in 1997 eventually granted almost 80,000 immigrants legal residency status. Priority was given to undocumented immigrants with family members who were citizens or legal residents of France. Some undocumented activists expressed great frustration with this outcome because it excluded recent immigrants and immigrants without family members. They directed this frustration at the human rights NGOs for having negotiated the terms of the agreement. "They [the associations] said they wanted the regularization of all undocumented immigrants but they really didn't. They just talked like that but their real focus was on the families. Everybody else was left out" (CNSP, personal interview). Another undocumented activist similarly attributed responsibility for this outcome to the human rights NGOs, "All these people [the *sans papiers*] accepted taking important risks but all they were doing was providing support for the strongest applicants, the parents. It is not fair that everybody takes the same risks but only a few benefit" (*Rassemblement Collectif Ouvrier*, personal interview).

In the months after the St Bernard campaign, the bad relations between these two clusters prompted some undocumented activists and the network of *collectifs* – National Coordination of Undocumented Immigrants (CNSP) – to seek alternative allies (especially among the extreme left) and sources of support. These moves intensified tensions with the human rights NGOs, with one human rights NGO reporting that:

> There is little information on what is happening with the CNSP. It is difficult to get reliable information from the group and other collectifs. We believe that the African groups are influenced by the extreme left. The Group of 10 has to reassert its relation to the *collectifs* because *we give these struggles their general character. Their struggles alone are not the same as ours.* (Minutes, FASTI, November 25, 1996, emphasis added)

Tensions blew up when the National Coordination was accused of fraud and charging high fees to assist undocumented immigrants with their residency applications. The immigrant activists denied the charges and argued that they were a pretext for reasserting associational control over the *collectifs*.

By the beginning of 1997, the power and momentum unfolding in Paris allowed activists to scale up their demands. However, the process of scaling up planted seeds of conflict that would eventually fracture the movement. The campaign of 1996 gave rise to new networks and stronger relations among some (human rights NGOs) but also powerful cleavages between others (human rights NGOs and the *collectifs*). Scaling up the campaign in 1996 increased the complexity of doing politics and required the specialized resources that the human rights NGOs had and that the undocumented immigrant activists didn't. As the human rights NGOs became better able to pool and deploy these resources, undocumented immigrant activists were pushed to the margins of their own struggle. Such a hierarchy in the division of political labor introduced powerful conflicts over who had the legitimacy to represent the interests and voice of undocumented immigrants in the public sphere. Activist stratification therefore arose in response to the rules of the game that demanded specialized resources for scaling up, and this introduced competition and conflict over legitimacy. The criticisms of leading human rights NGOs against *collectifs* only inflamed tensions and transformed structurally based cleavages into heated and "bad blood" conflicts.

These divisions between undocumented immigrant activists in the grassroots and Paris-based human rights NGOs were further deepened as successive governments emphasized that a strict distinction should be made between immigrants who deserve legal status and those who do not. Although the governments had different ways of drawing the line between deserving and undeserving immigrants, their discourses and policies emphasized that those who do not meet the requirements should be excluded from state services and deported. Those who had participated in the earlier campaigns of the mid-1990s but were left out of the mass regularization that followed, found themselves to be more "illegal" and excluded than ever. They were facing a reinforced immigration regime, and they felt betrayed and instrumentalized by their supposed supporters in human rights NGOs.

The Implosion of the Social Movement Space

Splintering grassroots networks

In spite of the problems that arose in the previous round of mobilizations, many undocumented immigrants continued to believe that self-organized and combative *collectifs* were effective tools to regularize their status. One leading undocumented activist remarked that "This result demonstrates a simple reality: When one fights, one proves that one wants to truly stay here. The administration has no other option but to regularize status" (Madiguene Cissé, cited in *Le Monde*, August 24, 1998). *Collectifs* continued to emerge in towns and cities across France. They continued to be made up of relatively small groups that embraced direct action tactics. They occupied high-profile buildings, tried to win public support through street protests, and occasionally used hunger strikes to escalate pressure. These mobilizations were also grounded in *local* political arenas. Department prefects continued to have authority and discretion over deciding the case of immigrants. This alone made these frontline state officials the immediate target of collective actions.

The year 1997 marked the return of a center-left government. By targeting cities controlled by Socialist mayors, *collectifs* tried to draw national attention to the new government's repressive immigration policies. In one action, an activist explained why his *collectif* chose to target a Socialist mayor: "We chose to occupy city hall of Limeil so that the Socialists get a little wet in this issue. We cannot accept that this government send us back into a clandestine situation, even though we submitted our file for regularization to get out of this impasse" (Brehima Niakate, cited in *Le Monde*, October 27, 1998). The National Coordination of Undocumented Immigrants added: "What is sad is that it is a left government that uses the same methods as a government of the right" (CNSP, cited in *Le Monde*, November 16, 1998). Similar direct actions were taken in Socialist Party strongholds throughout France, including Lille. In this case, the local Socialist Party took a stern line: "The Socialists of Lille firmly condemn the sectarian behavior of those who encourage men to put their lives in danger and direct them toward suicide" (cited in *Le Monde*, June 28, 2000). By targeting prefects and mayors, local arenas continued to be strategic arenas for these battles.

While *collectifs* were drawn into localities, weak mechanisms of coordination between *collectifs* spurred fragmentation. The CNSP had very limited resources, weak organizational capacities, and little legitimacy among many of the *collectifs*. It provided national coordination in name more than in practice. Conflicts appeared between *collectifs* because of differences in strategies and goals. Some were conceived as parts of broad political struggles against borders, capitalism, and neoliberal globalization. Others – and perhaps most – were conceived narrowly as pragmatic struggles for temporary or permanent visas for the members of the *collectif*. In addition to divisions, prefects often responded to them through divide and rule. They often promised the possible regularization of a handful of seemingly deserving cases in a *collectif* while enforcing the exclusion of others. This had the effect of splitting *collectifs* and introducing low-trust and competitive sentiment among these activists, contributing to a process of ongoing fragmentation. "Since 2000, the undocumented movement has exploded with 1,000 collectifs that cannot work with each other, that pass their lives in conflict with one another" (FASTI, personal interview).

The social and political networks holding these activists together were generally weak, but they were weaker in Paris than in the provinces. Paris contained many *collectifs*, often within the same neighborhoods. The number and density of *collectifs* in Paris contributed to intensifying competition over legitimacy and resources (i.e. members). Provincial cities, by contrast, contained one or two. Low density helped reduce situations of resource overlap, which reduced the levels of competition between undocumented activists. "The difference between the provincial cities and Paris is that in provincial cities, when there is a *collectif*, there is just one ... However in Paris, there have been many within the same district [*arrondissement*] ... The big divisions exist just in Paris" (FASTI, personal interview). The director of CNSP agreed, noting that "In Lille, all the undocumented immigrants are with one *collectif*. In Paris, no. In Paris, each *collectif* wants to be ahead all of the time" (CNSP, personal interview). Rather than spurring trust, solidarity, and cognitive convergence, organizational density in Paris spurred social-capital-sapping competition for resources and legitimacy ("wants to be ahead all of the time").

Undocumented activists in Paris *aggregated* but they did not *agglomerate*. Many were located in the city but conflicts between them limited their ability to become more than the sum of their parts. They lacked the capacity to coordinate their actions in the city. *Collectifs* in provincial cities did not look to Paris for guidance, inspiration, discourses, or resources. Outside activists turned to the big city because it was the easiest place to find others like themselves. Paris had become a simple container of many *collectifs* (aggregate) rather than a magnifier of productive relations between *collectifs* (agglomeration). The inability of Parisian activists to agglomerate undermined their capacity to assume certain coordination functions within the national social movement space. This contributed to the continued marginalization of *collectifs* in France's national immigrant rights movement.

Even in nearby cities, *collectifs* lacked relational and organizational mechanisms to coordinate campaigns. "We have had great difficulty joining cities that are close to each other. For example, there was a very big *collectif* in Angoulême. Several years ago, a *collectif* in Poitiers began a struggle with a hunger strike. They were all alone even though Angoulême isn't very far" (*Collectif de Montreuil*, personal interview). Bad relations between *collectifs* in Paris undermined the movement's ability to coordinate activities inside and outside Paris. This resulted in a national-level social movement space that was made up of hundreds of contentious and hard-hitting *collectifs* in disparate localities across the country. Bad or no relations in and across cities undermined the ability of *collectifs* to scale up from localities and become an offensive force within the national political field. They were trapped in hundreds of local trenches, lacking the relational and organizational means to overcome specific and particular battles and become an autonomous, potent, and *national* political force.

The enfeebled national center

The return of a center-right government in 2002 marked the return of professional human rights NGOs to the streets. The Minister of the Interior, Nicolas Sarkozy, announced his intention to introduce a law that would restrict the number of visas granted to families and asylum seekers, expand visas for high-skilled professionals, and impose more restrictions on associations working with undocumented immigrants. The human rights NGOs responded by calling for a demonstration in September 2002. The demonstration drew several thousand sympathizers and allies, making it the largest immigrant rights demonstration since the heady mobilizations of 1996 and 1997 (*Le Monde*, September 10, 2002). Many undocumented activists welcomed the return of human rights NGOs to contentious politics, but it revived past concerns over the legitimate representatives of the movement: "The members of the *Coordination 93 de lutte des sans papiers* welcomed the support [of the human rights NGOs]. However, we would have wanted to be at the head of the demonstration. It was us after all we who created all of that but, in the end, it was the big associations and personalities who passed in front" (Ali Mansouri, Coordination 93, cited in *Le Monde*, September 10, 2002). Efforts were made at some kind of reconciliation, but low levels of trust, tattered reputations, and high levels of competition for legitimacy made sustained collective work difficult if not impossible.

Rather than recreate the alliances of 1996, the human rights NGOs embarked on a project to create a new coalition. This effort would result in United Against Disposable Immigration (CIJ).[7] CIJ aimed to build a broad national coalition to fight against the Minister of the Interior's new immigration initiatives. The human rights NGOs felt confident about starting such a coalition because they had strong ties to one another and a deep well of collective knowhow and experience. The president of the LDH remembers:

> Yes, at the outset it was the League [LDH] that took the initiative. We launched an invitation … to our *habitual partners*: the antiracist associations, CIMADE, GISTI … After that, things unfolded quickly to 20 organizations, then 100, 200, 300. But at the beginning it was the habitual structure, with our constant partners on these subjects at the core … So, it was automatic; all of it was a reflex for us. (Personal interview, emphasis added)

The above statement reflects the thinking of the leading NGOs: the selection of the "habitual partners" (the human rights NGOs based in Paris) was "automatic" and a "reflex." Past relations and strong ties led them to an automatic selection of the leadership of the new coalition, laying down a framework in which the human rights NGOs would assume dominance from the outset.

LDH, GISTI, and CIMADE assumed a central position as the leading legal analysts of the movement. "Generally, all the legal work is done by the *Ligue* [LDH], GISTI, and CIMADE; because we have this expertise, and we work well together, *voilà*" (LDH, personal interview). In addition to developing effective and critical legal analyses of government measures, GISTI has also developed workshops in Paris to educate its allies in immigration law and how to develop legally informed political strategies. The other associations making up this cluster (MRAP, FASTI, Droit Devants) had expertise in campaigning and mounting mobilizations. They knew how to create compelling messages and frames, employ the media to diffuse frames, extend support in the public, negotiate with law enforcement, and broker relations with new allies. "We other associations provided information on what is happening on the ground and with different political contacts. *We mutualize our information and resources.* It's effective because it moves the campaign forward" (MRAP, personal interview, emphasis added). The director of FASTI concurred and noted, "That is where we complement GISTI. They are brilliant on legal theory but they have greater difficulty mobilizing people to confront the prefect or Ministry. That is easier for us" (FASTI, personal interview). The "habitual" working relations made it possible for them to reassert themselves as a central force in France's extremely fragmented and localized immigrant rights movement. They knew exactly which associations had resources and how these could be pooled in a national coalition to fight the Minister of the Interior.

The strength of ties (and some might say insularity) enabled the associations to form a new leadership group and coalition, but their ability to do so also contributed to reproducing past activist hierarchies and the conflicts associated with them. The "good blood" between human rights NGOs allowed them to quickly assemble a broad and national-level coalition. Smaller associations and the *collectifs* experienced this as another power grab, which revived the bad blood between the re-emergent center and the multiple peripheries. The strong ties and convergence between the leading human rights NGOs – the qualities that enabled them to create a new coalition and *lead* a national-level campaign – were the same qualities that alienated others from the coalition. The bad blood between the human rights NGOs and the *collectifs* making up the network meant that many did not trust the leadership from the outset of the campaign. The leader of one *collectif* noted, "It's a small milieu [the leading associations] where everybody knows one another, where everybody is in agreement on almost everything, where everybody is hostile to the self-organization of undocumented immigrants" (*Ouvriers Sans Papiers*, personal interview). Smaller associations and *collectifs* also criticized the centralized ways in which decisions were made. Weekly meetings of CIJ were open to all, but most of the decisions seemed to be made by the insider group. "We knew very well that decisions were taken internally by certain people. When we intervened to talk about other things, they politely listened to us, but then when we looked at the minutes, we realized that what we had said was forgotten, it did not even make it on to the minutes" (Rajfire, personal interview).

During meetings and demonstrations, more marginalized associations and *collectifs* talked to each other about these relations and shared their experiences. These interactions confirmed interpretations of insider-outsider dynamics and helped reinforce the negative perceptions and distrust of the leadership. Many undocumented activists found little reason to participate in the campaigns. "We had great difficulty finding our place. Moreover, because we are small, that represented a big effort for us, to attend those kinds of meetings. To have one of our members each week at one of their meetings was heavy [in terms of investment time] when ultimately it gave us nothing (*Ouvriers Sans Papiers*, personal interview). Other activists noted that they continued to show up to events but would not contribute more because of their deep-seated suspicion of the leadership.

The core human rights NGOs depended on the trust and loyalty of several close collaborators but trust fell precipitously the further one moved out from the inner circle. This resulted in mobilizations that tended to be shallow. They could not organize many actual undocumented immigrants to support CIJ events and they could not sustain campaigns over extended periods of time. In this way, there was a strong, capable, and smart core group of leaders but it was a leadership with tenuous connections to and legitimacy among locally entrenched grassroots groups.

The French immigrant rights movement in the 2000s was therefore deeply fragmented. There was a handful of associations located in Paris with excellent ties to one another. These stronger ties provided the organizational and relational basis for a national campaign. There were also countless grassroots and energetic groups that could reach deep into the everyday lives of immigrants and mobilize thousands in high-risk campaigns. However, relations that would enable connections between these two worlds had been torn asunder by the hierarchies, conflicts, and bad blood of past mobilizations in the same city. This made it very difficult for grassroots *collectifs* to scale up their campaigns through the assistance of the human rights NGOs, and for the human rights NGOs to scale down through the assistance of the *collectifs*. Competition between the *collectifs* for limited resources and legitimacy also limited their ability to construct an autonomous infrastructure to scale up on their own (in contrast to the Los Angeles case). There has been enormous energy on both sides but this kind of scalar fragmentation has made it difficult, if not impossible, to confront adversaries and protest repressive policies. In France, we therefore find high numbers of contentious and mobilized actors but the absence of a cohesive social movement network that could translate that energy and intensity into substantial wins.

Conclusions

The social movement space of the 2000s differed from that of the 1990s. This new space was driven by many high-energy and high-risk mobilizations of *collectifs* in localities throughout the country. While the mobilizations were geographically ubiquitous, there was no real force that could provide coordination and coherence between the different parts. The *collectifs* in Paris were too fragmented and the CNSP had limited geographical reach. The human rights NGOs made an attempt to recentralize the national social movement space and provide it with some coherence. Power struggles and bad blood relations with the *collectifs* and other grassroots associations limited their ability to do so. The social movement space was characterized by an enfeebled center with countless peripheries mobilizing independently and oftentimes in conflict with one another. This particular configuration meant that a specific mobilization could at times compel an occasional department prefect to legalize the status of a handful of immigrants. However, it undermined their capacity to achieve longer-term changes. As the country lurched further to the political right during the 2000s, the high number of skilled activists and advocates lacked the coordination needed to push back and demand immigrant rights.

We find important similarities to and differences from the case of the United States. There we find strategic divergences between national immigrant rights NGOs and local immigrant associations in Los Angeles. However, rather than splinter into countless localized battles, the grassroots immigrant activists were able to build up from localities and develop methods to coordinate their actions across different localities.

This network enabled them to develop a locally based but nationally oriented movement to demand the rights of immigrants in the country. While the national immigrant rights NGOs in the United States continued to claim leadership over the whole of the movement, it was actually the grassroots infrastructure, anchored by several urban activist hubs like Los Angeles, that permitted activists to move favorable immigration policies and struggles forward.

11

Divergent Geographies of Immigrant Rights Contention in the Netherlands

In 1997, the Turkish tailor Zekeriya Gümüş became national news in the Netherlands. The government was poised to deport Gümüş and his family to Turkey but a committee was formed to protest the decision. The committee was initiated by residents of De Pijp, one of the nineteenth-century neighborhoods where movements had proliferated in the 1970s and 1980s. While perhaps the sentiment of those turbulent years still hovered over the neighborhood, this time concerned individuals rather than movement organizations initiated the protests. The driving force was Anja Versnel, an assistant at the school Gümüş's two sons, Karaman and Samet, attended. Versnel had never been involved in activism before, but her concern for the two young pupils led her to form an impromptu committee – "Gümüş has to stay!" – with neighbors and friends.

Zekeriya Gümüş and his family had arrived in the Netherlands on a tourist visa in 1989 in the hope of building a new life. Amsterdam at the time had around 1,000 small-scale and informal textile businesses run by Turkish immigrants, including some of Gümüş's relatives (Van Oenen 1999). Gümüş entered the Dutch labor market as an informal worker at his cousin's business in 1989. After the two cousins had an argument and parted company, Gümüş moved in and out of jobs until he established his own tailor shop in De Pijp in 1995. Gümüş was a so-called "white illegal": although he did not have a residence permit, he had a social security number and paid taxes. The government decided

Cities and Social Movements: Immigrant Rights Activism in the United States, France, and the Netherlands, 1970–2015, First Edition. Walter J. Nicholls and Justus Uitermark.
© 2017 John Wiley & Sons, Ltd. Published 2017 by John Wiley & Sons, Ltd.

to no longer allow undocumented immigrants to participate in the economy but it offered a residence permit to white illegals, provided they could prove that they had worked for six consecutive years. In 1996, Gümüş received notice that he did not meet the criteria and got ready to leave. When Gümüş collected the school reports of his sons in preparation of his forced return to Turkey, Anja Versnel got involved in the case and organized the support committee.

Gümüş first hit the news in April 1996. Amsterdam's municipal council, the mayor, and several parliamentarians spoke out on his behalf. Camera crews and journalists flocked to De Pijp to speak to Gümüş and his support committee. The tailor was not exactly a poster boy. His Dutch was basic and he clearly felt uncomfortable performing on camera. His wife was heavily veiled and shunned attention. Gümüş nevertheless came to personify the tragedy of what happens when the line between illegality and legality is drawn more sharply. Since the laws demarcated legitimate immigrants on the basis of the financial contributions that were made, it is not surprising that much of the discussion focused on Gümüş's small but successful tailor business and his paying of taxes and social charges. But although the law emphasized financial contributions, the discussions also focused explicitly on civil integration. His support group emphasized how much the Gümüş family was embedded in the neighborhood and focused especially on the Gümüş boys – one of the sons had been born in the Netherlands, the other had been raised there, and neither had ever been to Turkey (out of fear of not being able to return to the Netherlands). Amsterdam's mayor urged the State Secretary to not only look at the financial contributions that immigrants had made but also take into account the degree to which they are rooted and integrated (*ingeburgerd*) into Dutch society. Gümüş generated widespread support, but in the end the mobilization was unsuccessful. One parliamentary motion that proposed bending the rules to allow people like Gümüş to stay failed to achieve a majority by a small margin, as did another motion proposing keeping the rules in place while making an exception for Gümüş and his family.

While Gümüş relied on his supporters, other immigrants took recourse to dramatic and desperate measures. In 1998, a group of almost 130 immigrants claiming they were eligible for the amnesty for "white illegals" started a hunger strike in a church in The Hague. The church leaders had reviewed their files and certified that the immigrants did indeed qualify for a residence permit. The hunger strikes continued until the State Secretary agreed to again review the files case by case, even though the hunger strikers had initially insisted they wanted to negotiate collectively. The hunger strikers' efforts by and large failed. The State Secretary expressed his disappointment with the evidence after reviewing the hunger strikers' files and granted only 13 a permit.

Their actions nevertheless inspired others to go on hunger strikes as well. A group of Moroccan "white illegals" engaged in a hunger strike at the head office of KMAN. KMAN had been established after the spectacular, and largely successful, hunger strike of 1975. While the hunger strikers of 1975 were embedded in strong movement networks and caught the nation's attention, the hunger strikers of 1998 suffered in isolation. Not a single newspaper reported on the start of the hunger strike and attention remained scant throughout the protest. As one of the hunger strikers noted, whereas the hunger strikes of 1975 had inaugurated a broad movement for immigrant rights, those of 1998 illustrated the dearth of support from politicians and allies (Krikke 1999: 196).

These events mark a new episode in immigration politics. Movements against discrimination and for immigrant rights had been severely weakened in Amsterdam in the 1990s and 2000s (see Chapter 8) at the same time as public anxiety over the inflow of asylum seekers increased. Especially after the electoral rise and subsequent murder of Pim Fortuyn in 2002, politicians and administrators insisted that there were too many asylum seekers, that they were often making applications under false pretenses, and that the government should promptly deport rejected asylum seekers. New laws were implemented and massive investments were made to manage and reduce the inflow of asylum seekers. However, the number of asylum seekers did not decrease, nor did the number of deportations increase (Leerkes and Broeders 2010). While these new laws and measures did not remove undocumented immigrants, they did change how immigrants are distributed over society's spectrum of deservingness – legitimate to illegitimate – and how their claims are channeled and viewed.

This chapter examines how different groups of immigrants become visible in public debates and especially looks into the networks that produce different types of images and claims. The chapter's empirical argument is that there has been a divergence in asylum politics between two different kinds of groups. The first group consists of people who are strongly integrated into local communities and receive substantial support in their quest to reverse a negative decision on their application. This group not only receives support from their local communities but also from large and professional NGOs, which use individual cases to create niche openings for specific categories of claimants. A second group consists of rejected asylum seekers who do not conform to the idealized image of the integrated immigrant. This group long remained invisible but has come into public view through a series of mobilizations starting in 2011. This group is embedded in very different sets of relations and places from those in the first group and relies strongly on movement networks in cities, especially Amsterdam.

Personalizing Immigration Politics

Ever since Gümüş was deported, the official government line has been that mediatized mobilizations should never have their intended effect lest others feel encouraged to adopt the same method. But former ministers and state secretaries retrospectively concede that the mobilizations do have effects. They describe how mobilizations put pressure on them and force them to more carefully review files. As Hilbrand Nawijn, a former Minister of Immigration and director of the Immigration and Naturalization Service (IND),[1] suggests:

> When an alien is in the spotlight, he receives more attention at the department. When a case is covered in the newspaper, the file ends up on the minister's desk. Then you start looking: Has everything been carefully weighted? Have mistakes been made? This is by definition to an alien's advantage. (Cited in *de Volkskrant*, February 8, 2014)

Considering the power of mobilizations to disrupt what has been designed and presented as a fully closed system, government officials have developed a range of measures to prevent mobilizations from scaling up and becoming visible, like relocating hunger strikers to different detention centers, putting hunger strikers under permanent camera surveillance, or imprisoning them in isolation cells (*NRC Handelsblad*, February 13, 2004; *NRC Handelsblad*, August 2, 2005; *NRC Handelsblad*, August 16, 2013). These strategies for making grievances invisible are to an extent successful: the vast majority of the approximately1,000 hunger strikers per year are immigrants (according to estimates of the Johannes Wier foundation, cited in *NRC Handelsblad*, July 15, 2002), but only a handful of cases are reported in the Dutch media. Even when hunger strikers do succeed in reaching the media, their actions may be answered with disapproval or apathy if they fail to win the support of mayors or respected civil society organizations (*de Volkskrant*, February 13, 2007).

In this politics of visibility, government-funded NGOs responsible for accommodating and guiding asylum seekers aligned with the government when it came to radical actions like hunger strikes or occupations. They advised against hunger strikes and insisted that only silent diplomacy on an individual basis has legitimacy and a chance of success (*NRC Handelsblad*, February 13, 2004). This stood in contrast to the approach taken by the national human rights NGOs in France. There, as discussed in Chapter 10, NGOs embraced open contention as a means to enhance their access to and influence with government officials. While respecting the framework in which decisions were made, government-funded Dutch NGOs did try to find niche openings for specific groups of immigrants through lobbying and campaigns. The most influential and resourceful among these organizations included churches and the NGO Refugees Work (*Vluchtelingenwerk*) with a budget of €50 million, which has been covered in large part by lottery money and government subsidies (*De Telegraaf,* April 22, 2014). Refugees Work was founded in the late 1970s by volunteers of Amnesty International, churches, and support groups when the number of asylum seekers was in the hundreds. The drastic increase in the number of asylum seekers and the intensification of government policies have resulted in the organization transforming from a federation of grassroots collectives into a professional NGO (*NRC Handelsblad,* September 18, 1999). Due to its resources, close ties to the government, and its cooperation with churches, Refugees Work has become the central organization in policies related to asylum. While Refugees Work has an office in Amsterdam and frequently discusses campaigns with other resourceful organizations like Church in Action (a large Protestant NGO), Defense for Children, and the Foundation for Support to Undocumented Immigrants (LOS),[2] it is largely disconnected from the urban grassroots. Refugees Work and its partners especially focus on policy discrepancies and emphasize that resolving these discrepancies contributes to the policies' legitimacy and efficiency. For instance, the director of Refugees Work emphasized that the new Asylum Law of 2001 should start with a "clean sheet" to give the new law "some chance of success" (cited in *de Volkskrant,* March 23, 2001).

Refugees Work and its partners especially pleaded for a group of circa 26,000 immigrants who had applied before the 2001 Asylum Law but had been in procedures ever since. Together with film directors and broadcasting associations, Refugees Work developed a campaign called 26,000 Faces. The directors made short clips showing the dire living conditions of people in this group and the partners in the campaign plugged selected stories into the media. In response, Minister Rita Verdonk leaked several files to right-leaning media, *HP/De Tijd* and *De Telegraaf,* insinuating that the asylum seekers were lying to appear more deserving and noble than they really were. Verdonk had made a name for herself as the Netherlands's "Iron Lady" and seemed determined not to give in to the pressure. The following cabinet, however, did regularize the status of almost all of the 26,000 people in 2007.

These amnesties and arrangements were meant to resolve problems inherited from older policies that had allowed immigrants to pay taxes or make numerous appeals. The Asylum Law of 2001 not only provided ways to keep immigrants out of the country, but especially ensured that undocumented immigrants and asylum seekers could not integrate into Dutch institutions and communities. The law was designed to prevent situations where immigrants without legal residence could contribute to and use state services (as in the case of Gümüş and other "white illegals") or where immigrants could integrate into society while waiting for the decision on their application (as in the case of the 26,000 faces).

A fine-grained infrastructure for monitoring, registering, and secluding immigrants has been developed. One tangible expression of this development is that the state's administrative detention capacity increased from circa 1,000 units in 1999 to almost 4,000 units in 2007 (Leerkes and Broeders 2010: 835). While all these measures were formally introduced to facilitate the immigrants' expulsions, they failed to do just this; the actual number of deportations decreased from an estimated 12,000 in 1999 to an estimated 6,000 in 2007 (ibid.). While this system is ineffective when measured according to its deportation output, it does serve to sharpen the dividing line between citizens and undocumented immigrants. When the government fails to deport immigrants, they are confined to informality and illegality. Undocumented immigrants are expelled from Dutch society but stay within Dutch territory: they cannot work legally or use state services and they are often detained in administrative centers. All these measures contribute to the weakening of linkages between immigrants and Dutch nationals, making it increasingly unlikely for them to mobilize supporters and claim they are "rooted" in the Netherlands. While undocumented immigrants are persistently present and scrupulously monitored, they are simultaneously excluded and made invisible.

Sahar and Mauro: Personalizing Immigration Politics and Opening Niches

While the new and more restrictive laws deprive many immigrants of entitlements, they also create new borderline cases that arouse contention. These new cases mostly concern children who have been going to school and participating in local communities in anticipation of the final decision on their (or their parents') asylum application. While the claims of adult immigrants falling under the Asylum Law of 2001 have hardly been heard, claims about immigrant children have resounded loudly. These claims have a specific geography and logic: they are produced by local communities and articulate around individual cases. Time and again local communities and political supporters have argued that these children are so rooted in Dutch society that it would damage them, as well as their communities, if they were forced to return. Take, for instance, Sahar Hbrahimgel, a 14-year-old girl from Afghanistan who had come to the Netherlands at the age of four. Her local community of Sint Anna Parochie, in the peripheral province of Friesland, mobilized against her deportation, emphasizing that she was strongly rooted and a stellar student in the highest track of high school. Pressured by parliamentary debates and intense media coverage, the responsible minister, Geerd Leers of the Christian-Democrats, conceded that he wanted her to stay but was neither willing to change the general rules nor to make exceptions. The solution was then to amend the rules in such a way that Sahar's case could be accommodated: he decided that Afghan girls aged between 10 and 18 were eligible for a residence permit if they had been living in the Netherlands for more than eight years. In addition, the girls should be "Westernized" in the sense that they speak their mind freely. And, finally, this process of Westernization should not be used by their parents to exploit legal loopholes to remain in the Netherlands – the girls were eligible only if the parents did not unduly frustrate the families' residence permit applications.

The Angolan Mauro Manuel was another child asylum seeker who came under the national spotlight. His mother had sent him to the Netherlands in 2003 in search of a better life, but Mauro's request for asylum was rejected in 2007. As is typical in these cases, a terse and complex discussion between the agency responsible for enforcing immigration laws, the Immigration and Naturalisation Service (IND),[3] and a team of legal advisors followed. Mauro's foster parents won one court case but the IND successfully appealed the decision. Since the route to asylum appeared blocked, his Dutch foster parents wanted to adopt Mauro, but a judge refused on technical grounds and because Mauro had been in contact with his mother in Angola. Mauro's foster parents then organized an online petition, started a case at the European Court for Human Rights, and initiated a media campaign. Mauro appeared on prime-time talk shows and was on the cover of newspapers; he became a household name. While Sahar was praised for her exceptional school results, the emphasis in Mauro's case was on his utter normality. Mauro wrote an open letter to parliament, and published in Dutch newspapers, saying that he had "become a symbol for all young, unaccompanied asylum seekers in the Netherlands" but that this is not what he wanted; "I would much rather be a symbol of integration in Dutch society ... I want to celebrate Queen's Day every year and, as a footballer myself, I want the Dutch team to be champions" (cited in *The Guardian*, November 1, 2011). A picture of the young man with closed eyes and tears running down his face was published widely and went viral on social media.

Defense for Children helped organize a demonstration at parliament in The Hague and arranged buses for the local community of Oostrum, a small village in the peripheral province of Limburg where Mauro lived with his foster parents. In addition to emotional speeches by his football coach and Mauro himself, the demonstration involved a football match between Mauro's team and several supportive politicians. The event underlined just how integrated Mauro was: a protester carried the sign "Mauro is 100%NL" (in reference to the radio station that plays only music produced on Dutch soil). A Christian-Democratic politician said that it was Mauro's "personal achievement" to integrate into a tight-knit "Limburg community" and he called Mauro "a neat guy" and "the type of guy we'd all like to have here" (cited in *de Volkskrant*, September 24, 2011). Although a parliamentary majority expressed support for Mauro, Minister Gerd Leers refused to use his discretionary power to give him a residence permit, citing fears of creating a precedent. Although Minister Leers persisted in his refusal to grant asylum, a compromise was found in the form of a renewable study visa, which allowed Mauro to stay in the Netherlands for the duration of his studies.

As in Sahar's case, the minister's refusal to grant an individual exception in turn led to the creation of a new, more general rule. Mauro's case set in motion a new policy arrangement, the "children amnesty" (*kinderpardon*), which affords a residence permit to children (and their parents) who have been in the country for more than five years and are "rooted" (*geworteld*) in the Netherlands.[4] After reflecting on the situation, Gerd Leers stated he had been caught up in the "media war." He claimed that a ghost writer had authored Mauro's letter and that the iconic tears had been edited into Mauro's picture (cited in *de Volkskrant*, February 8, 2014). Another former Minister of Immigration, Rita Verdonk, blamed lawyers, celebrities, journalists, and politicians for pushing individual cases to create "a hurricane" in the media around exceptional immigrants while ignoring less mediagenic immigrants (ibid.).

Exactly because immigrants in the media are often portrayed as alien, self-interested, disingenuous or mendacious, it is essential for them and their supporters to carefully craft representations that help to shed stigmas. They must demonstrate that they are not free riders, poor, unassimilated, foreign, or extremist. They do not engage in a frontal critique on discriminatory policy regimes but instead attempt to demonstrate that the stigmas do not apply to them personally. When such idealized immigrants are victimized by the rules, administrators might be persuaded to revise the laws and regulations so that they deter and punish unwanted aliens without victimizing immigrants who take part in and contribute to the community. While de-stigmatization requires well-placed immigrants to distance themselves from the polluting attributes of unwanted immigrants, it also requires them to show that they conform to national values and stand to make an important contribution to the country. They must publicly demonstrate that they no longer have attachments to their sending countries and cultures and that their tastes, values, aspirations, and commitments align with those of nationals. Their hard work ethic, love of family, and civic engagement build upon core national values and reinvigorate the moral and economic life of the nation (Honig 2006).

Crafting these representations requires communities willing to collectively express their support and commit their specific expertise when it comes to lobbying and communication. Such communities can be found in cities, as the example of Gümüş attests, but it nevertheless seems that the focus on well-integrated individuals under threat of deportation moves immigrant rights activism from the metropolitan centers into the province. While cities, especially Amsterdam, historically provide fertile soil for immigrant rights mobilizations, villages and towns form the canvas for the media campaigns of individual immigrants like Sahar and Mauro. There are at least two reasons for this new geographical dimension to immigrant rights politics.

The first is that policies by the Dutch government have distributed asylum seekers, especially underage asylum seekers, all over the Netherlands as a matter of policy. The centers for asylum seekers (AZCs) are located throughout the Netherlands. These institutions house families seeking asylum and their children go to local schools and participate in local sport clubs. Sahar, for instance, lived in a trailer park that functioned as a center for asylum seekers but she also attended the local school. Children who come to the Netherlands without their parents, like Mauro, are placed in the care of Dutch families. Through these arrangements, thousands of children are placed in different localities throughout the Netherlands every year. The bonds between the children and their local communities grow deeper over time, creating a social base from which opposition to a possible deportation may eventually emerge. Opposition emerges as local communities resist the deportation of a child from their midst and as the media, NGOs, and politicians (from the opposition) make the child into the iconic victim of brutal and arbitrary policies. Very few immigrant children come to play this role, because the carrying capacity of the media is limited and most asylum seekers either achieve a positive outcome or resign themselves to their fate. NGOs and politicians also often try to achieve results through silent diplomacy, knowing that administrators are eager to prevent a mediatized struggle and are unlikely to give in once the struggle takes off. But in a few cases – those of Sahar and especially Mauro being the most prominent examples – foster families, local communities, and NGOs are desperate and confident enough to confront ministers and government policy directly. The policy to spread (underage) asylum seekers throughout the country and restrict their access to legal residency thus creates seeds of contention that may, under certain circumstances, result in open resistance.

A second reason has to do with the parameters set by the debate on immigration and immigrant integration. Media campaigns can only be successful if immigrants can credibly claim they fully belong to Dutch society and not to their sending countries. This requires specific types of performances: dark-skinned children who declare their love for the Netherlands in regional accents and are supported by all-white communities. The main players in these struggles are not movement organizers but provisory support committees composed of school teachers, football coaches, and neighbors who "avoid politics" by keeping their campaigns "close to home" (Eliasoph 1997). Instead of addressing the injustices inherent in policies or states in general terms, they emphasize that it is outrageous to tear loved and integrated immigrants out of their local communities. While NGOs and political parties based in big cities play important roles in these campaigns by providing consultation and capitalizing upon niches that open up, they leave the front stage to local communities who are best placed to argue that the immigrants are truly Dutch and undeserving of the hardship that befalls immigrants who fail to meet the policy's eligibility criteria.

"We Are Here!"

Most asylum seekers are not as mediagenic as Sahar or Mauro and cannot claim to be as "rooted" in local communities as they are. This is especially true for adult immigrants whose applications have been rejected. According to policy, these immigrants should leave the country soon after receiving a negative decision on their application but often they cannot be forced to do so. Some countries refuse to welcome back immigrants who do not want to return and no country of origin accepts undocumented returnees (Leerkes and Broeders 2010: 831). To pressure immigrants to leave, the government introduced a range of measures. Engbersen et al. (2006: 211) list some of the most important ones:

> [The Benefit Entitlement Act] came into force in July 1998 in order to exclude illegal immigrants from all public services (social security, health-care, housing and education). The Benefit Entitlement Act was preceded

by several other measures that affected the position of undocumented immigrants, such as tying social-fiscal numbers to a valid residency status (1991), the Marriages of Convenience Act of 1994, the Compulsory Identification Act of 1994, the Employment of Aliens Act of 1994 and the revised Aliens Act of 2001. (See also Van der Leun 2003)

Undocumented immigrants have always faced difficulties finding work and social protection, but these laws and their increasingly sophisticated enforcement exacerbated the difficulties of remaining in the legal and legitimate institutions of society. As noted above, this does not mean that asylum seekers disappear but it renders them invisible. They concentrate in "shadow places" (Leerkes et al. 2007) where it is easier to access informal work, engage in subsistence crime, and remain unidentifiable (Engbersen and Broeders 2009). Irregular immigrants thus have incentives to remain hidden and for a long time it indeed seemed as if rejected asylum seekers disappeared from the public's view.

However, this changed when a small group of Somali asylum seekers set up a protest camp in Ter Apel on November 29, 2011. Ter Apel is a small village on the northeastern periphery of the country, in a rural area very close to the German border, far away from where most immigrants and immigrant activists live. The reason a protest erupted here is that Ter Apel has a "removal center" where immigrants are registered upon arrival and kept until their deportation. Since the protesters could not be deported, they were removed from the center, a practice known as *klinkeren*, which means that they were put on the street. The police arrested the protesters, but a judge ruled that their detention had been unlawful given the lack of prospects for a (forced) return to Somalia. In December 2011, the protesters returned to Ter Apel, wrapped in layers of thick clothes and blankets protecting them against the blistering cold. They again set up tents at the center's entrance and unfurled banners ("We are humans, we need human rights"), demanding to be provided with food and shelter. In response to (the coverage of) the protests, the IND suggested a bureaucratic solution to which the protesters reluctantly agreed: they could submit another asylum application and would receive food and shelter pending the decision. A third camp was set up on May 8, 2012 by Iraqis, who were quickly followed by Somalis. This time the encampment grew to several hundred people and attracted activists from around the country, who set up organizations, created communication channels (though wifi and radio), and carried banners protesting against the state with slogans like "no person is illegal." The minister persuaded many of the asylum seekers to leave the camp with a promise of shelter for a month, but more than 100 asylum seekers and supporters stayed and were arrested (*Trouw*, May 24, 2012).

The encampments, the evictions, and the arrests attracted considerable attention from the media. For the first time the dire conditions of rejected yet undeportable asylum seekers hit the national news. The encampments also provided some tangible results. Help from local residents and activists in the form of food and blankets allowed the homeless asylum seekers to fulfill their basic needs and their occupation also provided them with a (still very weak) bargaining position to wrest (minimal) concessions from the minister and the IND.

From the perspective that we outline in this book, the protests at Ter Apel may appear anomalous; Ter Apel is a hamlet far removed from the urban centers where many immigrants live and much of the activism takes place. The only reason the protests took place in Ter Apel is that this is where refugees happened to find themselves when they were put on the streets. However, while early disturbances and small resistances sprout up everywhere, they tend to gravitate to places with richer contexts of mobilization. Whether small acts of resistance grow into larger, more sustained, and forceful campaigns depends on the presence of organizations and potential supporters that can harness a mobilization and relays that help to diffuse its messages and connect its components. While mobilizations for rejected yet undeportable asylum seekers started in Ter Apel, they took off in cities and especially in Amsterdam. Activists based in Amsterdam had attended the demonstrations in Ter Apel and invited the protesting asylum seekers to come to Amsterdam for a small demonstration, which would snowball into a long series of mobilizations. The small demonstration took the form of an encampment of around 15 people in Amsterdam's city center, next to a Protestant welfare center. After they were told to leave the premises of the Protestant welfare center, they moved to a square in Osdorp, in the western part of the city. While in Ter Apel the refugees and their supporters had been isolated, here the encampment served as a hub. Organizations that provide services to asylum seekers referred people they could not help to the camp. The camp also became a platform where different supporters and activists – veterans of the Occupy movement, Christians, Muslims, socialists, anarchists, and many people without clear ideological affinities – networked. The encampment grew rapidly as it attracted both refugees and activists.

Although the encampment was a hub of activity, the main players in asylum politics kept their distance from the mobilization. Refugees Work, LOS, and Amnesty did not openly and fully assist the mobilization because they had difficulty supporting the demand of the protesters to arrive at a comprehensive and collective solution. Whereas these organizations wanted to know about individual cases to see if they qualified for support (a strategy of stressing deservingness and exceptionalism), the asylum seekers insisted on operating as a collective and stressed universal rights. Although individual mosques and churches from the neighborhood did provide support to the encampment, the resourceful and influential Protestant NGO *Kerk in Actie* did not participate for much the same reason: the organization is opposed to tent camps. Given the absence of large and resourceful organizations committing support, the protesters relied mostly on pre-existing and emerging networks of informal groups and individuals without commitments to the government's procedures for accepting and treating immigrants.

The asylum seekers received massive attention and considerable support at their Osdorp encampment. An activist asylum seeker, explains the energy generated from the media and the mobilization: "You know in Osdorp ... people had energy to speak, go to the meetings, and so on. In Osdorp, the government came every day, TV channels came every day. Each day there were discussions, speeches" (personal interview). The asylum seekers and their supporters mobilized energetically, but at the same time the conditions in the camp became difficult to manage. Sleeping bags and clothes were damp. The influx of large numbers of destitute people speaking many different languages created communication and coordination problems. Some people screamed in their sleep or suffered from a lack of medication.

The expansion of the encampment and problems of order also created a pretext for the government to intervene. As he had done before with an Occupy encampment and a squatted social center, Mayor Eberhard van der Laan personally visited the encampment to ostentatiously express his concerns and to make clear that they should accept his offer because they would otherwise be arrested and handed over to the IND. Van der Laan's offer was to accommodate a total of 88 refugees, registered on November 15, 2012 (before the encampment grew to around 200 people), in 10 different locations for a period of 30 days, provided they would discuss their individual cases with Refugees Work. The asylum seekers did not agree and Van der Laan ordered the eviction of the encampment. Local activists blocking the entrance were removed by the riot police and 95 asylum seekers were arrested. However, the majority of protesting asylum seekers were not handed over to IND but put on the streets the same night. Images of refugees huddled together at a bus stop on a rainy night were circulated in the traditional and social media.

With the help of squatters, the asylum seekers occupied an abandoned church, dubbed the "Refugee Church." The group had fully seized upon the relational opportunities afforded by Amsterdam: Dutch supporters of the protesting immigrants had contacts with the media, squatters, a lobbying organization, mosques, and churches.

Each contact further down the relational chain helped to draw in new resources and extend the struggle. The asylum seekers and their supporters played music in a cultural center, joined meetings at the university, organized street protests, and reached out to the media. Through the various relays, their message was amplified and eventually reached the national media and the national parliament. Parliamentarians and national celebrities spent a night in the church and spoke out in support of the refugees. The group had consolidated and so had their message. Asylum seekers and activists converged around the "We are here!" slogan. As one of the refugee leaders[5] explains, "We don't have any relatives here, we don't know where we are going to go, we do not go back to our country because it is impossible. So here we are. If you want to help us, we are here. And if you don't want to help us, well, we are still here anyway" (personal interview). The slogan thus was meant to convey the basic message that the asylum seekers' presence had to be acknowledged and that the response to their presence reflected on Dutch society. The slogan also provided a collective frame to which all asylum seekers could connect regardless of their legal status. As one of the Dutch activists supporting the mobilization explained, "There are three basic principles to 'We are here!' We are together. Together you're more safe than when you're alone. And together we have the power to become visible, to demonstrate, to express, to stay. We are here means that we are together, that we are safe, and that we are visible" (personal interview). This is especially important given that the state's procedures were premised on individualization. In the case at hand, the mayor and organizations like Church in Action and Refugees Work also tried to convince the protesters that they were better off collaborating with the government on an individual basis. Leftist activists from various small organizations and informal collectives instead emphasized that the protesters should stick together as a group and make collective claims. Activists between the two different groups – compassionate activists (mostly Christians) working for Church in Action and Refugee Work versus radical leftists from anarchist, socialist, anti-imperialist, and squatter circles – were in constant struggle. For most asylum seekers in the We Are Here group individual strategies had been unsuccessful and they were convinced that they had to stick together to help each other and call attention to their plight. While the mayor, the NGOs, and the compassionate activists were pulling in the direction of individualized assistance and promised accommodation and a review of their asylum applications, the radical activists agreed to assist in squatting accommodations for the group as a whole.

The struggle between the strategies of individualization and collectivization continued after the asylum seekers had left the Refugee

Church after being given respite several times. With the help of squatters, they occupied an office building in New West, another office in the Center, and a set of houses in Old West. Unlike the owners of the Refugee Church, the owners of these buildings did not want to give respite to the refugees and used the anti-squatting ban (in effect since 2010; see Pruijt 2013) to remove the asylum seekers in a matter of weeks or months. Meanwhile, the mayor also made a more attractive offer. He agreed to accommodate registered asylum seekers together in one building for a period of six months. As they had no prospect of stable accommodation, a number of asylum seekers accepted the mayor's offer: they could stay in a former prison as a group on the condition that they would individually collaborate with the IND to achieve a final decision on their application. Asylum seekers not qualifying for this accommodation were resigned to living in squatted accommodation, which quickly became uninhabitable. The conditions in a squat dubbed the "Refugee Garage," remotely located in Amsterdam South East, became acutely dangerous as asylum seekers and others with no other place to go packed in together, resulting in high stress levels, fights, harassment, psychoses, and thefts. A journalist visiting the "Refugee Garage" describes what he found:

> A smelly, filthy place. Around a hundred men, most of them from Sudan, Eritrea, Somalia, and Ethiopia. Apathetic people, confused people, desperate people. One grabbed my arm and wanted to tell his refugee story, another pointed at wet spots in the ceiling. A young guy wanted to sell me a belt. Somewhere a person in a sleeping bag burped, outside on the parking deck were two people on stretchers. I was asked if I had an iPhone, or money or food. Somebody told about fights for food. (*NRC Handelsblad,* June 20, 2014)

This government's strategy thus divided the group among different locations and subjected the protesters to different regimes of repression and cooptation. Van der Laan publicly reprimanded the activists and sharply denounced political activism: "Here is a mayor [Van der Laan is speaking of himself in the third person] who wants to do everything for the refugees that can be done. But I will also do what I can to fight political activism. Your purpose is to contest Dutch laws, and that's the difference between you and me."[6]

Van der Laan and the State Secretary later expressed their disappointment about the asylum seekers in the former prison and decided to remove them on the grounds that they had not fully cooperated, something that was contested by the volunteers (of the compassionate group) who had assisted the refugees in the prison (Vrijwilligers

Vluchthaven 2014). Even though public attention rapidly diminished, disagreements among exhausted activists and desperate refugees were widely covered in the media and communicated via blogs. Christian and Muslim volunteers expressed their anger at leftists for using the asylum seekers for their own radical campaigns, while leftists blamed especially the Christians for speaking on the asylum seekers' behalf and cooperating with the authorities to remove them. What most stands out is the bitterness, desperation, and exhaustion of the volunteers as well as asylum seekers. When the mobilization had momentum and was in the public eye it was possible to manage tensions, but the amount of suffering and stress became unbearable as the group was split up and moved around. The originally tight-knit and energetic group of protesters had been worn out, split up, and relegated to remote locations. While the mayor and the State Secretary were initially forced to acknowledge and deal with the asylum seekers, they now could deal with different groups and specify the conditions for negotiation and assistance.

Conclusions

Putting the findings of this chapter in the context of earlier chapters on Amsterdam, we can discern three stages in the dynamics of struggles over the rights of (undocumented) immigrants. In the first period running from the 1970s into the 1980s, activism for undocumented immigrants was very much embedded in the urban grassroots; social movement organizations involved in a range of struggles also mobilized around immigrants under threat of deportation, like the 182 Moroccan hunger strikers discussed in Chapter 5. These campaigns were carried out by immigrant rights activists but they were embedded in broader struggles around equality and self-determination.

The second period commenced in the 1990s and continued into the 2000s when large-scale NGOs like Refugees Work became the main actors in campaigns around immigrants under threat of deportation. These organizations are intertwined with the government, do not have strong ties to social movement organizations (which are, in any case, severely weakened – see Chapter 8), mobilize exclusively within their own sector (i.e. asylum seekers), and design their campaigns to be effective in the national media. The concentration of power in a few major players is not only or primarily a consequence of these actors' strategies. A first structural cause is that the growing influx of asylum seekers in the 1990s and massive government investments have made detention, accommodation, and management into a big industry where some major, well-funded, professional NGOs crowd out others. A second structural cause is the dissolution of Amsterdam's movement milieu, which has disabled movement organizations embedded in the urban grassroots from initiating and coordinating large-scale campaigns.

The third phase started around 2010 and is characterized by a sharp divergence between two types of mobilizations. On the one hand, there are mobilizations involving local communities seeking media and political attention for individual immigrants who are under the threat of deportation. While in earlier periods struggles around these issues had focused on groups (like the 182 Moroccans or the 26,000 faces), these campaigns focus on individuals and specifically children. Although these struggles are taking place in, and are oriented to, the media, they are also firmly embedded in local communities, mostly in small towns and villages. "Rootedness" has become both a moral and legal crite- rion for inclusion and these local communities help to communicate the message that immigrants under threat of deportation are strongly rooted in Dutch society (see also Duyvendak 2011). On the other hand, there are collective struggles by immigrants who have been expelled from mainstream Dutch society. Their applications have been rejected and the government refuses to provide them with shelter or food. They are expected to leave and therefore cannot legally work, rent a house, claim benefits, enjoy healthcare, or study. In response to denial of their presence, these immigrants claim "We are here!" and cobble together a survival strategy to redeem their status as a rights-bearing subject, and in the distant hope of receiving formal recognition in the form of a residence permit. While personalized campaigns rely on intimate pictures of individual children rooted in small-town communities, the campaigns of the We Are Here group revolve around collective mobili- zations and rely on activist networks based in Amsterdam.

In sum, this chapter has examined the divergence of different types of immigrant rights activism. It shows that different types of coali- tions emerged and that they have different spatial underpinnings. Mobilizations in favor of individual immigrants with relatively favorable prospects rely on the support of local communities and professional NGOs. While these mobilizations may be partly coordinated from cities, they are not embedded in urban grassroots networks. Professional NGOs play important roles in these mobilization by focusing attention on individual cases but local communities, especially in small towns, have been particularly important in arguing that the generic image of the alien and parasitic asylum seeker does not apply to the well-integrated and highly regarded immigrant in their midst. The collective strategies by rejected asylum seekers are underwritten by very different types of networks. They cling together to cope with a collectively experienced expulsion from the official mainstream of Dutch society. Their mobilizations center on Amsterdam where they can call upon residual movement networks (especially squatters) and a relatively forthcoming civil society (of compassionate Christians and concerned individuals).

Beyond the specifics of mobilization networks, the chapter shows that contention surfaces even in a hostile discursive climate and a context of massive investments in managing immigrant flows. Our argument is not that the increasingly restrictive and repressive policies are inconsequential. They have had the (intended) effect of making life unbearable for many undocumented immigrants. However, these policies, too, generate borderline cases of immigrants who do not meet formal requirements yet can count on a lot of support from their communities. Moreover, even groups lacking such support do not disappear, often because they simply cannot be deported. Since it has become increasingly difficult for these immigrants to lead a life in the shadows, at least a number of them have taken to the streets to protest their treatment. Their mobilizations provide the asylum seekers with a lot of attention but rather minimal power – they can wrest concessions like temporary shelter or food in return for their invisibility.

12

Conclusion

Sparks into Wildfires

If scholars attend to the geographically uneven development of social movements at all, they often consider local, regional, and national differences as so many variations on the same theme. Upon this understanding, global movements adapt and respond to specific local, regional, and national conditions.[1] We propose to look the other way round. We consider movements as complex assemblages emerging from local interactions. We consequently examine the local bases from which movements do or don't emerge. Whether and how marginalized or stigmatized groups organize and raise their voice depends in part, perhaps even in large part, on the specific conditions they find in their immediate vicinity. It is for this reason that social movement scholars and not just urban scholars should be attentive to the local: it is a crucial site for the mechanisms through which movements form, disband, transform, or fail to form in the first place. By zooming in on the relational mechanisms in cities, we can show some (though by no means all) mechanisms through which grievances are created, articulated, relayed, and – ultimately – broadcast to the public at large. This conclusion first recounts how urban environments provide budding immigrant rights activists with the relational resources to transform small acts of resistance into sustained mobilizations. The second section discusses why some urban environments are more conducive to social movements than others. The third section argues that the growing importance of online mobilizations reinforces rather than negates

Cities and Social Movements: Immigrant Rights Activism in the United States, France, and the Netherlands, 1970–2015, First Edition. Walter J. Nicholls and Justus Uitermark.
© 2017 John Wiley & Sons, Ltd. Published 2017 by John Wiley & Sons, Ltd.

the importance of city-based movement networks. Finally, the chapter concludes by arguing how a geographically sensitive analysis can help to uncover both the micro-mechanisms and macro-patterns of social movement evolution.

The Transgression of Boundaries and the Urban Grassroots

In recent years, the line between legitimate and illegitimate immigrants has been accentuated through a multitude of enforcement practices distributed to and enacted by local state officials and professionals like doctors, teachers, and police officers. The production of illegality has been displaced from border enforcement to local police, state officials, universities, charitable organizations, and so on. While governments use the localization of immigration control to create a hermetically closed system, the engagement of a multitude of stakeholders also increases potential points of conflict. The attempts to confine unwanted immigrants in prophylactic spaces (Sennett 1994: 228) and harness their illegality through the multiplication of enforcement practices may have deterred some prospective immigrants they have also triggered countless attempts to challenge the line between insiders and outsiders. As immigrants established families and entered into relationships in schools, in workplaces, and in neighborhoods, they also began to challenge their invisibility and illegitimacy as political subjects and protested deportations and other restrictive immigration policies. Through appeals to human rights and family rights (Joppke 1998), and with the assistance of local sympathizers, immigrants transgressed boundaries in everyday life and destabilized divisions between insiders and outsiders.

This book has addressed these conflicts over the boundaries of the national community by attending to their local roots. Wherever the division between insiders and outsiders is reinforced, there is the possibility of transgression. As illegality becomes locally constituted and enforced, this is also where it is circumvented, comprised, or contested outright. Although social movement theory's mainstay assumption that grievances by themselves do not produce mobilization is correct, this does not mean that grievances are irrelevant altogether. Grievances spark resistances, however small or seemingly insignificant. For instance, raids on undocumented immigrants or deportations of rejected asylum seekers can generate anxiety and anger not only among their intended targets but also among friends, neighbors, and families witnessing the operation. Most of the time the resistances against immigration regimes remain invisible, small, and localized, but occasionally they snowball into large-scale mobilizations that challenge immigration regimes. Whether sparks turn into fires depends in significant part on how local networks are wired: grievances are likelier to set in motion chain reactions where dense and complex ties among activists can serve to transmit and amplify grievances. A geographical perspective therefore provides a strategic point of entry into the mechanisms through which resistances remain confined to localities or grow into sustained mobilizations.

Sustained mobilizations, first of all, require a critical mass. In the case of immigrants, such a critical mass is found in specific places: immigrants disproportionately reside in central cities and adjacent municipalities. This may seem trivial but it should be noted that such concentrations in cities illustrate the incapacity of states to channel immigrant flows by keeping immigrants out or isolating them. Our cases show how governments have attempted to incorporate immigrants into specific regimes and spaces outside of the national polity. In the United States in the postwar period, the Bracero Program channeled immigrants away from large urban centers with a relatively strong union presence and into agricultural regions where they came under the discretionary power of employers. France also developed differentiated rights regimes for immigrants and housed them in hostels, where they were put under the surveillance of veterans of colonial armies. The Netherlands similarly followed a strategy of separation by enveloping immigrants in a tutelary regime. Although the immigrants and regimes differed across these cases, they have in common that governments sought to extract labor from immigrants while extricating them from the body politic. These regimes of separation start showing cracks when immigrants break out of the confines of the spaces designated for them. Immigrants gravitate to cities, carving out niches for their communities and negotiating their incorporation into national societies in everyday city life. It would be a mistake to think that the presence of sizeable groups of immigrants is by itself a cause for mobilizations, but such a presence does certainly create conditions that might be seized upon. The concentrated presence of specific groups allows economies of size and scope to develop. The operation of various associations, periodicals, social centers, and so on requires a constituency and the numerical presence of minority populations provides opportunities to reach critical thresholds. This is especially true for radical activists who – at least initially – will have difficulty finding a critical mass to support their periodicals, maintain their accommodation, or attend their demonstrations. A concentrated critical mass of marginalized immigrants therefore facilitates the emergence of social infrastructure needed to transform an aggregate of individuals into relatively bounded groups. Without "groupness," it would be difficult for precarious immigrants to overcome the major barriers facing them and launch the high-risk battles recounted in this book.

Sustained mobilizations further require wide support from diverse constituents. We have seen over and over that immigrant activists do not mobilize only by themselves or for themselves. Squatters, labor union activists, anti-fascists, Christian humanitarians, and many others identify for various reasons with immigrants' cause and join or even initiate protests against their illegalization. These connections among different types of activism have traditionally received scant attention in the literature, which tends to focus on individual movements or, at most, considers waves of contention that are induced by specific macro-conditions (Koopmans 1993; Tarrow 1998). By focusing on the places of activism, we bring out something that may be – and indeed should be – trivial yet is structurally overlooked: the intense interactions between activists mobilizing around different causes and issues. While news reports and academic studies may make it seem as if it is possible to isolate specific movements – the peace movement, the immigrant rights movement, the squatter movement, and so on – in the daily practice of organizers and activists these are often just different moments in a continuous process of constructing counterhegemonic spaces. The example of Abdou Menebhi, discussed in Chapter 5 on Amsterdam's burgeoning movement space, illustrates well how indigenous activist networks help to accelerate and amplify immigrant protests. He initially came to the Netherlands on a one-off mission to disrupt the inaugural meeting of the *Amicales*, but Amsterdam-based activists convinced him to move to the Netherlands and cast him as a pivotal figure in Amsterdam's vibrant activist environment. Even before he had learned to speak Dutch or English Menebhi had developed strong relations with a range of activists including squatters, parishioners, and students, engaged in a romantic relationship with a community worker who had been campaigning for guest workers, and founded an organization whose goal was to mobilize and represent the "Moroccan masses." This example illustrates how activist networks can help to catalyze and amplify individual efforts and campaigns. Immigrant activists not only see their efforts reinforced by pre-existing activist networks but also further contribute to the political vibrancy of cities. All three cases show how activists coming from oppressive and authoritarian environments had cultivated radical ideas and practices of self-organization before their arrival in Los Angeles, Paris, and Amsterdam. Mobilizing underground on a syndicalist basis was a prerequisite for survival in their countries of origin but also was an innovative and powerful – if not always efficient and tactful – impetus to the movements they came to be involved in. We thus observe that immigrant rights activism is inseparable from other types of mobilizations. Just like economic agglomerations, activist agglomerations are characterized by economies of scale and positive externalities.

Agglomerations allow activists to specialize in niches like distinct groups or issues while at the same time providing opportunities for networking across different clusters. For instance, Los Angeles does not only have the scale necessary to sustain an organization for day laborers but also provides a wide range of potential allies and therefore opportunities to participate in mobilizations that transcend the particular interests of day laborers.

Lastly, mobilizations remain fairly inconsequential if they stay confined within specific localities. Agglomerations not only allow a highly developed division of labor within localities but also facilitate the concentration of resources required to coordinate extensive networks. It is for this reason that we emphasized that contentious urban areas in Los Angeles, Paris, and Amsterdam were not only localized counter-hegemonic spaces but also hubs in movements extending across local and national boundaries. MTA in France and KMAN in the Netherlands provide illustrative examples. The founders established these organizations in urban cores where they could benefit from the presence of resourceful and experienced sympathizers but subsequently they created offshoots in other parts of the city and the country. The organizations and their allies extended their mobilizations as they teamed up with leaders in other urban cores to organize Europe-wide campaigns for immigrant rights. The Not One More campaign in the United States illustrates the ongoing relevance of geographical proximity within geographically extensive campaigns. The Not One More campaign is based on a bold and radical premise: deportations are illegitimate and should be ended immediately. The campaign also involves high-risk direct actions, including blocking buses carrying deportees, hunger strikes, and sit-ins. Conceiving and initiating a campaign of this kind – with radical messages and radical actions – requires strong ties that are shaped through repeated interactions. The Not One More campaign emerged from activist networks that had been growing and consolidating for decades. The campaign was conceived by diverse yet proximate activists concentrating in urban cores (in Chicago and especially Los Angeles) and spiraled outwards to regional peripheries and secondary cities. The campaign also quickly engulfed (smaller yet tightly connected) activist clusters that had been forming in more peripheral locations, with direct actions in the name of Not One More taking place in cities like Dallas, Phoenix, Houston, and San Diego. Although the Not One More campaign involves new modes of communication – notably Twitter and Facebook – it exhibits the same patterns we have observed in other and earlier cases: their concentration in movement hubs enables organizers to mobilize a critical mass in the early stages of the campaign, generate the collective creativity and zeal to develop radical demands, and coordinate geographically diffuse direct actions carried out in the name of the campaign.

In sum, social movements are constituted through specific mechanisms – developing counterpublics, establishing coalitions, extending networks – that require specific relational environments. The cities that are central to our inquiry helped to cultivate the roots of resistance and nurture them into sustained mobilizations. While we studied the immigrant rights movements, we believe that other movements, too, have these sorts of spatial underpinnings. The squatting movement, the feminist movement, and the labor movement, to name a few examples, also have specific geographies that, to a fairly large extent, overlap with the movements discussed in this book, if only because these movements depend on one other in the creation of counterhegemonic spaces. Cities were the pinnacles of all these movements as cities offered a conducive environment for transforming sparks of resistance into wildfires of contention.

Considering the local roots of social movements makes us see urban processes in a new light. For instance, the process of gentrification is not simply about changes in the class composition of specific areas, it is also about the possibilities for challenging the status quo more generally. While gentrification has become a global urban strategy, researchers have mostly analyzed the process and the resistance against it in historical working-class districts just outside the city center. These areas have provided a rich tapestry of activism and were hotbeds for many of the struggles analyzed in this book. Their central location, low housing costs, high diversity, and high levels of tolerance provided the ideal conditions for the emergence of contentious ideas and practices. The historical importance of these neighborhoods in cultivating contentious practices and ideas goes a long way toward explaining why activists and scholars have devoted so much attention to these areas. This is where alternative futures were not only envisaged but also organizationally pursued and prefigured. The changes in these very specific areas brought about by gentrification thus close down opportunities for social change way beyond the parts of the housing stock most immediately at stake. Generations of government programs have sought to tame these neighborhoods and coopt challengers with mixed success. Gentrification, however, appears particularly effective in weeding out the types of contention studied in this book. Many of these neighborhoods continue to be at the cutting edge with respect to lifestyle or identity politics, but they have lost much of their importance with respect to working-class or immigrant rights struggles for the simple reason that they are no longer accessible to groups without a lot of capital and high incomes.

As gentrification reconfigures these areas, an urgent question is whether other types of spaces will become crucibles of social change. In this respect, a number of scholars have convincingly argued that suburbs are no longer, if they ever were, pinnacles of social order or conservatism (Hamel and Keil 2015). Others have pointed to the significance of rural areas as the origin of revolutionary insurrections (Merrifield 2011: 107). Yet others look at the worldwide web as a site for cultivating radical practices and projecting alternative futures. While all these various spaces contain within them the seeds of (progressive or regressive) radical change, we would suggest that the gentrification of historical and central districts of metropolises forecloses opportunities for radical change by relegating stigmatized and deprived groups to the urban peripheries where they are less visible, more dispersed, have less social and political infrastructure, and fewer chances of connecting and coordinating different types of struggles. Other spaces certainly matter but we would suggest that the rich relations and infrastructures within central districts have provided enabling environments for harnessing the political energies of marginalized populations like the precarious immigrants analyzed in this book.

Weeding the Local Seeds of Contention

While the social movements we studied always had their roots in cities, not all cities are always conducive to movements. On the contrary, our analyses have shown that, just as many conditions and mechanisms for sustained mobilizations can be found in the urban grassroots, so too can the conditions and mechanisms undermining mobilizations. For instance, concentration does not equal agglomeration: proximity can also increase competition for a common pool of resources (recruits, money, influence, etc.) that drain activist trust and goodwill. The case of Paris provides one example: from the late 1990s onwards the many different *collectifs des sans papier* produced a cacophony of claims and their collective efficacy suffered from strained relations among activists. The infighting among the many *collectifs des sans papier* in the Paris region illustrates that proximity and diversity can erode collective efficacy, creating a situation where the power of a movement in the city is less than the sum of its parts. This is just one example that illustrates how certain factors may precipitate mobilizations but never determine them. Movement organizers can intelligently use even the smallest niches or digress into infighting even under the most favorable of conditions. Chance and contingency are always at play. This is also what many of our interlocutors emphasized: they talk about how they were unwittingly drawn into campaigns or how they accidently stumbled upon people who would become their comrades. However, although movements are always the underdetermined and complex outcome of contingent interactions, they are far from random: some places are much more important in fostering contention and driving mobilizations than others. Finding out why, how, and when cities realize their potential to bring forth powerful movements has been this book's key challenge.

While we acknowledge that a range of factors can stifle resistances and undermine mobilizations, we have especially devoted attention to the role of governments in either suppressing or reinforcing social movements. Contentious urban areas represent threats to a government's monopoly of physical violence and the legitimacy of its rule. These areas are counterspaces where established norms and values have been rendered problematic and where alternative visions gain ground. On the one hand, the threats emanating from these areas are a cause for alarm to authorities, especially when contentious urbanites – like *jihadi* or anarchist extremists – reject the very foundations of the liberal state. States generally respond to these threats by increasing surveillance and repression in an effort to eradicate threats before challengers develop substantial organizational capacity. On the other hand, these contentious areas represent opportunities. The informal and formal organizations within them are potential bridges to groups that are out of reach to the state. The leaders and spokespersons representing marginalized and discontented groups are potential intermediaries. By incorporating them into governance structures, governments can rewire networks in civil society in such a way that movement organizations and representatives come to serve rather than challenge the status quo. Giving the governmentality approach a relational twist, we have investigated how governments attempt to rewire relationships so that civil society associations serve as an extension rather than a counterforce to the government. Their proximity to civil society organizations also makes it easier for local governments to extend their influence into local civil societies through regulations, subsidies, and consultations. Such control is especially effective when it is exercised by local governments but backed by the central state. France provides one example where decentralization precipitated tightening controls over civil society. In the 1990s, funding decisions were decentralized from the central state to department-level prefects directly appointed by the Minister of the Interior, the ministry charged with immigration policies. This meant that critical civil society organizations faced a difficult choice. Either they would forgo subsidies and lose out to more complacent civil society organizations benefiting from state subsidies or they would have to appease the local administrators and play by their rules. Although critical civil society organizations still found niches, their room for maneuver narrowed as local governments administered funding schemes. While critical civil society organizations may initially comply with funding demands for purely strategic reasons, over time their organizational rationalities change as they adopt vocabularies, time frames, and priorities set by the government. When government power is wired into the local grassroots, criticism remains confined and a strong coalition among critical civil society organizations is unlikely to emerge.

More generally, we observe a seesaw pattern of contention and control. Governments target the most contentious areas with a range of measures (from repression to cooption) and meanwhile other – previously pacified – areas start to show cracks in the maintenance of social order. In European cities like Amsterdam and Paris, central urban areas were hotbeds of contention in the 1960s, 1970s, and early 1980s. While native families had moved out of these areas, a new generation of urbanites as well as immigrants moved in. These areas provided an extensive infrastructure of cafeterias, social centers, bookstores, and university classrooms where new social movements mushroomed. They also provided points of contact where native activists could come into contact with immigrants. When these areas had been largely pacified (because of targeted government action as well as other reasons, like gentrification and loss of momentum), contention emerged at the urban edges as defiant and radical groups challenged the state in suburbs that had epitomized order and harmony in the immediate postwar period. Whereas before anti-imperialist militants based in central areas challenged state authority, now challenges emanated from the suburbs where religious fundamentalists and diffuse groups of youth signified the incapacity of the state to legitimately and effectively incorporate all denizens.

While Amsterdam and Paris show significant similarities, the dialectic of contention and control played out differently in Los Angeles, especially after the 1980s. The pattern of contention was similar in Los Angeles to that of its European counterparts in the 1970s: central urban areas where new immigrant groups concentrated became incubators for budding immigrant rights movements. East Los Angeles, in particular, was a concentration of activism. What Harlem was for the African American renaissance, East Los Angeles was for the Chicano movement. Organizations, periodicals, universities, and social venues provided a counterhegemonic space where people of Latino descent reinterpreted their identity and relation to the American mainstream. In response to the threats and opportunities afforded by this vibrancy, the government extended its reach into East Los Angeles and managed to rewire relations so that civil society became an extension of government instead of a counterforce. However, Los Angeles diverged from Amsterdam and

Paris in the 1980s. The extraordinary statist measures taken by successive French and Dutch governments stand in contrast to the laissez-faire approach taken by governments in the United States (Bloemraad 2006). Whereas France and the Netherlands constructed sophisticated institutional and discursive apparatuses to channel the political integration of immigrants, the United States partially dismantled the urban-based programs that had once governed associational life in large cities. The national rollback of the state in the 1980s reduced the local government's cooptative capacity over new immigrant populations. Central Los Angeles became a powerful relational incubator in the 1980s as academics, labor activists, and newly arriving dissident immigrants furnished new relations and reinvigorated the immigrant rights movement. The relatively weak presence of the state in these areas and sectors meant that radical activists could carve out a space. After activists had extended and consolidated their relations, they engaged directly with the state, but their powerful networks allowed them to do so on their own terms. Whereas immigrant organizations in Amsterdam and Paris had become disgruntled yet complacent service providers on behalf of the state, immigrant organizations in Los Angeles could design and deliver services – especially worker centers – in ways that strengthened their activist networks.

As these divergent trajectories illustrate, the processes through which contention emerges and wanes are never identical; the nature of the challenges and the nature of the responses differ significantly between periods. But there are nevertheless significant parallels: contention emerges in territories where states are weak and states attempt to build up capacity in territories where contention is strong.[2]

Contrasting Trajectories

Our cases show how different sets of factors condition the trajectories of movements within specific localities. Amsterdam in the 1990s demonstrates how previously energetic movement organizations can become confined in specific sectors and territories. Amsterdam's activist momentum of the 1980s had withered in the 1990s and the government intervened deeply in the urban grassroots, channeling former and potential activists into elaborate governance structures and acting swiftly on new disruptions emanating from, for example, suspected Muslim radicals. While gentrification of the nineteenth-century neighborhoods encircling the historical center helped to tame these neighborhoods, civil society generally came to function as an extension of the government rather than as a counterforce as immigrant organizations increasingly focused on government-identified problems and participated in government-dominated platforms. However, the local trap (Purcell 2006) is no necessity. Local governments can absorb contention and circumscribe claims but they can also serve as launchpads. Los Angeles provides perhaps the clearest example. Local movement organizations first mobilized outside and against city elites but eventually succeeded in electing an activist from their ranks – unionist Antonio Villaraigosa – to the mayoral office. While other mayors mobilized vigorously against unregulated immigration, Villaraigosa became one of the figureheads in the United States's immigrant rights movement and spoke out strongly against anti-immigration measures. Struggles around undocumented immigrants in the Netherlands provide an example of the critical role that local administrations play in confining or amplifying mobilizations. Undocumented immigrants who came into the spotlight of the national media invariably are backed by mayors and local governments who reject their roles in facilitating deportations and instead become ambassadors in campaigns for individual exemptions or general amnesties. Los Angeles in the 1990s represents a case where a range of favorable conditions worked together to provide a particularly conducive environment. As immigration from Latin America continued and government restrictions on immigration intensified, activists from a range of sectors worked in close proximity. In the absence of an intrusive and resourceful state, they could create a counterhegemonic space where radical discourses and practices could flourish. While these activists had their roots in specific neighborhoods within Los Angeles, they extended their networks well beyond the city as they fostered ties with activist clusters in other major cities. Here we see how activists formed specialized clusters, developed connections across those clusters, and used their collective capabilities to develop and coordinate national campaigns.

Conclusions

Assessing the development of the literature on social movements since the 1990s, James Jasper argued that "if there has been a trend in recent theories of protest, it has been toward the micro rather than the macro, and toward interpretive and cultural rather than materialist approaches" (2014: 9–10). This has been a welcome development but it also raises important questions, as Jasper acknowledges: "How can we acknowledge the felt experience of participants without losing the insights of the structural school? How can we trace the effects of global capitalism or neo-imperialist states at the level of individuals and their interactions?" (ibid.: 10). This book tries to give some part of the answer by developing two propositions.

The first proposition is that states and other dominant forces cause grievances and that these grievances spark resistance. While this may seem trivial to activists, social movement scholars have done much to relativize the importance of grievances by stressing framing and other processes of signification. We have suggested that the extension and consolidation of deportation regimes (Kalir and Wissink 2016) has severe repercussions for immigrants who are labeled as illegal, undeserving, and unwanted. Policies aimed at banishing these groups of immigrants have created "resisting residues": people who are stripped of their rights yet remain in the country. These people do not necessarily rebel (most do not) but there is always the possibility that they will. While structural processes – like the hardening of deportation regimes – do not determine the extent or shape of protest, they do set the parameters and generate seeds of resistance that may or may not grow into larger mobilizations.

The second proposition is that we can understand how local sparks of resistance develop into wildfires by considering the networks through which grievances are transmitted and expressed. While structural conditions – like grievances, movement constituencies, the cooptative capacity of the state, and so on – are important, this is only because activists act on them. Our strategy has therefore been to chart the chains of relations through which activists do or do not transform seeds of conflict into sustained mobilizations. While recent literature has welcomingly focused on the micro-interactions that constitute the ground zero of social movements, we are especially interested in how, when, and why these micro-interactions amalgamate into sustained mobilizations. Following recent theorizing on networks, we argue that the relational contexts are key to understanding how grievances do or do not spark mobilizations. Outsiders who are especially stigmatized need relations to assess resources and build campaigns that extend beyond their individual lifeworlds. We have seen that – under the right conditions – the city is a platform to articulate rights claims that extend way beyond the local level. The intense networking processes taking place in vibrant social movement hubs are place-based yet drive national and even international mobilizations. If we want to understand how movements gain or lose power in the national or international arena, examining their local bases and relations is a promising avenue of investigation. It is for these reasons that unpacking the geography of social movements is more than a mapping exercise: it allows us to open the black box of movement evolution and understand what enables seemingly powerless and excluded groups to claim their rights.

Notes

Chapter 3

1 LULAC was one of the first and most prominent Latino organizations of the time. It was created in Texas in 1929.
2 *Centro de Acción Social Autónomo.*

Chapter 4

1 *Fonds d'Action Sociale pour les Travailleurs Immigrés et Leur Familles.*
2 *Société Nationale de Construction de Logements pour les Travailleurs.*
3 *Amicale des Algériens en Europe.*
4 *Mouvement des Travailleurs Arabes.*
5 Respectively, *Association des Marocains en France, Union des Travailleurs Immigrés Tunisiens, Mouvement des Travailleurs Mauriciens,* and *Associations des Travailleurs Turcs.*
6 Respectively, *Ligue de Droits de l'Homme, Mouvement contre le Racisme et l'Antisémitisme et pour l'Amitié entre les Peuples, Fédération des Associations de Soutien aux Travailleurs Immigrés, Comité Inter-mouvements auprès des Évacués,* and *Groupe d'Information et de Soutien des Immigrés.*
7 *Comité de Défense de la Vie et des Droits des Travailleurs Immigrés.*
8 Respectively, *Association des Travailleurs Maghrébins de France, Associations des Tunisiens en France, Fédération des Tunisiens pour une Citoyenneté des Deux Rives,* and *L'Assemblée Citoyenne des Originaires de Turquie.*
9 As President Mitterrand faced an economic downturn and plummeting levels of public support for the government's early policies, his government initiated what many observers have called the "Great U-Turn." This consisted of deregulating markets, privatizing publicly held firms, embracing a

Cities and Social Movements: Immigrant Rights Activism in the United States, France, and the Netherlands, 1970–2015, First Edition. Walter J. Nicholls and Justus Uitermark.
© 2017 John Wiley & Sons, Ltd. Published 2017 by John Wiley & Sons, Ltd.

"law and order" position on security issues, and moving to the right on immigration issues (Hayward and Wright 2002).

10 The *Beur* identity would be equivalent to the Chicano identity in the United States.

Chapter 5

1 http://bureaudehelling.nl/artikel/andr-e-van-es-je-moet-het-moeilijke-gesprek-aan-willen-gaan
2 http://deduif.home.xs4all.nl/basisgem/toennu/bas20jr.htm#BBN
3 Ibid.
4 *Kommittee Marokkaanse Arbeiders Nederland.*
5 *Wet Arbeid Buitenlandse Werknemers.*
6 *Stichting Welzijn Buitenlandse Werknemers.*
7 *Association des Moroccans en France.*
8 A study in 1981 counted 9,000 squatters (Van der Raad, cited in Pruijt 2003: 139); a study in 1983 counted 20,000 squatters (Draaisma and van Hoogstraten 1983).
9 *Buitenlandse Arbeiders Kollektief.*

Chapter 6

1 Many explanations of CASA's demise focus on splits over ideology and police repression (Muñoz 1989; Garcia 2002; Pulido 2006). These factors played important roles in limiting growth but they cannot account for its demise. Many activist organizations face painful ideological disagreements but many also overcome disagreements and continue to exist in spite of them.
2 According to Stephen Coleman (2013), "The *Drain the Sea* strategy takes its name from a quote attributed to Chairman Mao, who suggested that in order to be successful a guerrilla must be able to move through the people like a fish through the water. The main idea of the strategy is to prevent this sort of movement by identifying the sections of the local population that are likely to support the insurgency and then relocating them to places where they can be closely watched or controlled, and thus where any insurgent activity among them will be easy to spot. Those insurgents who remain after the supporting population has been relocated will be much easier to locate and deal with due to their isolation," http://isme.tamu.edu/ISME09/Coleman09.html, accessed on November 17, 2014.
3 Also known as the Simpson-Mazzoli bill.
4 Los Angeles Alliance for a New Economy.
5 American Federation of Labor-Congress of Industrial Organizations.
6 John Friedmann, Rebecca Morales, Paul Ong, Allen Scott, Edward Soja, Michael Storper, Martin Wachs, and Goetz Wolff, among others.

7 Alan Heskin, Jacqueline Leavitt, and Gilda Haas.
8 The book was edited by Ruth Milkman, Victor Narro (project director of the Labor Center), and Joshua Bloom (PhD candidate in Sociology at UCLA).
9 Anthony Thigpen (AGENDA), Gilda Haas (UCLA), and Maria Elena Durazo (HERE Local 11).

Chapter 7

1 Respectively, *Touche pas mon Pote, Ni Puttes, Ni Soumises.*
2 Their primary religious demand was to have a space for prayer in the factory.
3 The Socialist Party during the 1970s consisted of several major factions. While the Jacobin/statist faction dominated the party, a bottom-up faction was also very prominent and had existed as an autonomous party (United Socialist Party) under the leadership of Michel Rocard. This faction embraced the French Girondist tradition, which stressed democratic governance, participation, and active community life. This latter faction spurred major state decentralization reforms during the 1980s and was the principal advocate of urban policy.
4 *Mouvement de l'Immigration et des Banlieues.*
5 *Un Logement d'Abord.*

Chapter 8

1 *Stedelijke Marokkaanse Raad.*
2 A memorandum published by the municipality of Amsterdam in 1989 was unusually explicit in expressing the frustrations of civil servants with the ethnic councils:

> Advocacy in our view does not only mean that one all the time and in the same way reminds others of the presence of migrants and arrogantly points out the implications without proposing solutions or strategies ... Where the interests of migrants are represented, one must be convinced by a well-informed and creative contribution that shows new ways to take into account Amsterdam's changing population. There is a lot of scope for improvement in this area. These considerations apply strongest to the participation at an institutional level. (Gemeente Amsterdam 1989: 46)

These frustrations already existed in 1989 and only grew stronger over the years.
3 *De kracht van een diverse stad.*
4 *Moslimjongeren Amsterdam.*
5 While the cooptative capacities of the Amsterdam government are still impressive, at the time of writing (2014) the government no longer has the ambition to use religion, and specifically Islam, as a tool of integration and governance. Cohen's successor, Eberhard van der Laan, has shown no

specific interest in Islam or Muslims. This does not necessarily mean that religion is no longer used to discipline Muslims but this is no longer a government goal. In interviews, meetings, brochures, and websites, Muslims routinely argue that Islam demands proper conduct and should prevail over ethnic culture. Religion is seen as God-given and making people pure and differentiated from ethnic culture, which has come to stand for that which is all too human. Islam has been used to argue against arranged marriages, gender inequality, and insolence. This kind of discourse not only has been in circulation among governmental elites and higher-class Muslims but has also found strong support among, for instance, isolated lower-class Muslim women (Van Tilborgh 2006) – an indication that this was not exclusively or not at all a government-instigated process. In any case, at the time of writing, radical challenges emanating from minority groups are virtually absent.

Chapter 9

1   http://www.immigrationpolicy.org/special-reports/guide-s744-understanding-2013-senate-immigration-bill
2   http://www.notonemoredeportation.com/2014/04/04/afl-cio-president-trumka-applauds-not1more-campaign
3   http://www.politico.com/story/2014/06/immigration-reform-obama-108468.html
4   "High rate of deportations continue under Obama despite Latino disapproval," Pew Research Center, September 13, http://www.pewresearch.org/fact-tank/2013/09/19/high-rate-of-deportations-continue-under-obama-despite-latino-disapproval
5   MotherJones, http://www.motherjones.com/politics/2012/03/anti-immigration-law-database
6   www.aflcio.org/Press-Room/Press-Releases/AFL-CIO-and-NDLON-Largest-Organization-of-Worker
7   See Gara LaMarche (2010) "A growing drumbeat from activists energizes drive for urgent immigration reform," http://www.atlanticphilanthropies.org/news/growing-drumbeat-activists-energizes-drive-urgent-immigration-reform
8   http://www.atlanticphilanthropies.org/grantees
9   See Gara LaMarche (2010) "A growing drumbeat from activists energizes drive for urgent immigration reform," http://www.atlanticphilanthropies.org/news/growing-drumbeat-activists-energizes-drive-urgent-immigration-reform
10 http://www.puenteaz.org/about-us/our-history
11 http://www.altoarizona.com/barrio-defense-committees.html
12 www.maldef.org/news/releases/supreme_court_dec_azcase
13 Neidi Dominguez Zamorano, Jonathan Perez, Nancy Meza, and Jorge Guitierrez (2010), "DREAM activists: Rejecting the passivity of the nonprofit,

industrial complex," http://www.truth-out.org/archive/component/k2/item/91877:dream-activists-rejecting-the-passivity-of-the-nonprofit-industrial-complex

14 Cedillo was also a long-time advocate of a bill that would allow undocumented immigrants a license (repeatedly vetoed by Governor Arnold Schwarzenegger) and another bill that ended the towing away of cars of unlicensed drivers (signed by Governor Jerry Brown in 2011).

Chapter 10

1 *Unie[e] Contre l'Immigration Jetable.*
2 *Parents Etrangers d'Enfants Français.*
3 *Collège de Médiateurs.*
4 *Confédération Française Démocratique du Travail* (French Confederation of Democracy of Work).
5 Respectively: *Confédération Générale du Travail* (General Confederation of Work); *Solidaires Unitaires Démocratique* (Solidarity, Unitary, Democracy); *Fédération Syndicale Unitaire* (United Union Federation).
6 *Coordination Nationale des Sans Papiers.*
7 *Uni(e) Contre l'Immigration Jetable.*

Chapter 11

1 *Immigratie- en Naturalisatiedienst.*
2 *Stichting Landelijk Ongedocumenteerden Steunpunt.*
3 *Immigratie- en Naturalisatie Dienst.*
4 In addition to these general criteria, there are a number of controversial supplementary conditions. For instance, parents suspected of war crimes do not qualify. The most controversial condition is that children should have been under continuous supervision of the national government. This means that children who have been under supervision of municipal governments do not qualify for the amnesty.
5 The asylum seekers adopted a governance structure that can perhaps be best described as ethnic corporatism: the groups are organized according to language and each group has a "leader" who represents the group at the meetings and informs the group of actions and developments. Although some activists and commentators expressed concern that this structure might silence people who do not subscribe to the leaders' viewpoints, in practice the position of a leader was not at all coveted given that leaders were living under the same hardships as others yet had to fulfill the obligation to attend meetings and explain complex strategic considerations and developments to a destitute and confused constituency.
6 Broadcast on AT5 (2014) "Felle burgemeester: 'Ik ben er voor de vluchtelingen,'" March 2.

Chapter 12

1   Scholars who hold this view include Kriesi et al. (1995); Adam et al. (1999); Ferree et al. (2001); Koopmans et al. (2005).

2   The uneven development of contention and control has interesting parallels to the dynamic of uneven development as theorized and examined by neo-Marxist literature since the 1970s (see especially Harvey 2006; Smith 2008). Neo-Marxists argue that the circulation and accumulation of capital relies upon a relatively fixed territorial organization in the form of states, the built environment, and territorialized interactions among firms. While such forms of territorial organizations facilitate capital's circulation and accumulation, technological and organizational innovations also make them slowly but surely obsolete in a process of ongoing creative destruction, creating a seesaw pattern of emerging and declining regions. In our study of social movements, we observe a seesaw movement where state structures extend into sectors and territories that are not fully integrated into governance structures, capturing the revolutionary surplus and putting it to work in maintaining social order. But while the state consolidates its hold over previously contentious sectors and territories, new kinds of contention emerge in different territories and sectors.

References

Acuña, R. (1996) *Anything But Mexican: Chicanos in Contemporary Los Angeles.* London: Verso Press.

Adam, B.D., J.W. Duyvendak, and A. Krouwel (Eds.) (1999) *The Global Emergence of Gay and Lesbian Politics. National Imprints of a Worldwide Movement.* Philadelphia, PA: Temple University Press.

Amara, F. and S. Zappi (2006) *Breaking the Silence: French Women's Voices from the Ghetto.* Berkeley: University of California Press.

Arendt, H. (1977 [1963]) *Eichmann in Jerusalem: A Report on the Banality of Evil.* London: Penguin Books.

Armstrong, E. (2002) *Forging Gay Identities: Organizing Sexuality in San Francisco, 1950–1994.* Chicago, IL: University of Chicago Press.

Artières, P. (2002) "1972: Naissance de l'intellectuel spécifique," *Plein Droit* 53–54.

BAK (Buitenlandse Arbeiders Kollektief) (1972) "Nieuwsbrief," July.

Bartels, D. (1986) "Can the train ever be stopped again? Developments in the Moluccan community in the Netherlands before and after the hijackings," *Indonesia* 41(1): 23–45.

Becher, D. (2010) "The participant's dilemma: Bringing conflict and representation back in," *International Journal of Urban and Regional Research* 34(3): 496–511.

Beck, U. (2000) "The cosmopolitan perspective: Sociology of the second age of modernity," *British Journal of Sociology* 51(1): 79–105.

Beck, U. (2007) "Beyond class and nation: Reframing social inequalities in a globalizing world," *The British Journal of Sociology* 58(4): 679–705.

Berezin, M. (2009) *Illiberal Politics in Neoliberal Times: Culture, Security and Populism in the New Europe.* Cambridge: Cambridge University Press.

Blandin, N. (2009) "Biographie: Qui est Malek Boutih?," *La République des Lettres*, January 2009, online version: www.republique-des-lettres.fr/10638-malek-boutih.php

Cities and Social Movements: Immigrant Rights Activism in the United States, France, and the Netherlands, 1970–2015, First Edition. Walter J. Nicholls and Justus Uitermark.
© 2017 John Wiley & Sons, Ltd. Published 2017 by John Wiley & Sons, Ltd.

Blin, T. (2005) *Les Sans-papiers de Saint-Bernard: Mouvement social et action organisée.* Paris: L'Harmattan.

Bloemraad, I. (2006) *Becoming a Citizen: Incorporating Immigrants and Refugees in the United States and Canada.* Berkeley: University of California Press.

Boëldieu, J. and C. Borrel (2000) "Recensement de la population 1999: La proportion d'immigrés est stable depuis 25 ans," *INSEE Première* 748: 1–4.

Bonacich, E. and G. Gapasin (2001) "Organizing the unorganizable," in P. Ong and J. Lincoln (Eds.) *The State of California Labor.* Institute of Industrial Relations: Los Angeles and Berkeley, CA.

Bonjour, S. (2009) *Gezin en Grens. Beleidsvorming inzake gezinsmigratie in Nederland, 1955–2005.* Maastricht: unpublished PhD thesis, Maastricht University.

Borge-Holthoefer, J., A. Rivero, I. García, E. Cauhé, A. Ferrer, D. Ferrer, D. Francos, D. Iñiguez, M. Pilar Pérez, G. Ruiz, F. Sanz, F. Serrano, C. Viñas, and A. Tarancón, Y. (2011) "Structural and dynamical patterns on online social networks: The Spanish May 15th movement as a case study," *PLoS ONE* 6(8): e23883.

Boudreau, J.A. and R. Keil (2001) "Seceding from responsibility? Secession movements in Los Angeles," *Urban Studies* 38(10): 1701–1731.

Bouras, N. (2012) *Het Land van Herkomst, Perspectieven op verbondenheid met Marokko, 1960–2010.* Leiden: unpublished PhD thesis, Leiden University.

Bourdieu, P. (1984) *Distinction: A Social Critique of the Judgement of Taste.* Cambridge, MA: Harvard University Press.

Bourdieu, P. (1994) *Language and Symbolic Power.* Cambridge, MA: Harvard University Press.

Brenner, N., M. Mayer, and P. Marcuse (Eds.) (2011) *Cities for People, Not for Profit: Theory/Practice.* Oxford: Wiley-Blackwell.

Brenner, N. and C. Schmid (2015) "Towards a new epistemology of the urban?" *City* 19(2–3): 151–182.

Buijs, F.J., F. Demant and A. Hamdy (2006) *Strijders van eigen bodem. Radicale en democratische moslims in Nederland.* Amsterdam: Amsterdam University Press.

Burt, R.S. (1995) *Structural Holes: The Social Structure of Competition.* Boston, MA: Harvard University Press.

Buruma, I. (2006) *Murder in Amsterdam: The Death of Theo van Gogh and the Limits of Tolerance.* New York: Penguin Books.

Calavita, K. (1992) *Inside the State: The Bracero Program, Immigration, and the INS.* New York: Routledge.

Castells, M. (1977) *The Urban Question.* London: Edward Arnold.

Castells, M. (1978) *City, Class and Power.* London: Macmillan.

Castells, M. (1983) *The City and the Grassroots.* Berkeley: University of California Press.

Castells, M. (1996) *The Rise of the Network Society.* Oxford: Blackwell.

Castells, M. (2009) *Communication Power.* Oxford: Oxford University Press.

Castells, M. (2012) *Networks of Outrage and Hope: Social Movements in the Internet Age.* Cambridge: Polity Press.

Chauncey, G. (1995) *Gay New York: Gender, Urban Culture, and the Making of the Gay Male World, 1890–1940.* New York: Basic Books.

Chavez, L. (2008) *The Latino Threat: Constructing Immigrants, Citizens, and the Nation.* Palo Alto, CA: Stanford University Press.

Coleman, J. (1988) "Social capital in the creation of human capital," *The American Journal of Sociology* 94: 95–120.

Coleman, M. (2007) "Immigration geopolitics beyond the Mexico-US border," *Antipode* 38(1): 54–76.

Coleman, S. (2013) *Good Strategy, Bad Tactics: Ethical Considerations in ROE for Counter-Insurgency Warfare*, unpublished manuscript, http://isme.tamu.edu/ISME09/Coleman09.html, accessed on November 17, 2014.

Collins, R. (2001) "Social movements and the focus of emotional attention," in J. Goodwin, J. Jasper, and F. Polletta (Eds.) *Passionate Politics: Emotions and Social Movements*. Chicago, IL: University of Chicago Press, pp. 27–44.

Collins, R. (2004) *Interaction Ritual Chains*. Princeton, NJ: Princeton University Press.

Cordeiro, A. (2001) "Les luttes de l'immigration, 1970–2000," unpublished manuscript (ATMF archives), presented at États Généraux de l'Immigration et des Quartiers, Strasbourg, France.

Corona, B. (1994) *Memories of Chicano History: The Life and Narrative of Bert Corona*. Berkeley: University of California Press.

Cottaar, A., N. Bouras, and F. Laouikili (2011) *Marokkanen in Nederland. De pioniers vertellen*. Amsterdam: Meulenhoff.

Coutin, S. (2000) *Legalizing Moves: Salvadoran Immigrants' Struggle for U.S. Residency*. Ann Arbor: University of Michigan Press.

Coutin, S. (2003) *Legalizing Moves: Salvadoran Immigrants' Struggle for U.S. Residency*. Ann Arbor: University of Michigan Press.

Cox, K. (1995) "Globalisation, competition, and the politics of local economic development," *Urban Studies* 32, 213–224.

Cox, K. (1997) "Globalization and the politics of distribution," in K. Cox (Ed.) *Spaces of Globalization: Reasserting the Power of the Local*. New York: Guilford Press, pp. 115–136.

Cruikshank, B. (1993) "The will to empower: Technologies of citizenship and the war on poverty," *Socialist Review* 23(4): 29–55.

Cruikshank, B. (1999) *The Will to Empower: Democratic Citizens and Other Subjects*. Ithaca, NY: Cornell University Press.

Davis, M. (1990) *City of Quartz: Excavating the Future in Los Angeles*. London: Verso.

Davis, M. (1993) "Who killed L.A.? A political autopsy," *New Left Review* 197: 3–28.

Davis, M. (2000) *Dead Cities and Other Tales*. New York: The New Press.

De Barros, F. (2004) "From the local to the national, local governance and the genesis of the 'social mix' policy from 1950s to the 1990s," *French Politics* 2: 61–80.

De Genova, N. (2005) *Working the Boundaries: Race, Space, and "Illegality" in Mexican Chicago*. Chapel Hill, NC: Duke University Press.

De Genova, N. and N. Peutz (2010) *The Deportation Regime: Sovereignty, Space, and Freedom of Movement*, Durham, NC: Duke University Press.

De Liagre Böhl, H. (2010) *Amsterdam op de helling. De strijd om stadsvernieuwing*. Amsterdam: Boom.

Della Porta, D. and M. Diani (1999) *Social Movements: An Introduction*. Oxford: Blackwell.

De Telegraaf (2014) "Vrij spel voor de asielindustrie," April 22.

de Volkskrant (2001) "Begin uitvoering nieuwe asielwet met schone lei," March 23.

de Volkskrant (2007) "Geen pardon," February 13.

de Volkskrant (2011) "Angolese Mauro is Sahar niet," September 24.

de Volkskrant (2014) "Schrijnende gevallen," February 8.

De Wilde, M. (2015) *Brave New Neighborhood*. Amsterdam: unpublished PhD thesis, University of Amsterdam.

Dean, M. (2009) *Governmentality: Power and Rule in Modern Society*. New York: Sage.

Diani, M. (1997) "Social movements and social capital: A network perspective on movement outcomes," *Mobilizations* 2(2): 129–147.

Diani, M. (2004) "Social movements, contentious actions, and social networks: From metaphor to substance," in M. Diani and D. McAdam (Eds.) *Social Movements and Networks: Relational Approaches to Collective Action*. Oxford: Oxford University Press, pp. 1–19.

Diani, M. (2005) "Cities in the world: Local civil society and global issues in Britain," in D. della Porta and S. Tarrow (Eds.) *Transnational Protest and Global Activism*. Boulder, CO: Rowman and Littlefield, pp. 45–67.

Diani, M. and D. McAdam (2004) (Eds.) *Social Movements and Networks: Relational Approaches to Collective Action*. Oxford: Oxford University Press.

Dikeç, M. (2004) "Voices into noises: Ideological determination of unarticulated justice movements," *Space and Polity* 8(2): 191–208.

Dikeç, M. (2007) *Badlands of the Republic: Space, Politics, and Urban Policy*. Oxford: Wiley-Blackwell.

Donzelot, J. and P. Estèbe (1993) *L'Etat animateur*. Paris: Harmattan.

Draaisma, J. and P. van Hoogstraten (1983) "The squatter movement in Amsterdam," *International Journal of Urban and Regional Research* 7(3): 406–416.

Dreby, J. (2015) *Everyday Illegal: When Policies Undermine Immigrant Families*. Berkeley: University of California Press.

Durand, J. and D. Massey (2003) "The cost of contradiction: US border policy, 1996–2000," *Latino Studies* 1(1): 233–252.

Duyvendak, J.W. (1995) *The Power of Politics: New Social Movements in an Old Polity. France, 1965–1989*. Boulder, CO: Westview Press.

Duyvendak, J.W. (2011) *The Politics of Home: Nostalgia and Belonging in Western Europe and the United States*. Basingstoke: Palgrave.

Dziembowska, M. (2010) "NDLON and the history of day labor organizing in Los Angeles," in R. Milkman, J. Bloom, and V. Narro (Eds.) *Working for Justice: The L.A. Model of Organizing and Advocacy*. Ithaca, NY: Cornell University Press, pp. 141–153.

Eisinger, P. (1997) "Cities in the new federal order: Effects of devolution," *The La Follette Policy Report* 8(1): 1–24.

Eliasoph, N. (1997) "'Close to home': The work of avoiding politics," *Theory & Society* 26(5): 605–647.

Engbersen, G.B.M. and D.W.J. Broeders (2009) "The state versus the alien: Immigration control and strategies of irregular migrants," *West European Politics* 32(5): 867–885.

Engbersen, G., M. van San, and A. Leerkes (2006) "A room with a view: Irregular immigrants in the legal capital of the world," *Ethnography* 7(2): 205–238.

Entzinger, H.B., C. Ivanescu, P.W.A. Scholten, and S. Suvarierol (2013) *The Impact of Restrictions and Entitlements on the Integration of Family Migrants.* Rotterdam: EUR/Faculty of Social Sciences.

Eribon, D. (1991) *Michel Foucault.* Cambridge, MA: Harvard University Press.

Essed, P. and K. Nimako (2006) "Designs and (co)incidents: Cultures of scholarship and public policy on immigrants/minorities in the Netherlands," *International Journal of Comparative Sociology* 47(3–4): 281–312.

Estèbe, P. (1999) *L'Usage des quartiers action publique et géographie dans la politique de la ville.* PhD dissertation, Université de Paris X – Nanterre.

Estèbe, P. and J. Donzelot (1999) "Reevaluer le politique de la ville," in R. Balme, A. Faure, and A. Mabilieu (Eds.) *Les nouvelles politiques locales: dynamiques de l'action publique.* Paris: Presses de Science Po.

Estèbe, P. and M.C. Jaillet (1999) "L'agglomération toulousaine a-t-elle jamais été moderne? Les formes du pouvoir locale a l'épreuve des mutations urbaines, " *Sud-Ouest Européen* 4: 5–14.

Estèbe, P. and P. Le Galès (2003) "La métropole parisienne: à la recherche du pilote?," *Revue Française d'Administration Publique* 107: 1–9.

Eyerman, R. (2001) *Cultural Trauma: Slavery and the Formation of African American Identity.* Cambridge: Cambridge University Press.

Fainstein, S. and C. Hirst (1995) "Urban social movements," in D. Judge, G. Stoker, and H. Wolman (Eds.) *Theories of Urban Politics.* London: Sage, pp. 181–205.

Fassin, D. (2012) *Humanitarian Reason: A Moral History of the Present.* Berkeley: University of California Press.

Fennema, M. and J. Tillie (1999) "Political participation and political trust in Amsterdam: Civic communities and ethnic networks," *Journal of Ethnic and Migration Studies* 25(4): 703–726.

Ferree, M.M., W.A. Gamson, J. Gerhards, and D. Rucht (2001) *Shaping Abortion Discourse: Democracy and the Public Sphere in Germany and the United States.* Cambridge: Cambridge University Press.

Fischer C. (1975) "Toward a subcultural theory of urbanism," *American Journal of Sociology* 89(6): 1319–1341.

Florida, R. and A. Jonas (1991) "US urban policy: The postwar state and capitalist regulation," *Antipode* 23(4): 349–384.

Foucault, M. (1976) *Discipline and Punish: The Birth of the Prison.* New York: Pantheon.

Foucault, M. (1978) *The History of Sexuality I: The Will to Knowledge.* London: Penguin Books.

Foucault, M. (1984) "Truth and power," in P. Rabinow (Ed.) *The Foucault Reader.* New York: Pantheon, pp. 51–75.

Foucault, M. (1991) "Governmentality," in G. Burchell, C. Gordon, and P. Miller (Eds.) *The Foucault Effect: Studies in Governmentality.* Chicago, IL: University of Chicago Press, pp. 87–104.

Foucault, M. (2004) *Abnormal: Lectures at the Collège de France, 1974–1975.* New York: Macmillan.

Foucault, M. (2009) *Security, Territory, Population: Lectures at the Collège de France, 1977–1978.* New York: Picador.

Fraser, N. (1991) "Rethinking the public sphere: A contribution to the critique of actually existing democracy," in C. Calhoun (Ed.) *Habermas and the Public Sphere.* Cambridge, MA: MIT Press, pp. 109–142.

Fung, A. and E.O. Wright (2003) *Deepening Democracy: Institutional Innovations in Empowered Participatory Governance.* London: Verso.

Garbaye, R. (2005) *Getting into Local Power: The Politics of Ethnic Minorities in British and French Cities.* Oxford: Wiley-Blackwell.

Garcia, A. (2002) "Toward a left without borders: The story of the Center for Autonomous Social Action-General Brotherhood of Workers," *Monthly Review* 54(3): 69–78.

Gay, V. (2010) *From Dignity to Invisibility: Struggles of Immigrant Workers in Citroën's and Talbot's Factories, 1982–1984,* unpublished manuscript, presented at European Science Foundation Workshop on Migrant Legality in Contemporary Europe, University of Amsterdam.

Gay, V. (2014) "Lutter pour partir ou pour rester? Licenciements et aide au retour des travailleurs immigrés dans le conflit Talbot, 1983–1984," *Travail et Employ* 137: 37–50.

Gemeente Amsterdam (1989) *Raamnota gemeentelijk minderhedenbeleid.* Amsterdam: Gemeente Amsterdam.

Gemeente Amsterdam (1999) *De kracht van een diverse stad. Uitgangspunten van het diversiteitsbeleid van de gemeente Amsterdam.* Amsterdam: Gemeente Amsterdam.

Gerbaudo, P. (2012) *Tweets and the Streets: Social Media and Contemporary Activism.* London: Pluto.

Gielen, A.-J. (2008) *Een kwestie van identiteit.* Amsterdam: A.G. Advies.

Gonzales, R. (2011) "Learning to be illegal: Undocumented youth and shifting legal contexts in the transition to adulthood," *American Sociological Review* 76(4): 602–619.

Gonzales, R. and A.M. Bautista-Chavez (2014) "Two years and counting: Assessing the growth and power of DACA," Special Report, American Immigration Council, June.

Goodwin, J., J. Jasper, and F. Polletta (Eds.) (2001) *Passionate Politics: Emotions and Social Movements.* Chicago, IL: University of Chicago Press.

Gould, R. (1993) "Trade cohesion, class unity, and urban insurrection: Artisanal activism in the Paris Commune," *American Journal of Sociology* 98(4): 721–754.

Gould, R. (1995) *Activist Identities: Class, Community, and Protest in Paris from 1848 to the Commune.* Chicago, IL: University of Chicago Press.

Gramsci, A. (1971) *Prison Notebooks.* New York: International Publishers.

Granovetter, M. (1983) "The strength of weak ties: A network theory revisited," *Sociological Theory* 1: 201–233.

Gutiérrez, D. (1991) "'Sin Fronteras?': Chicanos, Mexican Americans, and the emergence of the contemporary Mexican immigration debate, 1968–1978," *Journal of American Ethnic History* 10(4): 5–37.

Gutiérrez, D. (1995) *Walls and Mirrors: Mexican Americans, Mexican Immigrants, and the Politics of Ethnicity.* Berkeley: University of California Press.

Haleber, R. and A. de Meijer (1993) "Revolutionairen in de moskee," *Grenzeloos* 6. Available at: http://members.chello.nl/rphaleber/int-abdou.html Hamel, P. and R. Keil (Eds.) (2015) *Suburban Governance: A Global View.* Toronto: University of Toronto Press.

Hamidi, C. (2003) "Voluntary associations of migrants and politics: The case of North African immigrants in France," *Immigrant and Minorities* 22(2–3): 317–332.

Hamilton, N. and N. Chinchilla (2001) *Seeking Community in a Global City: Guatemalans and Salvadorans in Los Angeles.* Philadelphia, PA: Temple University Press.

Hargreaves, A. (1995) *Immigration, "Race" and Ethnicity in Contemporary France.* London: Routledge.

Harvey, D. (1985) *Consciousness and the Urban Experience.* Baltimore, MD: Johns Hopkins University Press and Oxford: Basil Blackwell.

Harvey, D. (2001) *Spaces of Capital: Towards a Critical Geography.* Edinburgh: Edinburgh University Press.

Harvey, D. (2003) "The right to the city," *International Journal of Urban and Regional Research* 27(4): 939–941.

Harvey, D. (2006) *Limits to Capital.* London: Verso.

Hayward, J. and V. Wright (2002) *Governing from the Center: Core Executive Coordination in France.* Oxford: Oxford University Press.

Heins, J. (1991) "Immigrants, natives and the French welfare state: Explaining different interactions with a social welfare program," *International Migration Review* 25(3): 592–609.

Herod, A. and M. Wright (Eds.) (2002) *Geographies of Power: Placing Scale.* Oxford: Wiley-Blackwell.

Hmed, C. (2006a) *Loger les étrangers "isolés" en France. Socio-histoire d'une institution d'État : la Sonacotra (1956–2006).* Paris: unpublished PhD thesis, Université de Paris-I.

Hmed, C. (2006b) "Protesting in order to exit," paper presented at Research Committee 21 Annual Meeting, Paris, France.

Hmed, C. (2007) "Contester une institution dans le cas d'une mobilisation improbable: la 'grève des loyers' dans les foyers Sonacotra dans les années 1970," *Sociétés contemporaines* 65: 55–81.

Hondegneu-Sotelo, P. (2008) *God's Heart Has No Borders: How Religious Activists Are Working for Immigrant Rights.* Berkeley: University of California Press.

Honig, B. (2006) *Democracy and the Foreigner.* Princeton, NJ: Princeton University Press.

Huisman, C. (2014) "Displacement through participation," *Tijdschrift voor Economische en Sociale Geografie* 105(2): 161–174.

Inda, J. (2006) *Targeting Immigrants: Government, Technology, and Ethics.* Malden, MA: Wiley-Blackwell.

Ireland, P. (1994) *The Policy Challenge of Ethnic Diversity: Immigrant Politics in France and Switzerland.* Cambridge, MA: Harvard University Press.

Jasper, J. (1997) *The Art of Moral Protest.* Chicago, IL: University of Chicago Press.

Jasper, J. (2014) "Introduction: Playing the game," in J. Jasper and J.W. Duyvendak (Eds.) *Players and Arenas: The Interactive Dynamics of Protest.* Amsterdam: Amsterdam University Press, pp. 9–10.

Johnson, K. (2012) "Immigration and civil rights: Is the 'new' Birmingham the same as the 'old' Birmingham?" *William and Mary Bill of Rights Journal* 367: 367–393.

Joppke, C. (1998) "Why liberal states accept unwanted immigration," *World Politics* 50(2), 266–293.

Kalir, B. and Sur, M. (2012) *Transnational Flows and Permissive Polities: Ethnographies of Human Mobilities in Asia*. Amsterdam: Amsterdam University Press.

Kalir, B. and L. Wissink (2016) "The deportation continuum: Convergences between state agents and NGO workers in the Dutch deportation field," *Citizenship Studies* 20(1), 34–49.

Katznelson, I. (1981) *City Trenches: Urban Politics and the Patterning of Class in the United States*. Chicago, IL: University of Chicago Press.

Keck, M. and K. Sikkink (1998) *Activists beyond Borders*. Ithaca, NY: Cornell University Press.

King, L. and I. Szeléyni (2004) *Theories of the New Class: Intellectuals and Power*. Minneapolis: University of Minnesota Press.

Koopmans, R. (1993) "The dynamics of protest waves: West Germany, 1965 to 1989," *American Sociological Review* 58(5): 637–658.

Koopmans, R., P. Statham, M. Giugni, and F. Passy (2005) *Contested Citizenship*. Minneapolis: University of Minnesota Press.

Kriesi, H., R. Koopmans, J.W. Duyvendak, and M. Giugni (1995) *New Social Movements in Western Europe: A Comparative Analysis*. Minneapolis: University of Minnesota Press.

Krikke, H. (1999) *De valstrik van de hoop. Witte illegalen in hongerstaking*. Amsterdam: Van Gennep.

LA Weekly (2005) "The architect: Miguel Contreras, 1952–2005," May 12.

Le Galès, P. (2002) *European Cities: Social Conflicts and Governance*. Oxford: Oxford University Press.

Le Monde (1993) "Un entretien avec Charles Pasqua," June 2.

Le Monde (1993) "La révision constitutionnelle: Le PS et le PC ont voté contre la réforme du droit d'asile," October 29.

Le Monde (1994) "Le casse-tête des couples 'mixtes,'" February 7.

Le Monde (1994) "Le rapport de la Commission des droits de l'homme dénonce l'exclusion croissante des étrangers," March 22.

Le Monde (1994) "Des associations réclament une modification de la loi Pasqua," June 4.

Le Monde (1996) "Les Africains sans papiers tentent de relancer leur movement," August 29.

Le Monde (1998) "Les Saint-Bernard fêtent le deuxième anniversaire de leur mouvement," August 24.

Le Monde (1998) "Onze sans-papiers poursuivent leur grève de la faim dans une mairie socialiste," October 27.

Le Monde (1998) "Les neuf sans-papiers grévistes de la faim ont été évacués de la mairie de Limeil-Brévannes," November 16.

Le Monde (2000) "La grève de la faim des sans-papiers de Lille divise la gauche dans le Nord," June 28.

Le Monde (2002) "Plusieurs milliers de personnes ont défilé samedi à Paris pour soutenir les sans-papiers," September 10.

Le Monde (2004) "Le casse-tête des couples 'mixtes'," February 7.

Leerkes, A. and D. Broeders (2010) "A case of mixed motives? Formal and informal functions of administrative immigration detention," *British Journal of Criminology* 50(5): 830–850.

Leerkes, A., G. Engbersen, and M. Van San (2007) "Shadow places: Patterns of spatial concentration and incorporation of irregular immigrants in the Netherlands," *Urban Studies* 44(8): 1491–1516.

Lefebvre, H. (1991 [1974]) *The Production of Space*. Oxford: Basil Blackwell.

Lefebvre, H. (1996) "The right to the city," in E. Kaufman and E. Lebas (Eds.) *Writings on Cities*. Oxford: Blackwell.

Leitner, H. and C. Strunk (2014) "Spaces of immigrant advocacy and democratic citizenship," *Annals of the Association of American Geographers* 104(2): 348–356.

Lopez, M. and A. Gonzalez-Barrera (2013) "High rate of deportations continue under Obama despite Latino disapproval," Pew Research Center, September 13. Available at: http://www.pewresearch.org/fact-tank/2013/09/19/high-rate-of-deportations-continue-under-obama-despite-latino-disapproval

Los Angeles Times (1996) "Conversation with day labor activist, Pablo Alvarado," September 7.

Mamadouh, V. (1992) *De stad in eigen hand*. Amsterdam: SUA.

Mann, M. (1986) *The Sources of Social Power, Volume 1: A History of Power from the Beginning to AD 1760*. Cambridge: Cambridge University Press.

Mann, M. (1993) *The Sources of Social Power, Volume 2: The Rise of Classes and Nation States, 1760–1914*. Cambridge: Cambridge University Press.

Marcuse, P., J. Connolly, J. Novy, I. Olivo, C. Potter, and J. Steil (Eds.) (2011) *Searching for the Just City: Debates in Urban Theory and Practice*. London: Routledge.

Martin, D. (2003) "'Place-framing' as place-making: Constituting a neighborhood for organizing and activism," *Annals of the Association of American Geographers* 93(3): 730–750.

Martin, D. and J. Pierce (2013) "Reconceptualizing resistance: Residuals of the state and democratic radical pluralism," *Antipode* 45(1): 67–79.

Massey, D. (1994) *Space, Place and Gender*. Minneapolis: University of Minnesota Press.

Massey, D., J. Durand, and N. Malone (2003) *Beyond Smoke and Mirrors: Mexican Immigration in an Era of Economic Integration*. New York: Russell Sage Foundation.

Massey, D. and K. Pren (2012) "Unintended consequences of US immigration policy: Explaining the post-1965 surge from Latin America," *Population and Development Review* 38(1): 1–29.

Mayer, M. (2000) "Social movements in European cities: Transitions from the 1970s to the 1990s," in A. Bagnasco and P. Le Galès (Eds.) *Cities in Contemporary Europe*. Cambridge: Cambridge University Press, pp. 131–152.

Mayer, Margit (2007) "Contesting the neoliberalization of urban governance," in H. Leitner, J. Peck, and E.S. Sheppard (Eds.) *Contesting Neoliberalism*. New York: Guilford Press, pp. 90–115.

Mayer, M. (2009) "The 'right to the city' in the context of shifting mottos of urban social movements," *City* 13(2–3): 362–374.

Mayer, M. (2013) "First world urban activism: Beyond austerity urbanism and creative city politics," *City* 17(1): 5–19.

McAdam, D. (1982) *Political Process and the Development of Black Insurgency, 1930–1970.* Chicago, IL: University of Chicago Press.

McAdam, D., S. Tarrow, and C. Tilly (2001) *Dynamics of Contention.* Cambridge: Cambridge University Press.

McQuarrie, M. (2013) "No contest: Participatory technologies and transformation of urban authority," *Public Culture* 25(1): 143–175.

Menjívar, C. (1997) "Immigrant kinship networks and the impact of the receiving context: Salvadorans in San Francisco in the early 1990s," *Social Problem* 44(1): 104–123.

Menjívar, C. and D. Kanstroom (Eds.) (2014) *Constructing "Illegality": Immigrant Experiences, Critiques, and Resistance.* Cambridge: Cambridge University Press.

Mepschen, P. (2012) "Gewone mensen. Populisme en het discours van verdringing in Amsterdam Nieuw West," *Sociologie* 8(1): 66–83.

Mepschen, P. (2013) "De politiek van sloop. Stedelijke vernieuwing en de sociale constructie van 'gewone mensen' in Slotermeer," in E. Tonkens and M. de Wilde (Eds.) *Als meedoen pijn doet.* Amsterdam: Van Gennep, pp. 209–228.

Merrifield, A. (2011) *Magical Marxism: Subversive Politics and the Imagination.* New York: Pluto Press.

Milkman, R. (2006) *L.A. Story: Immigrant Workers and the Future of the U.S. Labor Movement.* New York: Russell Sage Foundation.

Milkman, R. (2010) "Introduction," in R. Milkman, J. Bloom, and V. Narro (Eds.) *Working for Justice: The L.A. Model of Organizing and Advocacy.* Ithaca, NY: Cornell University Press, pp. 1–22.

Milkman R., J. Bloom, and V. Narro (Eds.) (2010) *Working for Justice: The L.A. Model of Organizing and Advocacy.* Ithaca, NY: Cornell University Press.

Miller, B. (2000) *Geography and Social Movements: Comparing Antinuclear Activism in the Boston Area.* Minneapolis: University of Minnesota Press.

Miller, B. (2001) "Many paths forward: Thoughts on geography and social movements," *Political Geography* 20: 935–940.

Miller, B. (2004) "Globalization, sweatshops, and glocal organizing," *Antipode* 36(4): 575–580.

Miller, B. (2009) "Is scale a chaotic concept? Notes on processes of scale production," in R. Keil and R. Mahon (Eds.) *Leviathan Undone? Towards a Political Economy of Scale.* Vancouver: UBC Press, pp. 51–66.

Miller, B. and D. Martin (2003) "Space and contentious politics," *Mobilization*, 8(2): 143–156.

Mitchell, D. (2003) *The Right to the City: Social Justice and the Fight for Public Space.* New York: Guilford Press.

Mitchell, D. and L. Staeheli (2005) "Permitting protest: Parsing the fine geography of dissent in America," *International Journal of Urban and Regional Research* 25: 679–699.

Mollenkopf, J. (1983) *The Contested City.* Princeton, NJ: Princeton University Press.

Moody, K. (1988) *An Injury to All: The Decline of American Unionism.* New York: Verso.

Muñoz, C. (1989) *Youth, Identity, Power: The Chicano Movement.* London: Verso.

Munson, Z. (2001) "Islamic mobilization: Social movement theory and the Egyptian Muslim Brotherhood," *The Sociological Quarterly* 42(4): 487–510.

Musterd, S. (1981) "De huisvestingssituatie van Mediterranen in Tilburg," *Stedebouw en Volkshuisvesting* 62(7/8): 314–325.

Musterd, S. and W. Ostendorf (1993) "Stedelijke armoede en etniciteit in de verzorgingsstaat, Amsterdam als voorbeeld," *Sociologische Gids* 40(6): 466–481.

Narro, V. (2010) "Afterword," in R. Milkman, J. Bloom, and V. Narro (Eds.) *Working for Justice: The L.A. Model of Organizing and Advocacy.* Ithaca, NY: Cornell University Press, pp. 233–244.

Needleman, R. (1998) "Building relationships for the long haul: Unions and community-based groups working together to organize low-wage workers," in K. Bronfenbrenner et al. (Eds.) *Organizing to Win.* Ithaca, NY: Cornell University Press, pp. 71–86.

New York Times (2010) "In shadow of health care vote, immigrant advocates keep pushing for change," March 20.

New York Times (2010) "Immigration advocates rally for change," May 1.

New York Times (2011) "Arizona, bowing to business, softens stand on immigration," March 18.

New York Times (2012) "In Arpaio's Arizona, they fought back," July 21.

Ngai, M. (2004) *Impossible Subjects: Illegal Aliens and the Making of Modern America.* Princeton, NJ: Princeton University Press.

Nicholls, W. (2003) "Forging a 'new' organizational infrastructure for Los Angeles's progressive community," *International Journal of Urban and Regional Research* 27(4): 881–896.

Nicholls, W. (2006) "Associationalism from above: Explaining failure in the case of France's La Politique de la Ville," *Urban studies* 43(10): 1779–1802.

Nicholls, W. (2008) "The urban question revisited: The importance of cities for social movements," *International Journal of Urban and Regional Research* 32(4): 1468–2427.

Nicholls, W. (2009) "Place, relations, networks: The geographical foundations of social movements," *Transactions of the Institute of British Geographers* 34(1): 78–93.

Nicholls, W. (2011a) "Cities and the unevenness of social movement space: The case of France's immigrant rights movement," *Environment and Planning A* 43(7): 1655–1673.

Nicholls, W. (2011b) "The Los Angeles School: Difference, politics, city," *International Journal of Urban and Regional Research* 35(1): 189–206.

Nicholls, W. (2013) *The DREAMers: How the Undocumented Youth Movement Transformed the Immigrant Rights Debate.* Palo Alto, CA: Stanford University Press.

Nicholls, W. (2014) "From political opportunities to niche-openings: The dilemmas of mobilizing for immigrant rights in inhospitable environments," *Theory and Society* 43(1): 23–49.

Nicholls, W.J. (2016) "Producing-resisting national borders in the United States, France and the Netherlands," *Political Geography* 51: 43–52.

Nicholls, W. and J. Uitermark (2013) "Post-multicultural cities: A comparison of minority politics in Amsterdam and Los Angeles, 1970–2010," *Journal of Ethnic and Migration Studies* 39(10): 1555–1575.

Nicholls, W. and J. Uitermark (2014) "Giving voice: The ambivalent roles of specific intellectuals in immigrant and LGBT movements," in J. Jasper and J.W. Duyvendak (Eds.) *Players and Arenas: The Interactive Dynamics of Protest.* Amsterdam: Amsterdam University Press, pp. 189–210.

Nicholls, W.J., J. Uitermark, and S. van Haperen (2016) "The networked grassroots: How radicals outflanked reformists in the United States' immigrant rights movement," *Journal of Ethnic and Migration Studies* 42(6): 877–892.

NRC Handelsblad (1999) "Kritiek uit eigen kring op bestuur VluchtelingenWerk," September 18.

NRC Handelsblad (2002) "Hongeren soms succes: Hongerstaken een riskante actie met een kansje op resultaat," July 15.

NRC Handelsblad (2004) "Asielzoekers overwegen hongerstaking; Verzoeken bij organisaties," February 13.

NRC Handelsblad (2005) "Hongerstakers naar aparte opvangcentra," August 2.

NRC Handelsblad (2013) "Handig, de hongerstakers in de isoleercel," August 16.

NRC Handelsblad (2014) "Korte inspectieronde van de vluchtgarage," June 20.

Pallares, A. and N. Flores González (2011) "Regarding family: New actors in the Chicago protests," in K. Voss and I. Bloemraad (Eds.) *Rallying for Immigrant Rights.* Berkeley: University of California Press, pp. 161–179.

Patler, C. (2010) "Alliance-building and organizing for immigrant rights: The case of the Coalition for Humane Immigrant Rights of Los Angeles," in R. Milkman, J. Bloom, and V. Narro (Eds.) *Working for Justice: The L.A. Model of Organizing and Advocacy.* Ithaca, NY: Cornell University Press, pp. 71–88.

Péchu, C. (1999) "Black African immigrants in France and claims for housing," *Journal of Ethnic and Migration Studies* 25(4): 727–744.

Péchu, C. (2004) *Du Comité des Mal Logés à Droit au Logement, Sociologie d'une Mobilisation.* Paris: unpublished PhD thesis, Institute d'Etudes Politiques de Paris.

Peck, J. and A. Tickell (2002) "Neoliberalizing space," *Antipode* 34(3): 380–404.

Penninx, R. (1979) *Etnische minderheden. Naar een algemeen etnisch minderhedenbeleid?* The Hague: Staatsuitgeverij.

Pickvance, C. (2003) "From urban social movements to urban movements: A review and introduction to a symposium on urban movements," *International Journal of Urban and Regional Research* 27(1): 102–109.

Piven, F. and R. Cloward (1978) *Poor People's Movements: Why They Succeed, How They Fail.* New York: Vintage.

Polletta, F. (2006) *It Was Like a Fever: Storytelling in Protest and Politics.* Chicago, IL: University of Chicago Press.

Portes, A. (1998) "Social capital: Its origins and applications in modern sociology," *Annual Review of Sociology* 24: 1–24.

Portes, A. and J. Sensenbrenner (1993) "Embeddedness and immigration: Notes on the social determination of economic action," *American Journal of Sociology* 98: 1320–1350.

Pruijt, H. (1985) "Cityvorming gekraakt," *Agora* 1(4): 9–11.

Pruijt, H. (2003) "Is the institutionalization of urban movements inevitable? A comparison of the opportunities for sustained squatting in New York City and Amsterdam," *International Journal of Urban and Regional Research* 27(1): 133–157.

Pruijt, H. (2013) "Culture wars, revanchism, moral panics and the creative city. A reconstruction of a decline of tolerant public policy: The case of Dutch anti-squatting legislation," *Urban Studies* 50(6): 1114–1129.

Pulido, L. (1996) "Multiracial organizing among environmental justice activists in Los Angeles," in M. Dear, E. Schockman, and G. Hise (Eds.) *Rethinking Los Angeles.* Thousand Oaks, CA: Sage, pp. 171–189.

Pulido, L. (2006) *Black, Brown, Yellow and Left. Radical Activism in Los Angeles.* Berkeley: University of California Press.

Purcell, M. (2003) "Citizenship and the right to the global city: Reimagining the capitalist world order," *International Journal of Urban and Regional Research* 27(3): 564–590.

Purcell, M. (2006) "Urban democracy and the local trap," *Urban Studies* 43(11): 1921–1941.

Putnam, R. (1993) *Making Democracy Work: Civic Traditions in Modern Italy.* Princeton, NJ: Princeton University Press.

Putnam, R. (2000) *Bowling Alone: The Collapse and Revival of American Community.* New York: Simon & Schuster.

Raco, M. (2003) "Governmentality, subject-building, and the discourses and practices of devolution in the UK," *Transactions of the Institute of British Geographers* 28(1): 75–95.

Raissiguier, R. (2010) *Reinventing the Republic: Gender, Migration, and Citizenship in France.* Palo Alto, CA: Stanford University Press.

Rancière, J. (1993) "Early French socialism: Ways to construct social identity," *Labour History Review,* 58(3): 8–13.

Rath, J. (1991) *Minorisering: de sociale constructie van "etnische minderheden".* Amsterdam: SUA.

Rose, N. (1996) "The death of the social? Re-figuring the territory of government," *Economy and Society* 25: 327–356.

Rose, N. (1999) *Powers of Freedom: Reframing Political Thought.* Cambridge: Cambridge University Press.

Rose, N. and P. Miller (1992) "Political power beyond the state: Problematics of government," *British Journal of Sociology* 43(2): 172–205.

Routledge, P. (1993) *Terrains of Resistance: Non-violent Social Movements and the Contestation of Place in India.* Westport, CT: Praeger.

Routledge P. (1994) "Backstreets, barricades, and blackouts: Urban terrains of resistance in Nepal," *Environment and Planning D: Society and Space* 12(5): 559–578.

Routledge, P. (1997) "Putting politics in its place: Baliapal, India, as a terrain of resistance," in J. Agnew (Ed.) *Political Geography: A Reader.* London: Arnold, pp. 219–255.

Routledge, P. (2003) "Convergence space: Process geographies of grassroots globalisation networks," *Transactions of the Institute of British Geographers* 28(3): 333–349.

Sampson, R. (2013) *Great American City: Chicago and the Enduring Neighborhood Effect.* Chicago, IL: University of Chicago Press.

Sampson, R.J., D. McAdam, H. MacIndoe, and S. Weffer-Elizondo (2005) "Civil society reconsidered: The durable nature and community structure of collective civic action," *American Journal of Sociology* 111(3): 673–714.

Sassen, S. (1991) *The Global City: New York, London, Tokyo*. Princeton, NJ: Princeton University Press.

Sassen, S. (2004) "Local actors in global politics," *Current Sociology* 52(4): 649–670.

Saunders, P. (1986) *Social Theory and the Urban Question*. Second edition. New York: Holmes and Meier.

Schain, M. (1999) "Minorities and immigrant incorporation in France: The state and the dynamics of multiculturalism," *Multicultural Questions* 26: 199–224.

Scott, A. (1988) *Metropolis: From the Division of Labor to Urban Form*. Berkeley: University of California Press.

Scott, A. (2008) *Social Economy of the Metropolis: Cognitive-Cultural Capitalism and the Global Resurgence of Cities*. Oxford: Oxford University Press.

Seif, H. (2004) "'Wise Up!' Undocumented Latino youth, Mexican-American legislators, and the struggle for higher education access," *Latino Studies* 2: 210–30.

Sennett, R. (1994) *Flesh and Stone: The Body and the City in Western Civilization*. New York: W.W. Norton.

Shorto, M. (2013) *Amsterdam: A History of the World's Most Liberal City*. New York: Random House.

Sikkink, K. (2005) "Patterns of dynamic multilevel governance and the insider-outsider coalition," in D. Della Porta and S. Tarrow (Eds.) *Transnational Protest and Global Activism*. Lanham, MD: Rowman and Littlefield, pp. 151–173.

Silver, H., A. Scott, and Y. Kazepov (2010) "Participation in urban contention and deliberation," *International Journal of Urban and Regional Research* 34(3): 453–477.

Siméant, J. (1998) *La Cause des Sans-Papiers*. Paris: Presses Sciences-Po.

Sites, W. (2007) "Beyond trenches and grassroots? Reflections on urban mobilization, fragmentation, and the anti-Wal-Mart campaign in Chicago," *Environment and Planning A* 39(11): 2632–2651.

Slootman, M., J. Tillie, A. Majdy, and F. Buijs (2009) *Salafi-jihadi's in Amsterdam. Portretten*. Utrecht: Forum.

Smith, M.P. and M. McQuarrie (Eds.) (2012) *Remaking Urban Citizenship: Organizations, Institutions, and the Right to the City*. New Brunswick, NJ: Transaction Publishers.

Smith, N. (2008) *Uneven Development: Nature, Capital, and the Production of Space*. Athens, GA: University of Georgia Press.

Soja, E. (2000) *Postmetropolis: Critical Studies of Cities and Regions*. Oxford: Wiley-Blackwell.

Soja, E. (2010) *Seeking Spatial Justice*. Minneapolis: University of Minnesota Press.

Sonenshein, R. (1994) *Politics in Black and White: Race and Power in Los Angeles*. Princeton, NJ: Princeton University Press.

Stadsdeel Slotervaart (2007) *Actieplan Slotervaart: Het tegengaan van radicalisering*.

Steil, J. and I. Vasi (2014) "The new immigration contestation: Social movements and local immigration policy making in the United States, 2000–2011," *American Journal of Sociology* 119(4): 1104–1155.

Stone, C. (1994) "Urban regimes and the capacity to govern: A political economy approach," *Journal of Urban Affairs* 15(1): 1–28.

Storper, M. (1997) *The Regional World: Territorial Development in a Global Economy.* New York: Guilford Press.

Storper, M. (2013) *Keys to the City: How Economics, Institutions, Social Interactions and Politics Shape the Development of City-regions.* Princeton, NJ: Princeton University Press.

Storper, M. and A. Venables (2004) "Buzz: Face-to-face contact and the urban economy," *Journal of Economic Geography* 4: 351–370.

SWBW (Stichting Welzijn Buitenlandse Werknemers) (1973–1974) *Jaarverslag.* Amsterdam: Stichting Welzijn Buitenlandse Werknemers.

SWBW (Stichting Welzijn Buitenlandse Werknemers) (1975) "Nieuwsbrief," Autumn. Amsterdam: Stichting Welzijn Buitenlandse Werknemers.

Tarrow, S. (1998) *Power in Movement: Social Movements and Contentious Politics.* Cambridge: Cambridge University Press.

Tarrow, S. and D. McAdam (2005) "Scale shift in transnational contention," in D. della Porta and S. Tarrow (Eds.) *Transnational Protest and Global Activism.* Boulder, CO: Rowman and Littlefield, pp. 121–150.

Terriquez, V. (2014) "Dreams delayed: Barriers to degree completion among undocumented community college students," *Journal of Ethnic and Migration Studies.* DOI: 10.1080/1369183X.2014.968534.

The Guardian (2011) "Angolan teenager Mauro Manuel loses fight to stay in the Netherlands," November 1.

Tilly, C. (2005) *Trust and Rule.* Cambridge: Cambridge University Press.

Tonkens, E.H. (1999) *Het zelfontplooiingsregime: de actualiteit van Dennendal en de jaren zestig.* Amsterdam: Bert Bakker.

Trouw (2012) "Politie ontruimt tentenkamp Ter Apel," May 24.

Uitermark, J. (2003) "'Social mixing' and the management of disadvantaged neighbourhoods: The Dutch policy of urban restructuring revisited," *Urban Studies* 40(3): 531–549.

Uitermark, J. (2004) "Looking forward by looking back: May Day protests in London and the strategic significance of the urban," *Antipode* 36(4): 700–721.

Uitermark, J. (2009) "An *in memoriam* for the just city of Amsterdam," *City* 13(2–3): 347–361.

Uitermark, J. (2012) *Dynamics of Power in Dutch Integration Politics.* Amsterdam: University of Amsterdam Press.

Uitermark, J. (2014) "Integration and control: The governing of urban marginality in Western Europe," *International Journal of Urban and Regional Research* 38(4): 1418–1436.

Uitermark, J., U. Rossi, and H. van Houtum (2005) "Reinventing multiculturalism: Urban citizenship and the negotiation of ethnic diversity in Amsterdam," *International Journal of Urban and Regional Research* 29(3): 622–640.

Uitermark, J., J.W. Duyvendak, and J. Rath (2014) "Governing through religion in Amsterdam: The stigmatization of ethnic cultures and the uses of Islam," in N. Foner, J. Rath, J.W. Duyvendak, and R. van Reekum (Eds.) *New York and Amsterdam: Immigration and the New Urban Landscape.* New York: New York University Press, pp. 170–194.

Uitermark, J. and A.-J. Gielen (2010) "Islam in the spotlight: Discursive politics in an Amsterdam neighborhood after 9/11 and the assassination of Theo van Gogh," *Urban Studies* 47(6): 1325–1342.

Uitermark, J. and W. Nicholls (2014) "From politicization to policing: The rise and decline of immigrant social movements in Amsterdam and Paris," *Antipode: A Radical Journal of Geography* 46(4): 970–991.

Uitermark, J., W. Nicholls, and M. Loopmans (2012) "A relational approach to cities and social movements: Theorizing beyond rights to the city," *Environment and Planning A* 44(11): 2546–2554.

Valle, V. and Torres, R. (2000) *Latino Metropolis*. Philadelphia, PA: Temple University Press.

Van Beek, J.H. (2010) *Kennis, Macht en Moraal*. Amsterdam: unpublished PhD thesis, University of Amsterdam.

Van der Leun, J. (2003) *Looking for Loopholes: Processes of Incorporation of Illegal Immigrants in the Netherlands*. Amsterdam: University of Amsterdam Press.

Van Oenen, G. (1999) "Roodheet. Hoe restrictief immigratiebeleid de Nederlandse politiek ontregelt," *Migrantenstudies* 15(2): 113–127.

Van Tilborgh, Y. (2006) *Wij zijn Nederland. Moslima's over Ayaan Hirsi Ali.* Amsterdam: Van Gennep.

Vankatesh, S. (1997) "The social organization of street gang activity in an urban ghetto," *American Journal of Sociology* 103(1): 82–111.

Varsanyi, M. (2008) "Rescaling the 'alien', rescaling personhood: Neoliberalism, immigration, and the state," *Annals of the Association of American Geographers* 98(4): 877–889.

Varsanyi, M. (2011) "Neoliberalism and nativism: Local anti-immigrant policy activism and an emerging politics of scale," *International Journal of Urban and Regional Research* 35(2): 295–311.

Vermeulen, F. (2006) *The Immigrant Organising Process: Turkish Organisations in Amsterdam and Berlin and Surinamese Organisations in Amsterdam, 1960–2000.* Amsterdam: University of Amsterdam Press.

Voss, K. and I. Bloemraad (2011) *Rallying for Immigrants: The Fight for Inclusion in 21st Century America*. Berkeley: University of California Press.

Vrijwilligers Vluchthaven (2014) *Evaluatie Vluchthaven*, June 3.

Wacquant, L. (1993) "Urban outcasts: Stigma and division in the Black American ghetto and French urban periphery," *International Journal of Urban and Regional Research* 17(3): 367–383.

Wacquant, L. (2008) *Urban Outcasts: A Comparative Sociology of Advanced Marginality*. Cambridge: Polity Press.

Waldinger, R. and M. Bozorgmehr (1996) "The making of a multicultural metropolis," in R. Waldinger and M. Bozorgmehr (Eds.) *Ethnic Los Angeles*. New York: Russell Sage Foundation, pp. 3–38.

Waldinger, R., C. Erickson, R. Milkman, D. Mitchell, A. Valenzuela, and M. Zeitlin (1998) "Helots no more: A case study of the Justice for Janitors campaign in Los Angeles," in K. Bronfenbrenner, S. Friedman, R. Hurd, and R. Oswald (Eds.) *Organizing to Win*. Ithaca, NY: Cornell University Press, pp.102–120.

Walker, K. and H. Leitner (2011) "The variegated landscape of local immigration policies in the United States," *Urban Geography* 32(2): 156–178.

Weil, P. (1991) *La France et ses étrangers: L'aventure d'une politique de l'immigration, 1938–1991*. Paris: Calman-Levy.

Wihtol de Wenden, C. (1994) "Immigrants as political actors in France," *West European Politics* 17(2): 91–110.

Wihtol de Wenden, C. and R. Leveau (2001) *La beurgeoisie: les trois âges de la vie associative de l'immigration*. Paris: CNRS Editions.

Wolch, J. (1990) *The Shadow State: Government and Voluntary Sector in Transition*. New York: Foundation Center.

Wolch, J. (1996) "From global to local: The rise of homelessness in Los Angeles during the 1980s," in A. Scott and E. Soja (Eds.) *The City: Los Angeles and Urban Theory at the End of the 20th Century*. Berkeley: University of California Press, pp. 390–425.

WRR (Wetenschappelijke Raad voor het Regeringsbeleid) (1979) *Etnische minderheden. Rapport aan de regering*. The Hague: Staatsuitgeverij.

McCarthy, J. and M. Zald (1987) "Resource mobilization and social movements: A partial theory," in M. Zald and J. McCarthy (Eds.) *Social Movements in an Organizational Society*. New Brunswick, NJ: Transaction Publishers, pp. 161–180.

Zancarini-Fournel, M. (2002) "La question immigré après 68," *Plein Droit* 53–54. Available at: http://www.gisti.org/doc/plein-droit/53–54/question.html, accessed on May 1, 2010.

Index

*Cities and Social Movements: Immigrant Rights Activism in the United States, France,
and the Netherlands, 1970–2015*, First Edition. Walter J. Nicholls and Justus Uitermark.
© 2017 John Wiley & Sons, Ltd. Published 2017 by John Wiley & Sons, Ltd.